SEPTEMBER
SACRIFICE

BOOK YOUR PLACE ON OUR WEBSITE AND MAKE THE READING CONNECTION!

We've created a customized website just for our very special readers, where you can get the inside scoop on everything that's going on with Zebra, Pinnacle and Kensington books.

When you come online, you'll have the exciting opportunity to:

- View covers of upcoming books
- Read sample chapters
- Learn about our future publishing schedule (listed by publication month *and author*)
- Find out when your favorite authors will be visiting a city near you
- Search for and order backlist books from our online catalog
- Check out author bios and background information
- Send e-mail to your favorite authors
- Meet the Kensington staff online
- Join us in weekly chats with authors, readers and other guests
- Get writing guidelines
- AND MUCH MORE!

**Visit our website at
http://www.kensingtonbooks.com**

SEPTEMBER SACRIFICE

MARK HORNER

PINNACLE BOOKS
Kensington Publishing Corp.
http://www.kensingtonbooks.com

PROLOGUE

It was Sunday evening. Thirty-six-year-old Girly Chew Hossencofft was the only person inside her tiny Northeast Albuquerque apartment. That was no surprise. Ever since moving into the Valle Grande apartment complex eight months earlier, she kept its location a secret. Girly found refuge within her apartment.

And on the evening of September 5, 1999, she also found comfort.

While pressing the base of a newly lit joss stick into her palm, she knelt. Just five feet one inch tall and weighing ninety-five pounds, she slowly lowered her head, causing her long jet-black hair to cascade toward the crushed orange carpet.

With eyes now closed, the soft-skinned Malaysian woman directed her prayers to Kuan Yin, the Buddhist goddess of mercy. She believed that the thin trail of smoke rising from the incense carried her prayers to her bodhisattva.

Girly had carefully chosen her goddess.

She kept a small statue of Kuan Yin on the altar inside her living room.

Kuan Yin, according to Girly's belief, appeared in many

forms whenever a being needs her help, especially when someone is menaced by water, demons, fire, or sword.

What Girly ultimately prayed for was protection from the man who hunted her, the man who promised to have her killed. He had laughed as he bragged that no one would ever find her body.

That man was Girly's estranged husband, Diazien Hossencofft. It had been nearly seven years since she had arrived from Malaysia to marry him. During that time, she'd learned everything about the man was a lie.

Having finished her prayers to Kuan Yin, Girly sat at her desk and wrote a letter to her parents in Malaysia.

The sound of Buddhist chants to Kuan Yin came from her portable stereo, providing a soothing ambience. But the chanting was also intended to keep away any bad omens.

With the joss stick now burning on the altar immediately beside her desk, Girly wrote the numeral 1 in the upper right corner of the piece of paper before her and circled it.

She knew her parents enjoyed hearing the details of her life. She wanted to please them with a long letter.

"Dearest Mama and Daddy," she began the letter. Although she'd turned thirty-six just nine days earlier, Girly still enjoyed using the affectionate names for her parents. Mama was sixty-three-year-old Margaret Chew. Daddy was sixty-four-year-old Kheng Chew. Girly would always be their little girl.

She'd write nothing about the terror that gripped her life. She didn't want her parents to worry.

The letter was destined to arrive at her parents' home in Penang in mid-September. By that time, Girly would have already vanished.

1

At 8:00 A.M. on September 10, 1999, Kathy Semansky walked into the Bank of America in Albuquerque's Uptown neighborhood. Just as she had for the past two years, the successful forty-nine-year-old bank vice president looked forward to conducting her popular Friday-morning meeting with her dozen or so tellers and sales reps. It was always fun to give gift certificates to the employees who had recruited the most new customers during the week.

Semansky always began her day by walking straight to her desk, hanging her purse from her chair and logging into her computer. Not today.

Sales representative Terrie Gruen immediately spotted her boss entering through the glass double doors and wasted no time approaching her.

"Some man just called, asking if we've seen Girly," Gruen said as a phone rang nearby. "He didn't give his name."

Semansky felt immediate concern as she listened to Gruen's direct and brief report. It was not the sort of feeling that she *should* be concerned. No, this was genuine concern born from fear.

As well as anyone, Semansky knew her much-liked teller, Girly Chew Hossencofft, was being hunted.

"He keeps telling me I'm going to be murdered," Girly told her boss on four or five occasions during the year. "He even smiles and says no one will ever find my body."

Semansky wondered if the man who had called minutes earlier was Diazien Hossencofft.

"Kathy, it's some guy asking about Girly again," another employee, holding up a phone, blurted toward Semansky.

Semansky took the call.

"Has Girly arrived at work this morning?" the man asked.

Once again, Semansky wondered if the man was Hossencofft. She'd never spoken to him before, so she didn't know his voice. As the man kept firing off questions, Semansky detected a woman's voice in the background, prodding the man with more questions.

Finally the woman took the phone, telling Semansky, "Hello, this is Ernie Johnson."

Ernie Johnson. Semansky knew that name. Rosella Ernestine "Ernie" Johnson was Girly's close friend. They spoke every night on the phone before bed. Ernie always wanted to know that Girly was home and safe at night.

"No, Ernie. Girly's not here yet," Semansky told Johnson.

"Well, I called her last night, and she never answered the phone," Johnson said. "Do you know if she went out to dinner last night . . . or maybe a movie?"

Semansky said she did not know.

"Well, I even called her at six-thirty this morning, and she never answered," Johnson revealed.

Years later, Semansky said that "we both knew, right away, that he'd come through with his promise. That he'd killed her. The minute I knew that Ernie had called Girly that morning, I knew that he'd done it."

Semansky told Johnson she'd make some calls right away and wasted no time calling Girly's home number. No answer. Girly's cell phone. No answer.

Something's going on, she thought.

"I'm going over to her apartment." The voice came from Jesse Grove, a slender, soft-spoken teller in his twenties who was like a brother to Girly.

"He left immediately," Semansky recalled.

"Okay, I'm going to call police," she told Jesse as he walked away.

Shortly before 8:15 on the morning of September 10, 1999, Kathy Semansky called 911.

"I know they thought I was a lunatic. I know they thought, 'Here's this woman, it's not even eight-fifteen, and she's freakin' out,' " she recalled.

Still, Semansky managed to remain calm the first time she called police. The police operator, though, advised her to call the Albuquerque Police Department's nonemergency number. After all, Girly hadn't been missing for twenty-four hours, one of the prerequisites for a missing person case.

"Someone needs to get there. She didn't show up for work."

Semansky was now talking to the person who answered the phone at APD's nonemergency number. Struggling to maintain her composure while applying the forcefulness she felt the situation deserved, Semansky had just given the operator Girly's closely guarded home address. Not even Ernie Johnson knew where Girly had lived since leaving Hossencofft back in January.

As Semansky spoke on the phone, Girly's words played back in her mind.

"If I'm ever late for work, call police right away," Girly had told her.

And Girly was never late for work. She was usually the first one to show up. A model employee.

"We even gave her a nickname, 'Computer Chip,' " Semansky said.

The affectionate name came after Girly's early days at the bank. "She wanted to know *everything,*" Semanksy recalled.

"At first, asking so many questions was kind of irritating. But after a while, you watched the woman work, and you saw how efficient she was with everything: the way she handled money, the way she interacted with customers. The customers loved her. She usually had the most referrals."

Semansky soon realized she had an exceptional employee who wanted to be the best teller at the Bank of America. In time, Girly's outstanding work performance earned her trips to San Francisco and Hawaii in the bank's nationwide teller competitions.

"She didn't show up for work," Semansky stressed to the operator at the police nonemergency number.

"And they were like, 'Okay.' And that was the end of the phone call," Semansky said.

Everyone at the bank knew Jesse Grove had strong feelings for Girly. And although he was several years younger than Girly, the bank employees readily recognized that Jesse looked out for her as if he were her older brother, her protector.

Girly so trusted Grove that she allowed him to help her move into her apartment that January.

Grove, a soft-spoken young man, was one of the very few people who actually knew where Girly lived. When he arrived at the Valle Grande apartments shortly after 8:30 A.M., he drove directly to the remote area near the back.

Girly's apartment was supposed to be difficult for a hunter to find. But because it was removed from the complex's core population, there were fewer eyes to notice anything out of the ordinary.

Grove noticed Girly's green 1995 BMW still parked in the lot. A corner of the windshield was still smashed.

Someone had vandalized the car several weeks earlier while it had been parked near the bank. Everyone had suspected Hossencofft, intent on sending a message.

It was the car he *didn't* see outside Girly's apartment that troubled Jesse Grove, though. As he drove up beside Girly's Beemer, he grew annoyed because no squad cars were in sight. *Why aren't the police here yet?*

Perhaps they were on the other side of the building.

Grove didn't have to go far to reach Girly's first-floor apartment. It was only about thirty-five feet from the parking lot.

Grove repeatedly rang the bell and knocked on the apartment door, but no one answered. And no sound came from within. He attempted to turn the doorknob, but it was locked. He couldn't see through the window, either.

Grove next turned his attention to Girly's car. Looking through the windows of the BMW, he noticed that there was no sign of The Club on the steering wheel. Girly typically used this device to discourage anyone from stealing her car.

"She wouldn't answer the door. Where are the police?" Jesse asked his boss over the telephone.

"Well, Jesse, I've called," Semansky replied.

She felt frustration, too, after learning Grove found no sign of the Albuquerque Police Department or Girly.

"I'm going to get the manager, and we're going to go in," Jesse told Semansky.

Oh, my God, Semansky thought. *What is he going to walk into?*

2

More than 120 miles southwest of Albuquerque in the re-mote desert of central New Mexico, state highway worker Raymond Gabaldon drove westbound on Highway 60. This two-lane stretch of asphalt cuts across flat, arid land inter-rupted by occasional rolling hills. While the land is rugged and arid, juniper and piñon trees decorate the russet land-scape like scattered jacks on an old, hardwood floor.

It was just after 10:30 on Friday morning, September 10, 1999. The skies were mostly sunny, although it had rained overnight.

Gabaldon, thirty-nine, had set out to do the weekly job of picking up trash at local rest areas. Someone else had per-formed trash pickup duty the past two weeks, so the job hardly seemed bothersome to Gabaldon as he drove toward one of the more popular rest stops in the area, about eight miles west of the small town of Magdalena.

As Gabaldon's state vehicle climbed the steep hill that rises west of Magdalena, he was only a few hundred yards from the rest area when something suddenly caught his eye. It would have been hard to miss, actually.

On the south side of the highway, the land immediately

rises up a steep slope. About twenty feet up that embankment was the gray-colored object that caught Gabaldon's attention.

A blanket? he wondered. Whatever it was, it could be dangerous when the desert winds picked up, destined to blast along the flatland. And with cars, RVs and semis going up and down the hill, a wind-whipped blanket could be a hazard.

Raymond Gabaldon pulled over to pick it up.

It looked more like a tarp, he thought as he walked up to it. And in good condition. Why would someone throw it away? As Gabaldon inspected the tarpaulin, he noticed dark red stains on it. Dried blood. At first, he wasn't alarmed.

"It looked like one of those that you use for wrapping a deer after you hunt it," he said later.

It was, after all, hunting season. In fact, a local hunting contest was under way. The Magdalena area attracts a lot of deer, elk, mountain lion and bear hunters from throughout New Mexico as well as Texas and other states. A hunter might pay $8,000 to kill an elk on someone's private land. Hunting is big business here. The area's small hotels, restaurants and stores depend on it.

While holding the tarpaulin in his hands, Gabaldon discovered something that disturbed him. Hair. Long, dark strands of it. And just a few feet away, twisted clumps of duct tape. One piece had similar strands of hair stuck to it. Another piece of gray tape was twisted into a distinctive shape: a figure eight.

Alone in the desert, Gabaldon's eyes surveyed the landscape around him, but he needed to look only a little less than twenty feet away. At the bottom of the slope he had just climbed, right along the edge of Highway 60, he saw clothing.

"A small girl's top, shorts, underwear . . . it didn't look right," Gabaldon later told police.

What *really* didn't look right were the bloodstains, not

only on the tarp, but dried blood appeared on the blouse and panties, too.

Gabaldon tried to imagine how the tarp and clothing ended up alongside this stretch of Highway 60. The winds had been light overnight and were relatively calm now. It didn't seem as if the tarp and clothing could have all been blown here from some other location. Besides, the rain from the night before weighed a bit heavy on the tarp. It would have been difficult for the night wind to push it anywhere. No, it all looked as if it had all been dumped here.

Fearing the worst, Gabaldon's gut instinct told him where he had to look next. He knew the area well. And if someone wanted to hide a body nearby, the culvert about two hundred yards east of here would be a logical place to do so.

Gabaldon stepped into the sandy arroyo several feet below the south side of Highway 60. From there, he could clearly see the pipe that passes under the highway. Beneath the blue September sky, all seemed calm at this moment. Only the singing of nearby birds, occasionally drowned out by vehicles passing overhead, interrupted the tranquillity. But, many times, Gabaldon had seen an entirely different picture here.

Countless monsoons previously unleashed their stored-up energy upon this desert: the sporadic sounds of thunder, like random gunfire in a war zone, accompanied by lightning and the torrential downpour of a microburst.

At such moments, Gabaldon would never be standing there, in the arroyo. A raging wall of water could be snaking through the desert, following the entrenched path of the arroyo.

Now Gabaldon wondered if death passed through here. He peered inside the cylindrical passage, wondering if a body had been stuffed inside. He saw nothing. Gabaldon climbed back up to the highway, crossed it, then made his way back down into the arroyo. Now staring into the culvert from the north side of the highway, he still saw no sign of a body.

Gabaldon collected the bloodied clothing, tarpaulin, duct tape and a nearby washcloth and took it all into town. Looking at the suspicious items, a Magdalena lawman decided to contact the New Mexico State Police (NMSP).

An avid and competitive cyclist, forty-year-old Stephen Knight-Williamson had long ago developed a knack for noticing details along a road, things most people never notice. At noon on September 10, 1999, Knight-Williamson was driving his car southbound on Albuquerque's busy Tramway Boulevard when he spotted a wallet on the road, smack in the middle of the southbound lanes, twenty yards south of Tramway's intersection with Indian School Road.

Knight-Williamson pulled over, his distinctively English accent informing his passenger, business partner Linnah Neidel, that he'd be right back.

Waiting for a break in the steady stream of fifty-to-sixty-mile-per-hour traffic, Knight-Williamson found a safe moment and picked up the billfold.

At first the wallet seemed empty, but then Knight-Williamson noticed what appeared to be some sort of foreign identification card inside. It included a picture of a pleasant-looking Asian woman. The name on the card was Girly Chew Hossencofft.

Knight-Williamson didn't think much about his discovery and set the wallet aside in his car.

3

Just like any other shrewd predator, Diazien Hossencofft didn't waste his energy on elusive prey. Within thirty seconds of meeting someone, he usually knew if he could exploit the stranger's flesh for his gain. If not, he'd hunt elsewhere. If he saw an opening, he moved in. That's the trademark of a good con man, too.

"As far as his charisma and controlling and getting people to do what you want them to do, I think everyone in my family possesses that to a point," Stanley Chavez said of his half brother.

In the very early 1990s, Hossencofft was already spinning the web of lies that would ultimately take a woman's life.

As the late 1980s rolled over to the early 1990s, Girly Chew enjoyed working at the Bank of Hong Kong in Malaysia.

Now in her late twenties, she'd lived her entire life in Malaysia. Born and raised in Malaysia's "island state" of Penang, Girly's homeland reflected the very fiber of her being.

While predominantly Chinese, many of Penang's people also spoke English. The historic influence of Great Britain had had a profound influence on Penang. From its economy to its manners, the European influence was prevalent.

The island's outer edge was a thin band of coastal plains; luxurious hotels decorated brilliant, tropical beaches. The weather had a natural order, too. Alternating seasons of southwestern and northeastern winds delivered year-round monsoons.

At the center of Penang's 113 square miles were the mountains. The shifts in the wind against those mountains were responsible for separating rainy seasons from drier ones. When it rained, it poured. Much of Penang received more than one hundred inches of rain a year. The mountains, it is said, provide a shadow effect.

Girly lived among the water sports and near the world's largest butterfly field in the city of Tanjung Bungah in northeastern Penang. Her parents' house was the center of her universe. She'd lived there her entire life. The security of her home extended to her neighborhood.

In Malaysia, the crime rate was nearly nonexistent. Severe penalties, including death, had a lot to do with that. It was illegal to own a gun. It was a country where people felt safe walking the streets day or night. Girly not only felt protected in her hometown, she felt loved.

"The neighbors are nice, kind and extremely helpful. They're very concerned for each other. It is like a big family," Andrew Chew, her brother, later said.

Girly Chew was born August 27, 1963, in nearby George Town. It was the same year Malaysia had become a country.

In January 1985, at the age of twenty-one, Girly landed a job as a marketing representative at the Hong Kong Bank in Penang. It was surely a job to be proud of. The bank building, originally a post office built in 1883, was a popular tourist attraction.

Girly became close friends with her coworker, Susan Oh. In 1989, the pair traveled to the United States for a vacation. Visiting the United States became an annual holiday for Girly and Susan.

More important to Girly than any job, though, was her faith. She often visited the most popular Chinese temple in all of Penang, the Goddess of Mercy Temple. Girly found great comfort as she entered the cobblestone square in front of the temple, walking past the people feeding pigeons, then joining those praying to Kuan Yin while burning blue and silver paper called *kim* and *gin*.

It was a most peaceful place.

The equilibrium of Girly's life would not tumble out of control all at once. Rather, it would take years to destroy.

The parasite aimed at Girly Chew arrived in the early 1990s. Although it's not exactly known "how" it entered.

Some people believe Girly and Hossencofft had first been pen pals; others believe she had met him while on vacation.

No matter how their lives initially converged, there is plenty of evidence that he wasted little time manipulating her with a grand performance of deception from half a world away.

The truth is, the man who called himself "Dr. Diazien Hossencofft" was really Armand Chavez (sometimes Armando). The official name change would come later as he reeled in his prey.

"My point of origin is Zurich, Switzerland . . . ," Chavez wrote in a three-page italicized letter to Girly's parents on April 20, 1992.

That letter appeared to be aimed at "apologizing" for not having asked Girly's father for his daughter's hand in marriage.

Girly was still living with her parents, but she had accepted Dr. Hossencofft's marriage proposal and planned to move to the United States at the end of the year.

In the letter, Chavez offered a fictitious name and introduced himself to Girly's mother and father, providing details about his exciting life.

"I work for NASA which has a National Defense Systems subdivision called NDS," he wrote in his epistle.

The letter appeared to have been carefully typed, entirely in italics, and was signed: *"Fondly yours, Diazien Hossencofft."*

With his fiancée scheduled to arrive from Malaysia at the end of the year, Armand Chavez launched his plan to create the world she'd come to expect.

On July 17, 1992, he succeeded in legally changing his name to Diazien Hossencofft. Case number CV-9206554 filed in New Mexico's Second Judicial District Court was the Petition to Change Name filed by his attorney, Rondolyn R. O'Brien. In the petition, the attorney provided no insightful explanation for the name change, only "that it is in his best interests to so change his name."

On December 28, 1992, Hossencofft visited Krugers, a jewelers, in Northeast Albuquerque and purchased an obligatory symbol of his affection, an eighteen-karat yellow gold wedding ring featuring a one-carat diamond placed between four smaller diamonds and four baguette diamonds.

One day after Hossencofft paid $7,500 for the ring, Girly arrived in the United States.

As 1992 came to a close, Girly looked forward to a new beginning. On December 29, despite forty hours of connecting flights between Malaysia and the United States, she must have felt alive with feelings of excitement, anticipation and joy. A new life awaited her as she stepped off a plane in Los Angeles, a future with a brilliant man. She was closing in on her final destination: Albuquerque, New Mexico.

4

The dead bolt wasn't locked. Even Bill Orth knew that was unusual. Orth, who'd briefly come out of retirement to manage the Valle Grande, knew that his tenant in 53-D feared her estranged husband and had a restraining order.

The sense of urgency intensified for Jesse Grove, too. As well as anyone, he also knew Girly would never leave the dead bolt unlocked.

At 8:30 A.M., Orth and Grove entered the apartment together.

There was only silence.

Grove immediately noticed three large spots on the crushed orange carpet, which stretched throughout the apartment. The smallest spot was about the size of a grapefruit, while the largest approached the size of a basketball.

It appeared as if someone had tried to clean up a mess. Perhaps something had been spilled.

Aside from those stains, the living room seemed intact. But with no sign of Girly, the men decided to venture to the back of the apartment.

What would they find in Girly's bedroom?

Walking down the short hallway, they called out Girly's name together.

While their concern was genuine, the moment also felt invasive. What if there was nothing wrong? What if she had overslept? Grove knew that was extremely unlikely. Girly had never been late for work.

"Girly? Are you here?"

Still, no reply.

They entered the bedroom. It was empty. Without exactly knowing why, but fearing the worst, the men looked inside Girly's bedroom closet. The clothes were all neatly hung. There was no sign of Girly or any foul play.

The bed was made, although the pillow was slightly askew. Had Girly made her bed earlier that morning? Or did she never make it to bed?

Only one thing could be certain: Girly was nowhere in sight.

At 9:45 A.M., Semansky made her fourth call to the Albuquerque Police Department.

"I have an employee; her name is Girly Hossencofft," Semansky told police operator 96. "She and her husband are going through a pretty horrible divorce. It's been a lot of domestic violence that has been reported. And there's a restraining order on him. She did not come in to work this morning, which is totally not like her at all."

Semansky tried not to panic. She didn't want to seem hysterical. She needed to connect with this police operator, to convey the seriousness without coming across as some loony caller.

"And I really . . . I have a really bad feeling that something has happened to her."

"Okay," replied the operator.

"Only because she's *always* told us, 'If I don't show up for work, please call someone. Something happened.' And I really do believe that this probably has happened because this guy is wacko."

"Have you notified any family members?" the operator asked.

"She has no family here. She is from Malaysia. And a friend of hers that she stays in close contact with calls me this morning because, every night, they talk. She always calls Girly, or Girly calls her to make sure everything's okay. And Girly never called her last night. And it's totally out of character for her not to go home. The girl, right, the only life is her work."

The police operator offered some suggestions.

"Do you want us to send you a police officer so you can file a report, or do you want to file the report with our Telephone Report Unit? What would you like us to do for you?"

Without hesitation, Semansky knew where the police needed to go next.

"Well, what I'd like is to have someone go to her house."

Semansky explained that Grove and the apartment manager had waited about a half hour for police to arrive at Girly's apartment, but no one ever arrived.

"Okay, what's the address where we're supposed to go?" the operator asked. Semansky gave the operator Girly's address. "I'm sure I have a copy of their restraining order here."

"Where does the boyfriend or the husband live?"

Semansky gave the address off the restraining order. She could only stare at the restraining form and wonder if the man ordered to keep away from Girly had followed through on his threat to have her killed.

One couldn't have blamed Tim Portwine if he had immediately turned around. The Albuquerque police officer was en route to Girly's apartment when the dispatcher's voice came over his radio advising him to "cancel."

The dispatcher told Portwine that the apartment manager had just called police, telling them that he had already entered the apartment and noticed nothing wrong. But because Officer Portwine had just entered the parking lot at the Valle Grande, he decided he might as well check things out.

The police investigation into the mysterious disappearance of Girly Chew Hossencofft was about to begin.

Officer Portwine soon found Orth, who explained that he and Girly's coworker had waited for police to arrive earlier that morning. When the APD hadn't shown up right away, he and Grove decided they'd better go inside 53-D themselves. Girly might have been hurt. Maybe she needed help.

Orth told Officer Portwine that nothing inside the apartment appeared to be in disarray, but added that it seemed odd that the dead bolt wasn't locked. He shared that Mrs. Hossencofft had also been a domestic violence victim, and that Mr. Hossencofft had previously "punched in" the windshield of Girly's BMW.

"Maybe she left with someone," Portwine speculated. Having just been told by Orth that everything inside the apartment appeared to be in order, Portwine decided not to go inside and drove away.

At 10:23 A.M., Albuquerque police sergeant Edward Ade was dispatched to a home on Moon Northeast. The dispatcher called it a welfare check, although the real purpose was to see if a missing woman's husband might be home.

When Ade arrived, he met up with another officer outside the home. Tim Portwine had also responded to the call.

Sergeant Ade had recently been to this very same home.

On August 27, 1999, two weeks earlier, Sergeant Ade checked on the welfare of Diazien Hossencofft. The call to APD came from a caseworker at the Triad Adoption Agency. Vonda Cheshire had been concerned that Diazien Hossencofft might be suicidal because of a volatile mixture of horrible circumstances.

"You see," Hossencofft had explained to Cheshire, "I'm dying of cancer."

Hossencofft had told Cheshire that his wife had recently divorced him and left him behind with a three-year-old son. Hossencofft had added that no relatives would step in and help out. And now—although he said it tore him apart to do so—an adoption seemed to be the best solution for little Demetri.

Cheshire had sensed a sadness about Hossencofft. Sadness oozed from him. As she'd left his home, the caseworker couldn't help thinking of something Hossencofft still had in his possession: guns.

Cheshire called police on that late August day. Minutes later, Ade arrived to check on the man feared to be suicidal.

"I'm not going to hurt myself," Hossencofft had assured Ade.

For safekeeping, Hossencofft had agreed to turn his weapons over to his neighbor directly to the north of his home, John Deyber.

"Where's your wife?" Ade had asked before leaving the house on August 27.

Hossencofft had responded without any hesitation, "She's dead."

The front door was open. As Ade and Portwine approached the entry of the single-story home on Moon Northeast, on September 10, 1999, Portwine peered inside and discovered the place was empty. Seconds later, a woman holding a cleaning cloth in both hands came to the door.

"No speak English," she told the policemen.

"The entire residence was empty. No furniture, no dishes, etc.," Portwine would write in his missing person report.

Hossencofft had left the neighborhood. Was he on the

run? The police didn't have to go far to find the next piece of the puzzle.

"The moving crew hauled all of his stuff out of here Wednesday night," neighbor John Deyber stated matter-of-factly after opening his front door. "The guy said he was moving to El Paso so he could shuttle back and forth to Mexico, where he was getting his cancer treatment. His last night in that house was Wednesday night. Place was flat-out empty. I offered him my air mattress to sleep on, but he wouldn't take it."

Sergeant Ade carefully measured the turn of events.

"Where are the guns you were holding for him?" Ade asked.

"Oh, I gave them back to him a few days ago," Deyber explained.

Portwine and Ade decided they'd better go to the Valle Grande and get a firsthand look at the inside of Girly's apartment.

As Bill Orth opened the door to Girly's apartment, both policemen immediately detected the strong odor of bleach. As he walked inside, Portwine noticed three large stains on the carpet.

Each stain had "a slight, reddish tint to it," Portwine wrote in his report.

Aside from the spots on the fiery orange carpet, there was no immediate sign of any struggle. To the contrary, Girly Hossencofft's home appeared quite tidy. The bed was made. Girly's clothes were neatly hung inside her closet. There were no dishes in the sink. An immaculate Oriental desk, embedded with carefully crafted illustrations of "traditional" Asian women, made the place seem only more peaceful.

A banana and a glass of water had been left on the desk along with some joss sticks. Girly had left the food and water as offerings to Kuan Yin, the goddess of mercy.

Girly didn't have many possessions after leaving her husband, but material things had fallen far below other priorities: peace of mind and the absence of fear.

There were no signs of Girly's purse or car keys. With hopes of tracking down a friend or family member, Officer Portwine looked for an address book. Instead, he found a copy of Girly's apartment lease agreement. On it, he noticed the name and address of a contact person, Ernie Johnson.

Portwine found another document, too. It included the name of an attorney, Traci Wolf. Officer Portwine wrote down the names and contact information for Ernie Johnson and Traci Wolf. He also noticed several documents addressed to Girly from the United States Immigration and Naturalization Service (INS).

Before leaving Girly's apartment, Officer Portwine wondered if bottles of bleach might be nearby. He found none.

Surveying the entire carpet, he noticed it appeared to have been cleaned recently. Then, before going out the door, he knelt beside the stains and pressed his knuckle into the discolored carpet.

It felt moist.

5

On September 10, 1999, Detective Michael Fox finished work early in the evening and arrived home knowing that the night ahead was a wild card. The thirty-three-year-old detective was the on-call lead detective, or "primary," that night.

In his six years with the Albuquerque Police Department, Fox had seen more than a fair share of violent crime. With a population approaching 420,000, Albuquerque's crime rate was well beyond the national average, and exceeded that of many larger cities.

Named after the Duke of Alburquerque, New Mexico's largest city was now a royal pain for those fighting the war on drugs. The tremendous flow of black tar heroin, cocaine and marijuana typically came up Interstate 25, into Albuquerque and on to points east, west and north throughout the United States and Canada.

No one doubted that the strong presence of drugs contributed to the area's murder rate, including high-profile cases with names like "The Hollywood Video Store murders" and the "Torreon Cabin murders."

Detective Michael Fox had never been the lead detective

on a murder case. But that all changed shortly after he arrived home from work on September 10, 1999.

Fox got the nuts and bolts from the dispatcher on the phone: A woman is missing. Her friends and coworkers feared her dead.

It was time to get to work.

Although it's located in a fairly busy part of town, the Valle Grande apartment complex at the intersection of Wyoming and Spain Boulevards was typically quiet right around midnight. Residents liked it that way and took comfort in knowing that a security guard located at the entrance to the gated complex helped keep the riffraff out.

However, there were obvious signs of trouble on the night of Friday, September 10. A large number of police vehicles had arrived at the back of the complex. Not just squad cars, but the APD'S Mobile Crime Unit, too. The large police presence had many residents believing something serious had happened.

Inside the Mobile Crime Unit, Detective Michael Fox reached for the phone and dialed the home phone number for Paul H. Spiers. Fox didn't know Spiers, but he knew the man was the on-call assistant district attorney.

It was nearly midnight, and the detective wanted the ADA to sign off on a warrant that would allow police to search apartment 53-D and a green BMW.

A woman was missing, Fox told Spiers.

Her name was Girly Hossencofft.

Paul Spiers didn't exactly have a positive reaction to the story of the missing Asian woman.

In his previous travels around the world as a judge advocate general (JAG) in the United States Navy, Spiers had seen many women overseas play American men for fools, leaving them with empty pockets and broken hearts, especially during his time in the Philippines.

After speaking with Detective Fox, Spiers hung up the phone and returned to bed. He wondered if the missing woman had taken advantage of her husband, then run off. He would soon regret having ever considered Girly Chew Hossencofft in such a light.

At 1:56 A.M. on September 11, 1999, Albuquerque police executed search warrants on Girly's apartment and car.

Presumptive tests for blood conducted on the large stains on Girly's carpet only heightened the concern; the results were positive.

6

Is Girly alive? Is she trapped and in desperate need of help? Where is she?

The questions ate away at Detective Michael Fox.

The lead detective had another worry in the back of his mind. He hadn't had any luck locating one of his witnesses, the woman whose name appeared as an emergency contact on the adoption papers signed by Hossencofft a month earlier, authorizing the relinquishment of his three-year-old son.

The woman's name was Linda Henning. And Detective Fox hoped she hadn't fallen in harm's way, too.

On September 11, 1999, Fox knocked on the front door of Henning's Northeast Albuquerque town house. Located at the back end of a cul-de-sac, the white single-story home was located in Albuquerque's foothills area. The view to the west overlooked the entire city and beyond, to include Mount Taylor, sixty miles away.

This was a great location to watch one of those magical New Mexico sunsets or simply enjoy the twinkling lights of a city at night.

Directly east of Henning's home were the fast-rising desert

hills, which quickly climbed and became the sides of nine-thousand-foot mountaintops.

There was no answer at the door. Concerned about Henning's safety, the detective jumped over a fence and looked through a window. With no sign of anybody inside, Fox noticed a woman's purse on the kitchen countertop. He filed the memory of the purse into the back of his mind and left.

Intent on finding his missing witness, Detective Fox returned to Henning's town house later that evening. Once again, there was no answer at the door. And, just as he had done earlier that day, he jumped the fence and peered through the window.

There was still no sign of anyone. But the purse was gone.

7

Linda Theresa Henning was born in Hollywood, California, on October 10, 1953, and grew up in San Fernando, California, without her father. Her mother married an aerospace engineer when Henning was nine. Many years later, and against her mother's wishes, she reclaimed the Henning name.

If a boyfriend told young Linda that the moon was made of green cheese, she'd believe it, Henning's mother, Diane Booth, once said.

"Then she was devastated when she learned it wasn't."

"She lived and died on the words and acts of her boyfriends," according to a report on Henning's background written by attorney Robert Babcock and quoted in the *Albuquerque Tribune*.

In her excellent article headlined THE OTHER LINDA, *Albuquerque Tribune* reporter Joline Gutierrez-Krueger also further quoted the Babcock report: Henning's "friends speculate such romantic gullibility came from her fervent desire to find the mystery father she lost as a child. . . ."

Still, Henning was driven, a doer who always got things done, and a woman who took in stray cats and rushed to save spiders from being squished.

Babcock was a nationally respected defense attorney and the former assistant United States attorney for New York's southern district. He was hired by Henning's longtime friend Steve Zachary in an attempt to prove that she was a good person who'd been psychologically victimized by Diazien Hossencofft.

Zachary believed Henning was innocent.

"It's like a Manson thing," Zachary told the *Albuquerque Tribune*.

To hire the prestigious Babcock to investigate Henning's case required money and love for Henning. Zachary had both.

By the summer of 1999, Zachary had been a close friend of Henning's for sixteen years. They had also been lovers. But like all of the red-hot romances throughout Henning's life, this one fizzled out, though they remained friends.

"The Linda I knew was loving and caring with consistent behavioral patterns of decency," Zachary told the *Albuquerque Tribune*. "After she met Hossencofft, she became crazy as a loon, someone who believed in reptilian aliens taking over the world, cryogenic pods and government conspiracies. That was not Linda."

Zachary's story of Henning's rapid and dramatic change was simply chilling. He told the *Albuquerque Tribune* that Henning had revealed that she was already allowing Hossencofft to give her injections that Hossencofft told her would keep her young and vibrant.

For Zachary, Hossencofft's seven-page curriculum vitae immediately raised eyebrows, too. And it sure had a lot of typos and misspellings.

In his résumé, Hossencofft listed numerous academic degrees, awards and more than forty medical research papers. Among his lengthy detail of professional employment, Hossencofft's résumé stated he'd worked as a "cryogenics laboratory research chemist" at Stanford University and as the associate director of the "Neocarzinostatin project" at the University of Utah.

Zachary hired a private investigator to check it all out, then urgently faxed the investigator's findings to Henning:

"The guy's a fraud! His name isn't even real. It's Armand Chavez."

But Henning refused to believe it. In fact, Zachary said she went berserk. It was a far cry from the bright, gentle and attractive woman whom Zachary had known when she moved to New Mexico in the early 1990s.

In Albuquerque, Henning had previously teamed with another lover, Michael Harvey, and started their Running Horse clothing line.

Harvey was destined to become an ex-lover, too. But he also remained a close friend. He, too, noticed sudden changes in Henning's behavior after she met Hossencofft.

"Started going to these UFO meetings," Harvey told the *Albuquerque Tribune*. "She said she met this wonderful guy, and that when they made love, he'd turn into a cat. I told her, 'Linda, let's not go there.'"

Henning started telling coworkers that she and Hossencofft were engaged. She'd met him only two weeks earlier. And never mind that she was already living with Greg Ott, her coworker at 21st Century Resources, whom she had planned to marry in November.

That August, according to police records, Hossencofft and a friend, Bill Miller, physically forced Greg Ott out of Henning's home . . . and her life.

"He was weak," Henning later stated.

While there was no obvious sign of foul play in Girly's apartment, police slowly examined the area to make sure nothing was overlooked.

Over a period of days and weeks, it became clear that

there was much more in that tiny apartment than what had initially met the eye.

It all started as Detectives Nick Gonzales and L. T. Gunther slowly crawled upon the crushed orange carpet looking for any clue, no matter how small. As they approached the front of Girly's couch, something stood out as far from ordinary: a stain at the bottom of the skirt of the couch. The smear of dark red appeared to be blood.

Preliminary—or "presumptive"—tests for blood on the moist carpet stains also raised suspicions. They had been positive.

8

Girly told the FBI that she and Diazien Hossencofft became acquainted by corresponding through *Pen Pal* magazine. But Girly's close friend Ernie Johnson said Girly told her that she first encountered Hossencofft while vacationing at Sea World in San Diego, California.

While Girly Chew was a single woman when she arrived in the United States in late December 1992, her status changed just ten days later. The Hossencoffts married on January 8, 1993, in Albuquerque.

Here's this little gal who comes from clear across the world. She deserves a chance, Rosella Ernestine Johnson thought in April 1993.

Johnson had worked for the Bank of New Mexico's branch at Montgomery Boulevard across from the Red Lobster restaurant for about a year. That changed shortly after the bank hired a new employee, Girly Hossencofft.

Johnson, a strong employee, was reassigned to a branch where all other employees had failed: a tiny space tucked away inside a large building.

"It was like a huge warehouse with about four or five stores inside," Johnson recalled.

Since the "in-store" branch opened a year or two earlier, pairs of workers were assigned to it. But most fell to the temptations that idle time produces. The Renaissance Boulevard branch averaged only about twenty customers each day. Employees who'd worked there had often slacked off, killing time on the phone, goofing off, or getting on each other's nerves.

In April 1993, Ernie Johnson and the new kid on the block, twenty-nine-year-old Girly Chew Hossencofft, were sent to the branch.

"She was always immaculate. The way she carried herself, always so neatly dressed, her hair, everything to perfection. You could have put an old sack on her, and she still would have looked cute. She was just so . . . perfect," Johnson recalled.

But it was still a recipe for conflict. The branch was no larger than an average kitchen. Working thirty-five hours a week with the same person inside that small space might seem like some sort of experiment on the human temperament.

Johnson, fifty-five, knew the branch's troubled history but aimed to make it a success.

"They put us both out here, and they're trusting us to do our work. I like to have fun, yet I do my work before I have fun," Johnson told her much younger coworker.

She needn't have worried.

Girly brought a no-nonsense attitude to work. Though the young woman was from the other side of the world, she and Johnson were cut from the same cloth.

"[Even] if she was my daughter, I don't think Girly and I could have been so much alike," Johnson said.

Once the cash was counted in the morning to make sure that it matched the balance from the end of the previous business day, reports still had to be completed, the store had to be cleaned and customers assisted.

Chitchat was the lowest priority. But because the women were so hardworking and the customers so few, they had a lot of time for banter.

Johnson learned that personality bubbled from Girly with laughter and cheer.

"That's what made Girly, her personality. Always happy . . . always laughing."

Within a week of their time together, Johnson learned that Girly loved food and had an eager appetite for learning how to make New Mexican cuisine.

"You have to teach me how to make all this New Mexican food," Girly told Johnson.

Johnson explained how to make cheese enchiladas as Girly meticulously wrote every detail on a piece of paper. Later that week, Girly brought her first homemade enchiladas to work.

"They were good!" Johnson recalled with a smile. Johnson told Girly that several foods could be added to enchiladas: chicken, red or green chili.

Soon she was telling Girly how to make tacos, salsa, even a hominy stew called *posole*. "I'd tell her how to get the hominy, and how to wash it and cook it, and then how to mix it all together," Johnson recalled. "She would always cook a big ol' Crock-Pot of *posole*."

Girly's favorite dish, though, was *pico de gallo*, Spanish for "beak of the rooster," or "tip of the cock's comb." It's a Mexican relish (some prefer to call it a salsa) made with bits of jalapeños, tomatoes, onions, cilantro and lemon juice. Many people put *pico de gallo* on burritos or tacos. It's also a popular dip.

"That's what Girly liked to do. So, my husband got her one of those choppers and she really went to town," Johnson said, laughing.

As is often the case in life, food helped bring these two people closer together.

"We got to know each other. She told me about her life in Malaysia and her family. I told her about mine."

Girly cherished her homeland and spoke about its beauty as if it were a treasure.

"You have to come back with me," Girly would say.

"Sure, Girly, we'll just close down the branch and go," Johnson would tease.

Years later, Johnson recalled the moment with the unspoken *if only* hanging in the air:

"As a matter of fact, I think I probably would have gone back with her for a visit. . . ."

Johnson and Girly did make a less distant trip, though.

"I sort of felt that she was so far away from home, she didn't have anybody here for her," Johnson recalled.

"Doesn't your husband want to go places? Have him show you New Mexico," Johnson told Girly.

"Well, he's already been around here. He doesn't like to get out," Girly replied.

"I'll take you places. I'll take you to Taos!" Johnson said. And she did.

Beneath the laughter, a dark concern took seed within Girly's inner being. Her husband, she began to conclude, was a sick man. Mentally sick—a man with secrets, odd behavior, mysterious disappearances, and an increasing temper behind closed doors.

She wouldn't mention this to her trusted friend, Ernie Johnson. "Because she probably felt like she didn't want to impose stuff like that on me," Johnson said.

So the smiles and cheer continued. Girly and Diazien Hossencofft even began spending Thanksgivings and Christmases at the Johnson home.

Girly did share one deeply personal concern, though. She had not been able to get pregnant. She told Johnson that she'd been going through a variety of medical tests with hopes that she could one day bear the child her husband desperately wanted.

"It never turned out to be," Johnson remembered.

Clearly, Girly was infertile. She was heartbroken. Johnson suggested adoption.

"No, I don't think I want to because, what if the biological mom would ever want the baby back? I don't think I could handle that; getting used to the baby and then having it taken away from me," Girly said.

Johnson assured Girly that the odds of an adopted child's biological mother returning to pluck away the child were slim.

Adoption just seemed to make good sense to Johnson. Girly would make a wonderful mother, and Hossencofft was already a successful doctor, she thought.

"Why can some people have children and they abuse them? They don't want them. And here I want a child so bad, and I can't have one," Girly said.

"Only God knows the reason why things happen," Johnson responded.

One by one, most of the stores around the tiny bank branch on Renaissance Boulevard went out of business. Ultimately, the branch shut down in October 1995. Girly and Johnson were there until the end. Their 2 ½-year tenure far exceeded all other employees' time at the branch.

Their friendship would last until the very end, too.

9

Three days after the last-known sighting of Girly, police finally caught up with their elusive witness, forty-five-year-old Linda Henning.

Investigators were relieved that Henning had not been harmed, that she was not another victim.

In a videotaped interview with detectives on September 12, 1999, Henning shared that she was a caretaker for the ailing Dr. Diazien Hossencofft. She explained that her relationship with the doctor was strictly a professional one. Quite frankly, she said, she didn't even know how to pronounce his unusual name and simply called him "D."

Henning said she had met Hossencofft at a David Icke UFO symposium at the University of New Mexico's Continuing Education Center.

She said that Hossencofft told her that he was dying of leukemia and that he was obviously ill because blood was "gushing out of his mouth." She wanted to help.

Henning explained that she was well versed in the powers of holistic medicine and was confident that natural remedies would benefit Hossencofft. She said she also helped care for Demetri, Hossencofft's three-year-old son.

As he listened to Henning, Detective Fox sensed that she might have been "played" by Hossencofft, that she might have been conned.

But Henning also seemed to have lived her life a professional distance from Hossencofft.

It wouldn't be long, however, before Henning distanced herself from police.

Having provided police with a statement, Henning commenced a game of cat and mouse. She had no intention of speaking to them again. Not now. Not ever, if possible.

Suddenly Henning stopped going to work and stopped living at home.

10

In 1985, thirty-seven-year-old Steve Zachary had life by the balls. Now making $500,000 a year, he was a proven performer in the high-stakes world of selling apparel to the nation's major department store chains, mass merchandisers and discount chains. This included high-end stores ranging from Saks Fifth Avenue, Neiman Marcus and Bergdorf Goodman, and midlevel stores such as JCPenney and Sears, to the well-known discount retailers K mart, Wal-Mart and Target.

And now Zachary had his own business, Steve Zach, Intl., that brokered closeout apparel deals for stores all across the county.

In addition to his house on the beach in Marina del Rey, California, Zachary had two boats, five cars, a condo in Key Biscayne, Florida, and a winter house in Lee, Massachusetts.

The spoils of his success also meant Zachary could greatly indulge in his passion of watching live sporting events. He traveled the world to watch title fights ringside; he went to Super Bowls, Yankee Stadium and Madison Square Garden to watch his beloved Knicks.

He did all of this with "the guys": the other six fellows, who alongside Zachary, started their careers in the world of apparel at Bloomingdale's executive training program in 1967. They called themselves "the Magnificent Seven."

These were days to enjoy cigars and the finest restaurants in New York and Los Angeles. Zachary's live-in girlfriend just happened to be a gorgeous cheerleader in the National Football League.

In these times of splendor, it was not unusual for entrepreneurs to approach Zachary, asking him to finance their businesses. Such was the case in 1985 when two business partners sat across a table from Zachary.

"There's no *meeting* without *eating*," Zachary often proclaimed with his booming voice.

Just as he had done as a child growing up in a Jewish household, Zachary enjoyed people, food and good conversation. This made for the gusto in his life.

This was the Zachary now sitting directly across the table from two business partners inside The Cheesecake Factory restaurant in Marina del Rey.

Zachary listened as thirty-two-year-old Linda Booth (née Henning) and her associate shared their business plan and hopes of securing his financing. The upstarts explained that they specialized in designing women's lingerie and robes. But women's apparel wasn't Zachary's interest. He'd always specialized in what he knew best, men's fashion.

Still, Zachary was intrigued by Booth's enthusiasm, her choice of words, and her enthusiasm for her vision. A quick study, he could tell the woman was intelligent.

And she was striking. "Five feet eight, dark hair, dark eyes, beautiful features. Absolutely beautiful and the intelligence irradiated from her eyes," Zachary recalled.

"And she spoke with authority and confidence, which I love," he added.

Over the course of the two-hour lunch, the conversation branched out to a variety of topics, many not even related to the apparel industry. Zachary was impressed that Booth had a strong opinion about most anything: current events, fashion, health and more. This was no flimsy, indecisive woman simply letting the world pass her by.

Unwittingly, Zachary became nearly entranced by Booth's every move. It was as if she were the only other person in the entire restaurant. Her facial expressions, that intelligence, even the way she moved her hands and arms as she went about cutting her food and eating. So fluid and graceful, "both appendages working in unison like a praying mantis," he thought.

He noticed her habit of inspecting her food by tapping it with her fork. He found it fascinating.

Booth was so damn feminine, and Zachary loved it.

Deliciously interested in this woman sitting directly across from him, Zachary started slowly to cut his steak into thin strips; he pressed his fork into one piece of the sliced meat and presented it to Booth, who leaned forward and took his offering with her mouth.

As Zachary continued to feed Booth thin strips of steak, they continued to discuss their interests and passions.

As the end of the meeting approached, Zachary told Booth and her associate, who also happened to be Booth's boyfriend, that he didn't have much of an affinity for lingerie or bathrobes. But he knew this much: he wanted Linda Booth in his life.

It was love at first sight. And Zachary never hesitated to set out to get what he wanted.

"I am terminating my relationship, and should there be any change in your life, I would be vitally interested," Zachary told her.

Indeed, over the course of a week or two, Zachary set about delicately ending his relationship with his current girlfriend. Always the gentleman, he found her a nice apartment and paid the first six months' rent.

Linda Booth hadn't heard the last from Zachary, though.

A month or so passed with no word from Booth before Zachary had a friend reach out to her on his behalf.

Booth agreed to call Zachary.

"I thought that you were an intelligent girl," he told her over the phone.

If Zachary thought he was being cute when he explained that an intelligent girl would have contacted him after the dinner at The Cheesecake Factory, Booth didn't see it that way.

When Zachary asked her out during their phone conversation, she promptly turned him down.

Finally Zachary decided he had to make a final gesture. He sent a special delivery to Booth: a weed, some rocks and a note. The note said that he'd preferred to have sent a beautiful bouquet of spectacular flowers, but somehow the weed and rocks seemed more appropriate.

Booth laughed. She decided to call Zachary and decided she would go out with him.

"If you ever want to find Steve Zachary, look behind a menu," Booth later said.

And true to form, Zachary took her to a fine restaurant in Malibu, called Splash, for their first date.

After a delightful dinner, Zachary and Booth were in his car when he said that he wanted to swing by the airport to say hello to a friend.

"On our first date?" Booth stated, more like a reprimand than a question.

"It won't take long," Zachary assured her.

Zachary parked in the short-term lot at LAX. The pair went through security and right up to the gate for an Eastern Airlines flight.

"We can't go on the plane," Booth protested.

"My friend's a pilot," Zachary answered.

While Booth first made a quick call from a nearby pay phone, Zachary could be seen speaking with the ticket taker at the gate.

Moments later, Zachary and Booth boarded the jet.

"We'll sit right here on the plane and wait for him. He knows we're here," Zachary said of his friend.

But Booth wasn't comfortable, at all. "Steve, there are people getting on this plane. It's going to leave. We don't belong here," she said.

"Linda, he's in the cockpit. He's got to push buttons, throw levers, prep the plane. He'll be out as soon as he's finished. He knows we're here."

Zachary did his best to distract Booth with constant conversation as the final boarding announcement was heard. And there was no hiding the sound of the entry door sealing, even though Zachary continued to press on with trivial bits of unrelenting conversation.

Then the plane moved; its taxi to takeoff was now under way.

Zachary gently put his left arm around Booth, then his right hand over her mouth.

"Linda," he began, "did we have a nice time tonight?"

"Yes, no doubt," came the reply from beneath the hand.

"Do you think you want to go out with me again?" Zachary asked.

"Up until now, I did" was the soft-spoken reply.

"We've discussed many things, one of which is that we both love Gloria Estefan."

Booth shook her head in agreement.

"Would you like to see Gloria Estefan tomorrow night?"

Booth shook her head as if to say yes, the plane still in slow motion as it moved toward the runway.

"Great. We have tickets to see her in Miami tomorrow night, and we're going there."

After Booth's immediate muffled scream, Zachary removed his hand and revealed the details of his surprise getaway.

He explained that they'd be staying in his three-bedroom condo in Key Biscayne, where Booth could have her complete privacy.

Hoping to reassure her, he explained that he'd already

spoken to her mother and given her a phone number where Linda could be reached.

"But I have no clothes, no makeup," Booth said.

"Whatever clothes you need, I'll buy them. Get all the makeup you want."

When the plane finally touched down at 6:30 A.M. in Florida, Booth was exhausted from the travel and shock of surprise.

Arriving at the condo, Zachary provided Booth with a bathrobe and a room, where she promptly settled in and fell asleep. Zachary left her a cell phone number before leaving to a nearby restaurant for breakfast. A bit later, he returned and enjoyed the new day from his swimming pool while Booth continued to sleep much of it away.

By the time she awoke at 4:30 that afternoon, Booth was well rested and looking forward to the Gloria Estefan concert, where, it turned out, she and Zachary had a wonderful evening. They even got to go backstage and meet the singer and her husband.

For the next two weeks, Zachary and Booth enjoyed the bliss of sun and ocean at the condo. Residents of Key Biscayne tout the area as "the island paradise." They wouldn't get an argument from Zachary, who continued to fall deeper in love with a warm, beautiful and intelligent woman.

11

"Oh, *Caaaatheriiine*," came the long drawn-out query from down the hall inside the Albuquerque Police Department's crime laboratory.

APD forensic scientist Catherine Dickey knew the voice and the implication of its tone. Detective Nick Gonzales always called out for her like that when he had something for her to look at.

Oh, God, what does he want now? Dickey thought.

"I've got the carpet from the Hossencofft case upstairs," Detective Gonzales began.

Enough said. Dickey knew he'd like her to take a look at what he had. And that's exactly what she did that morning of September 14, 1999.

The entire living-room carpet had been taken from Girly Hossencofft's apartment. It now appeared before Dickey, rolled up, in the brightly lit triage room at the crime lab.

Dickey and Detective Gonzales unrolled the carpeting to a point just beyond what was necessary to reveal the three large stains on it.

Investigators had already tested the stains for blood with luminol, a colorless chemical that turns bright blue when mixed with blood. It was actually the oxygen atoms in hemoglobin that triggered the reaction.

While their test results were positive, the detective knew the possible presence of bleach could have produced false positives. And at this early stage, investigators wondered if any crime had even taken place.

"Yeah, she's probably met some guy and she went to Las Vegas and she'll come back Monday morning with a heck of a hangover. And this case will be done," Dickey overheard Detectives Gonzales and Gunther stating.

Still, Dickey knew she faced a daunting task. If any blood had been on that carpet, someone apparently tried very hard to remove it with bleach or some other cleaning agent.

Dickey carefully cut out the three stained sections of carpet so that she could conveniently examine and test the material. And that's when something else caught her eye.

Dickey noticed, away from the three major stains, an extremely tiny and dark stain. As she looked closer, she could see that it was composed of only three or four carpet fibers. And this stain was in a section of carpet that would have been much closer to where Girly's couch had been located.

Because she wondered if the tiny spot was blood, Dickey cut it out and immediately tested it. True to protocol, she took a Q-Tip and dampened it with distilled water. Next she touched the stained fibers with the Q-Tip, which absorbed some of the stain. Finally Dickey completed her presumptive test for blood by applying drops of leucomalachite, a colorless chemical compound, to the swab.

The swab turned teal green, a reaction that happens when oxidation occurs as the chemical reacts with hemoglobin found in blood. The test was positive.

That same day, Dickey focused her attention on strands of hair that came from Girly's hairbrush and wastebasket.

The hair was long and jet black.

Running it through the analyzer would be the first step toward acquiring a possible "standard" for Girly's DNA. If

DNA could be extracted from blood on the carpet, investigators would be able to determine if it matched that standard.

While Dickey examined the living-room carpet taken from Girly's apartment on that Tuesday morning, trace evidence expert Donna Arbogast was asked to take a look at the inside of Linda Henning's Honda Accord.

Had Hossencofft used his girlfriend's car to commit a crime? Investigators considered the possibility.

Arbogast found two items of possible interest: a windshield visor, which appeared to have a few tiny spots of dried blood on it, and a pair of slightly bloodstained panties in a small sack. Henning explained the panties were hers and that they'd been stained during her recent menstrual period.

Arbogast removed a "cutting" from the panties and passed it on to her colleague Dickey, who would analyze the blood's DNA. Indeed, the blood on the panties found inside the Accord turned out to be Henning's blood.

Not that anyone suspected Henning of anything.

"Early on, Linda was really thought to be just the unfortunate girlfriend," Dickey said later. "She's probably going to be the alibi for Hossencofft. She's probably not involved."

12

In the summer of 1992, taking the trash out each morning soon became an engaging prospect for seventy-year-old Pedro Tirado. The HUD home next door had sat vacant for about two years. Suddenly it had someone living in it.

Initially peeking out the window, Tirado caught glimpses of the man working in the yard. In fact, he suspected the stranger was a hired hand.

But it was the conversations that evolved as Tirado took out the garbage each morning that revealed a fascinating new addition to the Delamar Northeast block.

The new neighbor lived alone, at first. When he wasn't mowing the lawn, he was often seen tending to his bonsai, plants he'd claimed to have sculpted personally.

Tirado was six feet one inch tall, with a slim build, a long face and a kind smile. Before moving to Albuquerque in 1976, Tirado lived in his native Puerto Rico. His career as an agronomist for the United States government had taken him to several South American countries.

Tirado spoke with a thick Spanish accent, which oozed with the passion he felt for life. A former professional trumpet player, once called "the Harry James of Puerto Rico," Torado's words now formed melodic sentences.

He was also a man who saw the best in everyone. He moved slowly in his advanced years, but he always moved, and often did so toward an interesting conversation.

He didn't have to go far after the bonsai-growing, charismatic neighbor moved into the two-story green fixer-upper directly next door.

The new neighbor said that he was a scientist. Tirado felt a friendship taking hold.

"Why don't you come over to the house and we'll exchange ideas," Tirado eventually offered.

"Fine, that's fine," said the man who called himself Dr. Diazien Hossencofft. It was a strange name, and difficult to pronounce, at first. Soon, everyone simply called him D.

Hossencofft made his first visit at the Tirado home around 11:30 one morning. He arrived wearing a gleaming white shirt, tie and black jacket.

"He was very well-dressed, impeccably. Per-son-*ALI-TEEE!* He wanted to give the *best* impression," Tirado remembered later.

Tirado was also taken aback by his neighbor's entrance for another reason: Hossencofft bowed to him.

"You don't have to do that in the United States of America," Tirado explained, obviously uncomfortable with the notion that his guest seemed to put him on a pedestal.

"I thought he was freshly from China!" Tirado explained later. "So, I had to tell him how to behave in the U.S. I told him all you have to do is shake hands, and if you are real good friends, you just hug each other."

In short order, Tirado and Hossencofft became good friends, often passing the time together by playing dominoes. Hossencofft came to call Tirado by the affectionate nickname "Papa."

Hossencofft shared that he once had a wife who was severely injured in a horrible car crash. His two little children died in the crash, he said. In time, Tirado observed that his neighbor was a man with many interesting "connections."

On one occasion, a fellow who appeared to be Asian came by the Hossencofft home to discuss a grand moneymaking scheme. Hossencofft and his accomplice spoke of acquiring "forbidden" ingredients that could be "mixed and cooked" into a narcotic.

"For getting high, and this or that or the other things," Tirado recalled.

It wasn't long before Tirado noticed some people keeping a close eye on Hossencofft.

"Two months after he moved into that house . . . there were two FBI people [parked outside in a car]. They said they'd been investigating him for a long time, that he had a long history of crimes, but they had never been able to prove it."

Despite the intriguing, darker side of Hossencofft, Tirado remained enamored with the man's engaging charisma and brilliant scientific mind. "He told me he had graduated from the University of Japan when he was twelve years old. I tell you, he talked in such a way; he had such a vast capacity to absorb information and keep it in his mind. And then he knew how to use it. We talked like scientist to scientist," Tirado remembered.

After a few months, Hossencofft's fiancée, Girly Chew, arrived from Malaysia and married him a few days later.

"She was like a saint. . . . I don't want to talk about her right now because it touches my heart," Tirado said.

The Hossencoffts seemed like a very happy couple. And they wanted a family. That wasn't about to happen any time soon, though. On April 27, 1994, Girly began seeking medical attention for infertility.

Hossencofft kept giving birth to fantastic tales, telling Tirado that he was the "last of the Hossencoffts"—with the exception of an uncle in Germany.

Pedro's wife, the softspoken Luz Tirado, eventually heard

a different story. "He told me that his father was married and living in New York with two daughters," Luz said.

Hossencofft told Luz that he was raised in Switzerland.

"And that one time his grandfather who lived in Switzerland bought him a ticket to visit his father in the U.S. But his father said, 'Well, I cannot have you.' So the next day, he bought him a ticket and sent him back to Switzerland. That's what he told me," Luz said.

Unlike her ever-trusting husband, Luz had a skeptical eye for Hossencofft. She was particularly weary of his statement that he was dying of leukemia.

Hossencofft often said that he only had six months to live. But six months would always come and go. Luz's skepticism only grew as Hossencofft continued to look "the picture of health."

Pressed by Luz for an explanation, Hossencofft said that he went to see a doctor who gave him a treatment that would put the leukemia into remission for up to five years. When that time passed, the next treatment would only give him up to three more years of life. A third such treatment would only offer limited life extension.

While Luz remained unconvinced, the deceit continued to chip away at Pedro's trusting heart.

13

In the second half of the 1980s, Steve Zachary relished the pleasures extracted from the merging of bachelorhood and wealth: sporting events, Friar's Roasts, a buffet of self-indulgence.

"Somehow, I didn't fit in the mall shopping. . . . Women call it quality time," he recalled later.

The constant diet of "guy time" was "not consistent with relationship success," as Zachary later put it.

"She's a very hardworking, very intelligent, very independent woman. But she's also somebody who wanted to have somebody by her side," Zachary remembered of his former girlfriend Linda Booth.

Zachary's money and the security he offered were always present, though. He opened a checking account for Booth when she first moved in with him. Each month, he deposited a thousand dollars into it. After one year, Booth sent Zachary a letter and a check for $12,000.

"I never loved you for your money," Booth wrote.

For seven months, Zachary and Booth enjoyed an unusually quiet time as they cared for a six-year-old girl named Ashley.

Ashley's father was Zachary's friend, a bookie who had gotten into some trouble with the law and was sentenced to seven months in prison. Zachary agreed to take care of Ashley in the meantime. The mother had run off.

Caring for the little girl changed their lives. Nights were at home and quiet. They sent her off to school in the morning, enrolled the child in dance lessons and bought her a pony. A highlight came on Christmas, when Ashley awoke to the excited greeting she'd long wanted: an Akita puppy. Ashley named her Samantha.

The day Ashley returned to her father was both good and bad. It was surely nice to see her joy at the reunion, but sad for Zachary and Booth to let go.

With Ashley no longer in their home that first night, the couple just stared at one another. Booth cried.

"How foolish that Linda and I didn't go forward. She would have been a great mom. I certainly loved kids," Zachary said later.

Soon the constant stream of phone calls, beepers and people revisited Zachary.

"I was deficient in quality time, alone time, holding-hands-and-walking-in-the-park time."

Booth especially grew tired of Zachary's time spent with the late Sam Kinison, then a rising comedic star.

It is not surprising that the romance between Zachary and Booth ran hot and cold. And so it was for four years. Until August 1989.

That's when Zachary got the sobering news that he had multiple sclerosis. A month later, he found himself in hospitals, seeing a variety of doctors, bedridden. Booth remained a friend and offered support. She would have remained his girlfriend, too, if he had let her.

Zachary struggled to walk, a result of poor balance. He required a stool in the shower. He still loved Booth, but he felt it would be selfish of him to maintain a romantic relationship with her. He didn't want her to have to "baby-sit" her man.

In September 1991, Zachary moved back to his native Long Island, New York, and continued to receive medical attention.

His disease went into remission. He had good days and bad days. He even dated. Still, the multiple sclerosis robbed Zachary of all feeling in his left arm and leg. He was given a cane and walker, but he refused to use them.

Zachary required constant therapies. Three times a week, he went to the swimming pool and walked a hundred times across the pool in four feet of water. To fit in with the old ladies in the physical therapy class, Zachary wore a flowered swim cap. The ladies laughed and enjoyed his sense of humor.

Still in the early 1990s, doctors performed a delicate operation on Zachary, hanging him upside down, draining all of his spinal fluid, and then shooting air into the spine so that any tumors could be detected. At the end of the treatment, the spinal fluid was put back in the spine. The procedure was excruciatingly painful.

So were the cluster headaches brought on by the multiple sclerosis. Cluster headaches push outward from directly behind the eyeballs. They are so forceful, they can actually push the eye or eyes outward. Zachary often had one protruding eye and mucus dripping from one nostril. Many people with cluster headaches have lost an eye. Suicide is not uncommon, either.

At night, Zachary slept with the constant, staccato sound of *sshhhh . . . sshhh . . . sshhh . . . sshh*. It was the sound made by a Bi-PAP. Looking like a mini-refrigerator, the Bi-PAP's compressor delivered oxygen to Zachary's body. It was necessary because his diaphragm no longer worked when he was horizontal, yet another complication from multiple sclerosis.

During this time, Booth often flew from California to New

York to visit Zachary. No matter whom they were dating, it remained as if things had never ended.

In 1996, Zachary learned he had sarcoid tumors in his chest and head. Doctors successfully removed the tumors from his chest, but the egg-size sarcoid tumor at the top of his spinal cord had wrapped itself around the medulla, the "motor strip" at the base of the brain that controls the heartbeat and other motor functions.

"It dropped me, totally. Just decimated me," Zachary said.

While living through hell on earth, Zachary continued to listen to Booth as she shared the highs and lows concerning the men who came in and out of her life. Inside, though, he was also listening to his heart.

"She was the girl that owned my soul. She unlocked the combination of what was inside of me. We shared a special relationship that I'd never had with anyone else," Zachary recalled.

Linda Booth loved dolls. She had a passion for collecting Barbies. In 1995, she joined Barbie Friends of Albuquerque and happily paid the $10-a-month club dues.

To members of the Barbie club, Booth really seemed to have it all together: dressed to the hilt, nails always perfect, an extremely attractive, professional woman—a walking billboard for a successful woman.

It was during this time in her life that Booth returned to using her father's last name, Henning.

Pamela Hutton (an alias) joined Barbie Friends of Albuquerque in 1993 and served as its president for two years.

"She always seemed like she had everything going for her. The kind of woman you'd be envious of, in a way," Hutton recalled.

One day, Henning brought Greg Ott, her fiancé, to a Barbie club meeting. Club members found it odd.

"She came to a doll house meeting with this handsome man. When we did doll club things, you didn't bring a guy. We debated whether the club should pay for his meal. Other women didn't bring their men. It's just not real cool to bring a man. It's kind of amusing, though, that she'd bring a guy," Hutton remembered.

Early in her four years with the Barbie club, Henning decided to collect toys for the organization Children of Chernobyl. She had read about a teacher in Ohio who had started the project, and thought it would be great to pitch in.

Once a year, between 1995 and 1999, Booth urged club members to bring in their old "junk" Barbies, then fixed the dolls' hair and gave them new clothes. Matchbox cars were collected for boys.

"Linda spearheaded it. She did all of the packaging and shipping. We sent tons of toys," Hutton remembered.

In August 1995, a new fashion doll was born. Very loosely based on the 1940s actress Gene Tierney, the Ashton-Drake Galleries' new Gene doll became popular nationwide.

Eventually a Gene doll club was formed in Albuquerque. Many members of the Barbie club joined the Gene club, including Hutton and Henning. So did Henning's close friend, Mary Alice Thomas.

"Linda pretty much hung out with Mary Alice all the time. They stuck together like glue," Hutton said.

When the West Coast Gene convention was held at the Roosevelt Hotel in Hollywood, California, several club members from Albuquerque attended. Most flew to California. Henning drove her car because she was from the Hollywood area and wanted to have her own wheels.

The first Academy Awards had been held at the Roosevelt Hotel, and it looked much the same inside for the Gene convention. Everyone dressed in '40s-era attire. A big band blasted tunes from the stage.

Wearing an ivory, low-cut, beaded gown with spaghetti straps, Henning was beautiful.

But as is often the case with doll conventions, this one had about six hundred women and nearly no men.

With the band so loud it was hard to hear, Henning asked Hutton if she'd like to move out to the lobby, where they could hold a conversation.

While sitting in the lobby and sipping drinks, a few hotel guests stopped from time to time to ask Henning and Hutton what was going on inside the ballroom. The women explained it was a dance for a doll convention.

When a handsome man made a similar inquiry, it appeared he might be hitting on the women.

"Linda got so rude. This guy asked the same questions everybody else did. She was just immediately nasty to this guy," Hutton recalled.

The man just happened to be a friend of the hotel manager.

"I'm sorry for upsetting your friend. I don't know what I did wrong," the man told Hutton when they bumped into each other later that evening.

Hutton expressed her surprise, too.

"I don't know why she bit your head off."

One of the last times, if not the last time, Hutton saw Henning was at the Albuquerque Doll Museum.

"She complimented me on my dress. We talked about makeup. She gave me the name of a facial person. She said she was going to get her eyeliner tattooed and said she was going to stop spending money on dolls and start spending it on herself."

14

With no immediate hope that they could have children, the Hossencoffts decided to get a dog.

A blondish red chow seemed to be the picture of health. Once it was weaned, Girly and Diazien provided a home for the dog. It was during this time that Girly Chew Hossencofft turned up on Ernie Johnson's doorstep at seven o'clock one morning.

Right away, Johnson knew something was wrong. She could always see any sign of trouble on Girly's face.

"My girl died!" Girly said of her beautiful puppy.

Girly explained how the young dog suddenly started to convulse and shake. It died before her eyes.

Later, the Hossencoffts got a second puppy, yet another chow. This one disappeared. The animal apparently managed to escape from the backyard.

In February 1996, Diazien and Girly Chew Hossencofft moved into a new home. They didn't move far, just 264 yards. The new house on Moon Northeast was just around the corner from their former home on Delamar.

In addition to his furniture, Hossencofft brought along his wild stories, curious behavior and old habits.

The "doctor," now living on Moon Street, continued to take many trips out of town, going away for days, even more than a week at a time.

It was all part of his calling, he explained. Like it or not, he was the one blessed with the incredible skills to save lives where all others had failed.

Hossencofft returned from trips out of state, explaining that he'd been rushed to operating tables across the country, spending twelve, sixteen or more hours performing life-saving operations on women and children who'd been in horrible car crashes.

Girly continued to enjoy working as a bank teller.

And the Hossencoffts seemed to be financially well-off. Girly was driving a green 1995 BMW, and Hossencofft drove a beautiful Jaguar. Hossencofft told his neighbors he'd paid cash for both cars.

The inside of the Hossencofft home was but lightly furnished, though. There were no signs of luxury, just the modest items of necessity.

One room remained off limits to everyone—even Girly.

"Never go into that room," Hossencofft told Pedro Tirado on more than one occasion.

Hossencofft spent much of his time alone inside the forbidden room and would not reveal what was inside.

After six months in his new house, Hossencofft decided it was time for an addition. He arrived home one day with an infant, a baby Asian boy less than a month old. He informed his wife that they were adopting the child and that his name would be Demetri.

Johnson was blown away by the news of the adoption.

"Ernie, I have a baby," Girly said on the phone.

From all of her previous conversations with Girly, Johnson thought it evident that Girly did not want to adopt.

"A baby? Girly, what are you talking about? Did you get another puppy?" Johnson replied.

"No, it's a baby."

"Girly, where did you get it?"

Girly continued to talk in a hushed voice. "He got it."

"Where did he get it?"

"Through his lawyers."

"Well, okay, what is it?"

"It's a boy."

"Can I come over and see him?"

"Sure! Come on down."

And when Johnson arrived that Sunday morning, she discovered exactly what Girly had reported.

"How old is he?"

"Three weeks."

While she carried on with the child as grandmothers do, a flood of thoughts raced through Johnson's mind.

None of this made sense. Girly had been opposed to adoption. D was dying of leukemia. Maybe he wasn't really dying. Or perhaps his lawyers had pulled some strings. Money talks. And D had money.

During their three years of friendship, Girly had explained that D had inherited a huge trust fund left by his grandparents. The grandparents had raised him in a mansion in Switzerland, and they also owned a large home in San Francisco.

Over time, though, Johnson was finding it more difficult to believe Hossencofft's stories.

In the beginning, back in 1993, Hossencofft had said he was a recent medical school graduate. He explained his frequent trips away from home by stating that he was attending graduate school. Later, he said he was on the lecture circuit. And then, suddenly, he was a member of a team of doctors that traveled the country to perform heart and lung transplants.

No wonder questions were racing through Johnson's mind

as she admired the infant now in the trusted care of Girly and Diazien Hossencofft.

He probably paid someone off, Johnson thought. Careful not to offend or impose on Girly's business, Johnson kept her suspicions to herself.

15

On September 14, 1999, Detective Fox called prosecutor Paul Spiers with a confession of his own.

"Look, I'm not sure what to do. We're getting some resistance from witnesses," Fox revealed.

This was quite a statement from an up-and-coming detective. A more seasoned, crusty cop would rarely admit to such a thing. Concede that you can't do everything? Allow the DA's office to know that the guy over at APD was having difficulty? Never!

But Fox wanted to find Girly. He refused to let his ego stand in the way.

The prosecutor wondered which witnesses were being difficult.

"Like who, in particular?" Spiers asked.

"Linda Henning," the detective replied.

Spiers paused and gave careful consideration to his next move. He knew full well that when push came to shove and witnesses decided not to talk, he couldn't make them. Except with the power of subpoena. And the only way to get that advantage would be to take the case to a grand jury.

"Well, we're going to convene a special grand jury investigation, investigating the disappearance of Girly Hossencofft," Spiers finally said.

Initially Fox's decision to let the DA's office take command of the engine that was controlling the Hossencofft investigation created a bit of friction for him. Within the ranks of APD, a few officers felt the DA's office was usurping the police department's investigation. Fox, though, took comfort in knowing that he had an important ally, his commanding Sergeant Ron Hettes.

Throughout this complex and mysterious case, Sergeant Hettes stood by his detective, signing off on Fox's reports.

Less than a week after Fox told Spiers about his uncooperative witness, district court judge Albert "Pat" Murdoch granted Spiers's request for a grand jury investigation. It was a stroke of great fortune to get approval so quickly. It usually takes at least two months to get approval for a grand jury and three months before that jury even hears the case.

And this grand jury would begin hearing the case in just eight days, September 22, 1999. The investigators felt as if some divine force was overlooking their investigation.

First, bank manager Kathy Semansky had taken the bull by the horns when Girly didn't show up for work. Semansky made sure police knew the situation was extremely serious just minutes after 8:00 A.M., September 10. On that same morning, state highway worker Raymond Gabaldon found Girly's bloodied clothing more than 120 miles from Albuquerque on a remote stretch of Highway 60. All of this good fortune helped the investigation move forward while time was precious. The colder a case gets, the harder it is to solve.

And now a grand jury would hear it all in just days.

There's a scene in the movie *Mississippi Burning* when FBI agent Alan Ward (played by Willem Dafoe) wants to call a criminal investigation into the disappearance of three black men a civil rights case. Ward is a product of East Coast schools and a by-the-book kind of guy.

But FBI agent Rupert Anderson (Gene Hackman) prefers to call the investigation a missing person case. Anderson is from a small Southern town, relates well to common folk, and knows what plays well in Mississippi in 1964. He knows that Ward's approach will only alienate the community.

Spiers thought about that scene in *Mississippi Burning* as he considered naming this matter that he would put before a grand jury.

The investigation into the homicide of Girly Hossencofft was definitely out of the question. Sure, if you wanted a media splash, that would get the attention of local reporters. The state would automatically be on the defensive, too. It had no proof that Girly was dead.

But the biggest problem with that "homicide" word was that it would likely put at least one witness, Henning, on the defensive. And she was already quite an unsettled bird.

Spiers decided to call the matter *The Investigation into the Disappearance of Girly Hossencofft*. He intended to keep witnesses in a zone of ambiguity, feeling unthreatened.

On September 22, 1999, Linda Henning testified before the grand jury for the entire day.

16

Forty-six-year-old Paul H. Spiers had already built himself an impressive résumé.

He joined the United States Navy as a young man, where he served as a JAG from 1981 to 1986.

During his years as a JAG, Spiers started off as defense counsel and argued on behalf of service members charged under the Uniform Code of Military Justice and the United States Code. Later, he traded hats and prosecuted cases. The cases he defended and prosecuted as a JAG included sexual assault, drug importation, passport misrepresentation and kidnapping.

Ultimately, the navy promoted Spiers to senior defense counsel, where he became experienced in handling crimes related to top secret documents.

He held a great respect for the English language and enjoyed reading classic literature as much as he enjoyed *Sports Illustrated*.

Spiers especially admired Flannery O'Connor's short story "A Good Man Is Hard to Find," in which a serial killer approaches a grandmother with a con man's kindness. More than anything, O'Connor's story made Spiers aware that some of life's brightest moments contain seeds of darkness. He became adept at never getting too caught up in any bright moment; instead, a part of him remained wary and watched for signs of trouble.

It should not be surprising that Spiers's affection for words developed early. His father was a retired journalist, who had written for the army's *Stars and Stripes* before moving on and becoming a Pentagon reporter for *Nation's Business* magazine.

While growing up, Spiers noticed that his father always seemed to be reading books about popes and presidents. And he noticed the strong traits of his father's character: an admiration for government and public service, an appreciation for people along life's journey and an empathy for the human story.

Spiers's father also had a knack for selflessness. By observing his father, Spiers learned that if he achieved something good, it's proper to thank those who helped make it happen and remove oneself from the spotlight.

The competitive spirit thrived in Spiers since his boyhood. A lifelong Boston Red Sox fan, he knew that being the very best didn't come easily. Spiers's determination to cross finish lines applied quite literally to his own athletics, namely distance running.

He'd run Albuquerque's Duke City Marathon six times, and tackled the La Luz Trail Run in Albuquerque's Sandia Mountains three times. La Luz is a nine-mile, 4,500-foot climb into thin air and named by one trail-running magazine as one of the twelve most grueling trail races in North America.

"He was very much a gutty guy who liked a challenge," recalled William Copeland.

Copeland, who fought crime for twenty-seven years before his retirement, worked as an investigator at the district attorney's office in Albuquerque from 1982 to 1999.

"His integrity is beyond reproach. And I've been through the fire with him several times," Copeland said of Spiers.

Back when they were investigating several violent crimi-
nals together, Copeland noticed that Spiers welcomed the
"radioactive" cases that other prosecutors would run from.

"He walked that fine line, following the regs, but he kind
of liked it on the edge . . . doing what was necessary to ac-
complish the mission without compromising his integrity,"
Copeland said.

It was those qualities, and the fact Spiers had been a JAG,
that prompted Copeland to nickname Spiers "Maverick"
after the character in the movie *Top Gun*.

Copeland also admired Spiers's stealth approach to the
media. While some in the DA's office sought out reporters
and cameras, Spiers preferred to fly low.

The Hossencofft case converged upon Spiers by chance,
but he was one prosecutor who would not simply walk away
from a daunting "no body" case.

And he aimed to win.

17

At 9:58 A.M. on Thursday, September 23, 1999, forensic scientist Catherine Dickey loaded her first batch of DNA samples from the Hossencofft case into a machine that would analyze it and eventually spit out a unique code.

This initial batch included stains from the panties found in Henning's car and the tiny spot of blood found on Girly's living-room carpet. That spot was so small, Dickey used a machine in the lab's polymerase chain reaction (PCR) room to amplify it, effectively growing more of that DNA until she had an adequate amount for testing.

Before going home that Thursday night, Dickey placed a second batch of DNA into the analyzer at 10:24 P.M. It contained blood found on the blouse, the panties and the tarp found near Magdalena.

When she returned to work Friday morning, Dickey looked at the results from the first batch of DNA. It included the results for what was believed to be Girly's hair. The samples had been taken from Girly's hairbrush and from her bathroom trash. This was how investigators first established a DNA profile, or "standard," for Girly's DNA.

Girly's profile did not match the DNA results for the

bloodstained panties found in Henning's Honda Accord. Nor did Girly's DNA match the blood found in the tiny stain on her carpet. The source of those other stains remained a mystery.

But the ambiguity surrounding the bloody clothes and tarp found near Magdalena would end on that Friday, a time when many people were still praying for Girly's safe return.

Dickey knew that the results from her second batch of DNA would be extremely critical to the future of the investigation. As the results for that second batch began to emerge from the analyzer, Dickey recognized the DNA profile right away.

"I was elated, because I had fit a piece into the puzzle, but I was also horrified because I had basically just confirmed everyone's worst fear, and I was the only one who knew it," Dickey remembered.

"With all that blood, I knew, 'Crap, she's dead.' She really is dead. It's not a missing person case. It's a homicide."

Dickey shared the information with her boss before going home that night, but she didn't tell anyone else.

Why ruin everyone's weekend? she thought.

Catherine Dickey worked through the weekend. On Saturday, September 25, 1999, she set out to identify the DNA profiles for Hossencofft and Henning. Investigators had already taken hair and saliva samples from Hossencofft after his recent arrest.

Henning, while not a suspect, had agreed to come downtown and willfully provided hair and saliva samples after signing a consent form. Also that Saturday, Dickey began to extract DNA from two of Girly's toothbrushes, one from her apartment, the other from her workplace.

Dickey returned to work on Sunday and loaded another batch of DNA into the analyzer at 7:58 that evening. More hard data, the solid type required by courts, emerged from the crime lab on Monday, September 27, 1999. Dickey was stunned by two results.

She now knew whose blood was on Girly's couch and on that tiny stain on the living-room carpet. That it came from the same person was no great surprise.

Everybody had suspected it was Hossencofft's blood.

But it was not.

18

In 1990, the U.S. Department of Energy teamed with the National Institutes of Health and began an ambitious program called the Human Genome Project.

For the men and women in the world of white lab coats and beakers, this was their version of the race to put a man on the moon.

There are about thirty thousand genes in human DNA; the Human Genome Project intended to identify every last one. It also aimed to determine the sequences of the 3.1 billion chemical base pairs that make up human DNA, each pair essentially a step in the DNA ladder of the human blueprint.

The implications for the project's success were mind-boggling; scientists would have the raw ingredients for life. Billions of dollars were at stake. As a result, the government said it would also study the project's ethical, legal and social implications.

Initially the government allotted fifteen years, or until the year 2005, to complete the project. By the mid-1990s, Diazien Hossencofft claimed he'd already figured it out by himself.

Over their many games of dominoes in the mid-1990s, Hossencofft revealed to Pedro Tirado the details of his scientific breakthrough. He had invented a machine that successfully mapped out the entire human genome. Hossencofft said he was on the cusp of making billions of dollars.

To say that Tirado felt Hossencofft was letting him in on something important would be an understatement. Tirado knew that scientists in different countries were racing to map out the genome.

Hossencofft explained that he had protected his invention by separating it into five parts and storing each component at five separate universities across America. Now the time had come to move forward. Hossencofft said that he recently had all five parts taken out of the storage sites and transferred to a laboratory at the University of New Mexico.

Hossencofft told Tirado that the financial return for anyone who invested in his machine would be phenomenal. Everyone would soon be rich. Tirado quietly began investing his savings into Hossencofft's most awesome invention to date.

It would be many years before Tirado learned he had been scammed. "He always had me fooled. He could fool you! He could fool anybody," Tirado stated.

19

Thirty-seven-year-old Catherine Dickey had already seen a lot of death in nearly two years as a forensic scientist at the Albuquerque Police Department. It came with the territory.

While she respected a job that could bring a killer to justice, she equally revered her profession's ability to exclude suspects from suspicion, keeping the innocent out of prison and away from the death chamber.

In addition to science, Dickey enjoyed other passions, too. As a Valencia County volunteer firefighter, Dickey helped save lives. She also served as a mentor for children interested in both forensic science and fighting fires. She volunteered her time with Habitat for Humanity and helped build homes for disadvantaged families. And because she was a master gardener, that meant she also volunteered to answer the public's questions about gardening.

In the early and mid-1990s, Dickey somehow managed to earn two master's degrees while also competing in competitive cycling. The broken bones she suffered in three road races ultimately led to a greater toll: a total hip replacement. After a few years, the prosthetic came loose; its metal shaft already jammed into Dickey's thighbone now rattled as she walked with her newly acquired limp.

Dickey, five feet nine inches, slim, bespectacled, her shoulder-length blond hair usually pulled back to form a no-nonsense ponytail, was very much a student of life.

If she were, on occasion, to enjoy a glass of beer, it would certainly be a stout, rather than a Bud. "I like my beer like my men: warm, dark and with a good head on 'em," she'd once joked.

The discovery of a spot of Linda Henning's blood on Girly's living-room carpet had been a huge turn in the investigation. Since that find, Dickey had also found a small spot of Girly's blood on the carpet, too.

That carpet was now telling a story. How much more might it reveal?

On Friday, October 1, 1999, Dickey and her colleague, fellow forensic scientist Donna Arbogast, rolled out the entire living-room carpet and proceeded to look for every possible clue into Girly's disappearance and presumed murder. Hours upon hours were spent looking for—and removing—every tiny bit of potential trace evidence.

Dickey and Arbogast methodically executed the forensic practice of pressing strips of clear tape against the carpet, then peeling back and removing the tape to see what may have stuck to it. As is common, the tapings removed strands of hair, some of it black, some gray, some neither. Some of the hair appeared to be animal rather than human.

Did Girly have any pets? No. Perhaps a previous tenant did.

Piece by piece, each strip of tape with its sticky collection of hair, dust and other minute particles was applied to clear sheets of plastic similar to the transparency sheets used for overhead projectors.

Dickey and Arbogast amassed a huge collection of those transparent sheets filled with tapings from the carpet. Their efforts began to pay off in short order.

The scientists discovered four more tiny stains of blood scattered in different areas of the carpet. That blood would be analyzed for DNA on a later date.

To stand back and look at the entire carpet, knowing that it had just yielded more blood, Dickey began to consider a scenario for the aftermath of a crime.

Clearly, someone had worked hard to clean the carpet area near Girly's front door. That's where the three large, bleached-out stains were located. And there appeared to be streaky impressions in the carpet, going back and forth, possibly from a carpet cleaner, concentrated in that same front half of the carpet.

If someone had actually attempted to clean up blood, he or she had done an effective job at the front of the carpet. Despite numerous tries, Dickey still hadn't been able to prove the bleached-out areas ever contained blood. All of her presumptive tests had come back negative.

But now, isolated spots of blood were turning up in the back half of the carpet. To Dickey, it appeared someone had felt rushed to clean the carpet.

"They had a mess to clean up, and a body to get rid of," she considered.

And if that were true, the story in that carpet seemed to say something about the assailant's psyche.

Whoever's doing the cleaning is torqued-off because they weren't supposed to make a mess of the crime scene, she thought.

Another breakthrough in the crime lab also began to emerge on that first Friday of October 1999.

By this time, Dickey had seen the results for DNA that came from hairs found on Girly's hairbrush and in her trash, as well as the DNA on Girly's toothbrush. The unique peaks and valleys in the computer readouts had become familiar.

Dickey found the same unique profile on the bloodied items found near Magdalena.

But as she reexamined the results for the stain taken from the shoulder of Girly's blouse, Dickey noticed signs of a "second contributor." In other words, someone else's DNA was mixed in with Girly's blood.

Dickey carefully cut out more tiny dots of blood from the shoulder of Girly's blouse, suspecting some of the drops came from a second person. Next she amped her samples in the PCR room again, growing the necessary amount of DNA for the analyzer.

But once again, the analyzer told her the DNA was mixed. There was more than one person's DNA in the drops of blood.

Over and over, Dickey got the same "mixed" result.

And that's when it all clicked.

Dickey considered the possibility that Girly's blood wasn't mixed with another person's blood, but a different source of DNA. *It's coming from something else,* she thought.

And that's when she tested the dots of blood on the shoulder of Girly Hossencofft's blouse for amylase, a digestive enzyme found in saliva. The presumptive test came back positive.

Dickey re-amped the sample, then programmed the analyzer to provide a DNA printout for saliva.

It turned out the sample still wasn't quite strong enough to produce a result that would hold up in court.

Still, a second DNA profile began to emerge: the saliva, it seemed, came from Diazien Hossencofft.

On the morning of Wednesday, October 6, 1999, top brass gathered outside the PCR room, eagerly waiting for Dickey's latest test results. Word that Hossencofft's saliva may have been on Girly's blouse, mixed in with her blood, had spread. It was not only a disturbing prospect, but, if true, it would be vital evidence in the case against Hossencofft.

Albuquerque police chief Gerald Galvin, APD criminalistics director Ann Talbot, and ADA Paul Spiers were just some of the people standing outside the PCR room, peering in and watching Dickey as she worked.

Feeling more than a little pressure to produce a definitive result, Dickey double-checked, and triple-checked, the results from the analyzer.

At 12:15 P.M., she emerged and told her audience that the results were conclusive. "It's his. The saliva came from Diazien. And these results are good and strong. It'll hold up in court," she told them.

ADA Spiers wondered how Hossencofft's saliva ended up on Girly's blouse, mixed with her blood.

He wondered if it had been some simple act of spitting on Girly. Worse yet, he thought, perhaps Diazien had performed some twisted sexual act on her before her death, or afterward.

20

From the time her husband first brought Diazien Hossencofft home, Luz Tirado never really liked him. Something about the guy just didn't seem to add up. And in due time, the curious man gave her only more reasons to raise an eyebrow.

Hossencofft established a daily routine: He'd take Demetri to the Tirados around noon each day. And seventy-five-year-old Luz would baby-sit while Hossencofft tended to his affairs. Luz found the boy to be a delight, although he did seem starved for attention.

For more than five hours a day and five days a week, Luz, already a mother of six grown children, cared for Demetri. She changed him and fed him. Hossencofft often remained nearby, playing dominoes in the Tirado home with Pedro.

At the end of each day, Girly usually arrived from work shortly after five o'clock.

"Mama, Mama, Mama!" Demetri shouted as Girly arrived.

Luz noticed how tightly the boy had bonded with Girly, and how Girly had grown to love him.

Luz became a keen observer of Hossencofft, too. He enjoyed reading the personal ads in the newspaper, explaining that he was trying to find a girlfriend for his buddy. Strange charges were showing up on the Tirado phone bill, including a dating service and a subscription to AOL.

As the months of caring for Demetri stretched into years, Luz witnessed her husband's attachment to Hossencofft intensify. Indeed, he seemed to be addicted to Hossencofft.

While taking a rest one day, she overheard Demetri ask his father for a glass of water. Hossencofft, who was playing dominoes with Pedro, had an instant reply: "Go ask Grandma."

Luz was near her limit. After 2½ years of caring for Demetri, she felt overworked and taken for granted. She shared her feelings with Pedro when they were finally alone.

A few days later, as Luz lay on her bed reading a book while Demetri napped beside her, Pedro informed Hossencofft about Luz's decision.

"Luz has decided that she can no longer care for the boy. She is tired," Pedro explained as the pair played dominoes.

"I don't believe it. I won't believe it unless she tells me herself," Hossencofft countered.

"Well, you know, D, I am no spring chicken anymore," Luz explained.

From that day forward, Demetri spent his days elsewhere. His father simply dropped him off at the house across the street from his home on Moon Street, and into the care of another elderly woman.

Kari Wyeth (an alias) typically cared for Demetri at her house from noon to 9:00 P.M. each weekday. Hossencofft would come over for dinner, then leave. Demetri would stay.

When the time arrived to take Demetri home, the 2½-year-old often screamed and cried.

"Don't wanna go. I don't wanna go. I like it here! I wanna stay here with you!"

Wyeth knew some of her neighbors must have felt she was crazy. She'd been caring for her stroke-stricken husband, Gary (an alias), for eight years when she took on the responsibility of caring for Demetri. But Wyeth didn't give a damn what the neighbors felt. She could never turn her back on a child.

Perhaps it had something to do with her childhood in Oklahoma. Her mother abandoned her, and her father never hung around, either. Until the age of eight, she was raised by her grandmother, living in a simple house, built by her great-grandfather, located near the railroad tracks. Just as it had existed while in Indian Territory, the home had no electricity or running water.

In 1941, a couple acquainted with her family took eight-year-old Kari into their home. They clothed her and fed her. And loved her.

21

That Diazien and Girly Hossencofft moved from an older home into a newer one might have suggested to some that the couple was doing well, that times were getting better. Any such appearance, however, would eventually unravel in dramatic fashion.

At 5:30 P.M. on January 17, 1998, Hossencofft launched into a violent rage against his wife. He had learned that Girly had sought out his mistress, letting her know that he was a married man.

Hossencofft, who was drinking at the time, began pushing and hitting Girly in the kitchen. He grabbed Girly and held her in a headlock, a move he'd often used in his high-school wrestling days. The grip on Girly's neck was so intense, she nearly passed out. All the while, her husband repeatedly punched her face.

The Hossencoffts' tenant, fifty-three-year-old Shelly Abrams (who briefly rented a room in the Hossencofft home), emerged from her bedroom to grab something from the kitchen and saw the fight begin.

Hossencofft had Girly in a "bear hold," Abrams later told police. Hossencofft pulled his wife by the hair, taking her from the kitchen to their bedroom. Somehow, a dresser fell over and landed on Girly.

Little Demetri could only watch and listen.

Abrams called Pedro Tirado, whose last name she'd always struggled to pronounce, on the telephone.

"Mr. Teedo! Mr. Teedo! Come over here immediately. He's going to kill her!"

Seventy-five-year-old Pedro Tirado didn't hesitate. He did his best to run around the block, where he found Abrams waiting for him outside the Hossencofft house.

"He's going to kill her. Get in there immediately."

Tirado ventured inside and found no sign of anyone in the living room, but he could hear commotion coming from the bedroom.

Thank goodness, it's not locked, he thought as he opened the bedroom door.

Inside, Tirado found domestic violence at its ugly core.

Hossencofft held Girly by her neck and repeatedly struck her against the wall.

"You bitch! You're a liar!" he said.

Hossencofft appeared surprised to see Tirado. But he was so incensed and enraged that he didn't seem to care. He kept pounding Girly's tiny body against the wall.

Tirado threw his frail body between the Hossencoffts. Somehow, that move allowed Girly to separate from the grip of her attacker.

"Run to my home, Girly. Run!" Tirado yelled.

For the moment, Tirado had managed to suppress the force of Hossencofft's rage.

"He respected me in many ways. I was a scientist," Tirado said later.

When police arrived, they found a beaten Girly Hossencofft, her lip cracked and bleeding, her left eye red and swollen shut, red marks visible around her neck, and a large scrape down her left leg, made by the dresser that fell upon it.

Hossencofft was immediately arrested and charged with

domestic violence, aggravated battery on a household member and assault on a household member. He was booked into jail at 6:30 P.M. Seven hours later, he posted bond and walked out.

In filling out the Domestic Violence Victim's Statement while inside the Tirados' home, Girly did not hold back from providing details of the attack. The form also asked if her attacker was using drugs.

"My husband suffers from leukemia and is on medication," Girly wrote.

The case dragged through the court system for more than a year before a judge granted the defendant's motion and dismissed all three charges on May 5, 1999.

The January 1998 incident would not be the only time Girly ran to the Tirados' doorstep in fear for her life.

22

The evening of January 24, 1999, started for the Hossencoffts as it did for many married couples: in bed, watching television.

But the average night began to change with an unusual remark. Hossencofft told Girly that he wanted her to drive downtown the following day and pick him up a menu from the restaurant at the Hyatt Hotel. And make sure you take the freeway, he told her.

Girly considered the request highly unusual, not to mention inconvenient. She had to work in the morning.

After voicing some resistance, she ultimately succumbed to her husband's insistence. Apparently at peace, the Hossencoffts returned their attention to the television. Moments later, Hossencofft got out of bed and started to leave the room.

"Where are you going?" Girly asked.

"To get a glass of juice."

Girly continued watching television. A moment later, the alarm from the garage sounded.

Girly got up to investigate. When she entered the garage, she saw her husband squatting beside her BMW's right rear tire. He had tools in his hands. It appeared to her as if

Hossencofft were attempting to loosen the lug nuts on the wheel.

"What are you trying to do? Are you trying to kill me? You want me to have an accident tomorrow on the freeway?" she asked.

And with that, the second domestic violence attack on Girly commenced. Hossencofft shoved Girly onto the front of the car. She managed to break free and hit the button that engaged the automatic garage door opener. She threw her body to the ground and slithered beneath the partially open garage door. Hossencofft chased after her. He fell down.

Girly repeatedly pounded on Kari Wyeth's wrought-iron door across the street. Wyeth was sewing at the far end of her home; her paralyzed, silent husband sat nearby and watched television. The frantic pounding frightened Wyeth.

By the time she peeked out a window, nobody was on her doorstep.

A moment later, Pedro and Luz Tirado responded to the pounding at their door. It was about 9:30 in late January when Girly appeared barefoot and wearing her nightgown.

"And there she was, shaking. And she said that she was running from D because he wanted to kill her. She said, 'Help me. Help me. He's going to kill me,' " Luz Tirado recalled later.

The Tirados offered a drink, thinking it would calm Girly down, a shot of rum or bourbon.

Girly wanted water. She tried to raise the glass to her mouth, but she trembled so badly, she could not drink.

Having spotted something unusual in her lawn, Wyeth ventured into her yard. She discovered a pair of pajama bottoms with grass stains. The next sight was even more unusual. Hossencofft emerged from the south, taking his time as he walked home. He had no pants on.

"What in the world is going on?" Wyeth asked.

"Nothing. Why don't you tend to your own business?" Hossencofft responded.

"Why don't you do that yourself some time?" Wyeth countered.

Meanwhile, inside the Tirados' home, Girly called the police. And she told the Tirados the events of that evening.

The detailed account was interrupted by a knock at the door. When Pedro opened the door, Hossencofft pushed him against the wall and threw several of Girly's dresses upon the floor.

Girly was already hiding. Luz stood in Hossencofft's way.

"I don't want to see you. Where is she?" Hossencofft asked with clenched teeth.

Hossencofft then revealed his hip and a scrape upon it. "See what she did to me? I don't want to see her again!" Hossencofft proclaimed.

"Well, you are going to see her again because she is going to come with the police and get her things," Luz responded. Hossencofft turned and left.

Girly emerged and expressed her concern about three boxes in the home that contained all of her vital records, including her immigration documents, birth certificate and medical reports.

"That's my life," she told police.

Two officers escorted Girly back to the house on Moon Street that evening so she could retrieve some work clothes, the boxes and some other possessions.

The boxes were missing. Hossencofft said he had no idea where they were stored. Finally an officer located the boxes in the backyard.

Inside the house, an officer reached for a jewelry box.

"That's mine," Hossencofft declared.

"Do you wear earrings?"

"No."

The officer handed the jewelry box to Girly.

She left her husband for good that night.

One day after finding her husband apparently loosening the lug nuts on her car, Girly filed for divorce. She began looking for an apartment. She got a restraining order. And she went to see a doctor.

A court-ordered examination at Presbyterian Hospital's urgent-care facility documented Girly's injuries: numerous cuts, abrasions and bruises. The words "Husband tried to kill her" appeared near the top of the medical evaluation. This domestic violence case would exist until October 10, 2000. Girly would not.

23

Girly hadn't moved far, only 1.29 miles. But the Valle Grande apartment complex was surrounded by a tall fence, and a nighttime security guard was stationed at the entrance gate, a move aimed at reducing crime.

The small, single-bedroom apartment located near the back of the complex had been considered remote and harder to find.

Girly told very few people where she lived, not even her close friend, Ernie Johnson. She allowed her coworker Jesse Grove to help her move in. Grove had vowed that he would protect her, that no one would ever harm her. The younger man acted much like a watchful older brother.

On February 9, 1999, Girly received the temporary restraining order she desperately wanted. The court order made it illegal for Hossencofft to have any contact with her. It was effective through February 2000. Girly provided a copy of her restraining order to her boss, Kathy Semansky.

Talking about the divorce helped. Girly would discuss it from time to time with Semansky, who was going through her own divorce. The two women had something in common, and they continued to bond. They even had a little running bet: whoever got divorced first would buy the other a margarita.

As days stretched into weeks and months, Semansky heard the stories.

Hossencofft wanted to keep their adopted son.

"My God, you've got to get that baby," Semansky urged Girly. But Girly felt only despair.

Whenever she arranged to see Demetri, there were angry phone calls: phone calls before she picked up the child and phone calls after she returned him because she hadn't followed Hossencofft's rules to a T.

On March 27, 1999, Girly signed papers that terminated her right to visit Demetri. She was crushed by her decision, but she hoped it would save her life.

Girly, who earned a modest $19,000 a year, also agreed to pay Hossencofft $100 a month in child support. It made Semansky sick.

"I mean, my gosh, the girl never spent a dime. The only time she'd perm her hair was when she would win a contest here and I would give her a gift certificate or money. She was very, very careful with her money," Semansky recalled later.

Although Girly's fears had compelled her to give Hossencofft what he wanted, she believed she did deserve some of the couple's financial assets. She was living on her own now, and money was tight. A share of the equity in the home on Moon would help her pay her attorney's fees and move on with her life.

Hossencofft also wanted Girly's ring.

"You can't give him that," Semansky said.

"Oh, but he keeps wanting it," Girly replied.

To Semansky, it seemed Girly was clearly rolling over for Hossencofft.

Despite the restraining order, the terror didn't stop. When Girly went to her car in the parking lot at work, she found her windshield shattered. She knew it was Hossencofft's handiwork. While driving home one day, she stopped at a red light. Hossencofft suddenly appeared out of nowhere, shouting and screaming as he stood outside her car.

Hossencofft's threats kept coming. Over and over, he told her she'd be killed and that no one would find her body.

He kept calling the Bank of America and asking to speak with Girly. Because her coworkers knew the situation all too well, they never transferred the calls. And they made excellent witnesses.

Hossencofft was charged with three counts of violating his restraining order. A trial date was set for July 8, 1999. With the possibility of putting Hossencofft away behind bars, the trial couldn't come soon enough for Girly.

Semansky even arranged for a temporary transfer so that Girly could work out of a different branch. The objective was to "hide her out."

24

In 1993, a radio program debuted on the U.S. airwaves and quickly became a huge hit. "Coast to Coast AM" gave its audience exactly what it wanted: thought-provoking discussions on UFOs, unexplained happenings and life after death. And it all came in the middle of the night, when its millions of listeners were usually alone with their radios, their thoughts and the dark.

From 1993 until the end of 2002, Art Bell, with his deep baritone voice, guided his listeners through the mysterious sojourn into the unexplained—broadcasting live from Nye County, Nevada. Bell soon became a household name.

In the beginning, "Coast to Coast AM" pondered conspiracy theories concerning a New World Order. But that line of discussion came to a sudden halt in 1995, after the Oklahoma City Bombing. Some people blamed Bell for feeding the minds of crazies like Timothy McVeigh. The critics included Steve Benson of the *Arizona Republic,* who pointed the finger at Art Bell in a political cartoon.

Bell did change the program's focus, leaving behind the New World Order for the exploration of UFOs, aliens and the unexplained. Instead of the New World Order, Bell latched onto a new term that held a sense of pending doom: the Quickening. When tragedies such as airplane crashes, floods and earthquakes unfolded, they were signs that the Quickening was closing in.

Just as he had legions of fans, Bell also had his critics, and they primarily existed in two camps. Some detractors believed he was a harmless kook providing insomniacs with a way to pass time in the night. Others feared that his program might propel his followers to act out in dangerous ways.

What could not be debated was Bell's commercial success. While he sat at the microphone in the Las Vegas suburb of Pahrump, Nevada, the number of radio stations airing "Coast to Coast AM" grew to an impressive 530. When he left the program at the end of 2002, he had more than 15 million listeners.

Bell's fans held UFO meetings around the country, including a group that gathered each Thursday more than six hundred miles east of Bell's Kingdom of Nye.

Minato's Japanese restaurant on Montgomery Boulevard in northeast Albuquerque provided a perfect setting for people who wanted to meet for lunch and discuss UFOs, conspiracy theories and the paranormal.

"It was an ideal place to meet and talk because we were screened from the public," group member Alexis Holland (an alias) recalled later.

The "UFO Group," as it came to call itself, met in the restaurant's Tatami Room, where members would close the sliding divider wall that afforded the group the privacy it wanted. Just pull the cord, and the partition slid into place.

Holland was a registered nurse whose work experience included caring for psychiatric patients. She'd recently returned to New Mexico after living in Durango, Colorado. She was about to celebrate her forty-fifth birthday when she joined the group in early 1999. She was curious about the subject matter and wanted to learn more.

"A lot of people in the group were big Art Bell fans," Holland said.

Members of the UFO Group removed their shoes before entering the Tatami Room. Once inside their private space, they could freely discuss UFOs and aliens without fear of being overheard.

On April 2, 1999, several members of the UFO Group attended author Chris O'Brien's book signing event. O'Brien was a nationally known author who wrote about cattle mutilations and other paranormal subjects. The UFO Group members didn't have to go far to see him, either. O'Brien signed his latest book at the Page One bookstore, less than 200 yards up the same street from Minato's.

The UFO Group was not only impressed with O'Brien, but also with a woman who had attended his book signing. The articulate woman had a sharp mind and spoke with passion about UFOs. Members of the group invited her to their weekly meetings. Her name was Linda Henning.

Holland vividly recalled the day Henning joined the UFO Group and remembered being extremely impressed with the new member. Henning was immaculately dressed. Her hair and makeup were perfect. To top it all off, she was very intelligent.

"I was almost intimidated by her. She seemed like a high-powered businesswoman," Holland remembered.

Henning was primarily interested in discussing the Free Masons, UFOs and aliens, especially reptilians.

"There were some other people in the group who had knowledge of the reptilians, but it was all new to me," Holland recalled.

Reptilians, according to their believers, are aliens who shape-shift between reptilian and human form.

Henning became a regular at the UFO meetings and continued to impress members with her knowledge, strength and beauty. That spring, she even brought her fiancé to a UFO meeting. Holland remembers the man was tall, blond, very good-looking and lived in Arizona. That man was believed to be Greg Ott. But he never returned for another meeting.

"And then she showed up with 'Dr. D,'" Holland said with a rising, emphatic pronouncement.

As Henning's guest, Hossencofft wasted no time making a memorable first impression.

Sitting directly next to Holland, Hossencofft spoke in a strange, high-pitched, almost boyish voice and declared his most impressive background.

"Which included that he had several Ph.D.s and that he was an M.D. and that he spoke a number of different languages," Holland recalled.

UFO Group member Rick Carlson later recalled that Hossencofft claimed to be a ten-thousand-year-old doctor of genetics who was warning that the world was about to be attacked by aliens. According to Carlson's statement to police months later, Hossencofft said the aliens would kill most of the world's population by poisoning the drinking water and that only a select few living within certain vortexes would survive. The vortexes were allegedly located in Colorado Springs, Colorado, Laramie, Wyoming, and Charleston, South Carolina.

The psychiatric term "very flat" came to Holland's mind as she listened to, and observed, Hossencofft. Though high-pitched, the man's voice was monotone. There was no joy in his voice or face; in fact, no emotion at all.

This guy is a wacko, she thought. *This guy's a psychopath.*

Still, the odd man dressed extremely well.

"He was like Mr. *GQ,*" Holland said.

At future UFO meetings, Holland noted Dr. D's expensive shoes just outside the Tatami Room. She could always tell if he'd arrived at the meeting ahead of her just by noticing his shoes among the sneakers, sandals and other less expensive footwear.

As turned off as she was by Hossencofft, Holland noticed that the strange man had the opposite effect on Henning.

"After she met him, she was in a state of euphoria."

Aside from Henning, no one in the UFO Group believed what Hossencofft was selling.

"She bought it hook, line and sinker," Carlson said.

The popular conclusion was that Hossencofft was a fraud. And that Henning was, among other things, his meal ticket. While most members spent about $8 for lunches at Minato's, Henning paid more than $60 to feed herself and the man she seemed to worship.

The guy who told the UFO Group that he was dying of leukemia also happened to eat like a horse.

The men and women in the UFO Group quickly became cautious when questioning Hossencofft's credentials. Henning would rush to his defense and was quite offended when anyone doubted Hossencofft's greatness.

But the rapture seemed to take a toll. Henning's appearance soon became disheveled. She didn't seem to be taking care of herself any longer. And the way she spoke became excited and intense. Holland, who'd worked with several psychiatric patients over the years, saw it in a more clinical way.

"She had a pressured speech."

25

As the owner of the Albuquerque Health Club, thirty-
seven-year-old Pat Nichols had seen a lot of interesting people come and go. None were quite like Diazien Hossencofft,
the diminutive Buddhist doctor who'd wasted little time in
sharing that he was dying of leukemia and only had three
months to live.

Hossencofft often spoke about his divorce; "she" was
doing it to "him," and it was costing thousands of dollars in
legal fees. Hossencofft was obviously very angry.

"Diazien, you've got months to live. My goodness, don't
waste it on this. I mean, spend time with your son," Nichols
advised.

Meek, sickly, sweaty and pale: That was Hossencofft. And
no matter how high the temperature, the guy always wore
sweatpants and a towel tucked around him.

By the summer of 1999, Hossencofft had been roaming
the health club for nearly a year. And he'd long told a grip-
ping tale that had the club owner's heart pumping with sym-
pathy: Hossencofft had shared that he was going through a
series of three blood transfusions, but he was running out of
money to pay for them. He said he needed $90,000 to stay

alive. He never directly asked Nichols for the money, but there was an unspoken request of sorts. Nichols gave Hossencofft about $300.

"And I guess he did get one of the three treatments from what he told me, which I guess explains why he didn't die within three months," Nichols later said.

Over many months, Hossencofft and Nichols shared intense discussions at the club. Nichols, a devout Christian, sensed a prevailing guilt and fear in Hossencofft. It came out as Hossencofft shared that he'd worked for the CIA and had killed tens of thousands of people in Third World countries with chemical warfare.

As Nichols explained that all sins can be forgiven through Jesus Christ, he felt Hossencofft walking a spiritual tightrope, an attraction to the notion of being saved tempered with a fear that he might burn in hell for his sins. Hossencofft said he could see it no other way; if what the Bible said was true, then he'd surely burn in hell for his war atrocities.

Overshadowing his moral dilemma was Hossencofft's grim pronouncement that in the year 2007, government authorities were going to destroy two-thirds of the world's population.

It was during this time and through this club that Hossencofft met Linda Henning.

Nichols's health club had a new sales rep from 21st Century Resources, the company that managed the club's payroll. The sales rep spent a lot of time, though, in Phoenix. So, he'd often send his coworker Henning to the health club to pick up the payroll.

As the weeks passed, Nichols learned Henning and the sales rep had become engaged.

Henning began to work out at the club. And in time, she confided in Nichols and shared her belief that "the end times" were closing in.

"You sound a lot like a guy that comes in here," Nichols said.

Henning listened as Nichols spoke of Hossencofft and his prediction of global doom.

She got noticeably excited. She asked a lot of questions about the man Nichols described.

Yes, yes! What she was hearing about Hossencofft's proclamations was absolutely true. She blurted something out about some group that really ruled the universe. She said she had proof. Could Nichols tell her where Hossencofft lived?

"No, I don't know where he lives. I haven't seen him in a couple of weeks, maybe a couple of months."

But Nichols did have Hossencofft's business card. He gave it to Henning.

"And she got very excited and kind of ended our conversation, got up, and I'd say ran out," Nichols later said.

Just how Henning first arrived at Moon Northeast is not clear. The story going around the UFO Group was that one of its members, Bill Miller, had given her a ride to the house. Miller, though, had his own exact version of how he and Henning came to meet Hossencofft. He said it all began in late July or early August of 1999 and went as follows:

"Can you come over here? Let's see if we can help this guy," Henning told Miller on the telephone.

Miller went to join Henning at Moon Northeast and found the object of her dire concern: a guy on his deathbed who was hooked up intravenously, and bleeding, and throwing up blood. Henning said she'd heard about Hossencofft at the health club. The club owner had given her his address.

Miller discovered a little boy named Demetri. His heart went out to the child.

"This guy's in bad shape, he has no money, his wife deserted him, and they have no food," Henning told Miller.

Miller chipped in with some cash to help buy food. He brought over videos for Demetri: *The Lion King, Beauty and the Beast,* some John Wayne flicks, and *Braveheart.*

Over time and between heaves of blood, Miller listened to

Hossencofft's stories: he was dying of leukemia, he was an alien from the Gigaplanet and he was thousands of years old.

Heck, Miller thought, *this guy's like that fella in that* Highlander *movie, a man who just keeps living forever.*

Hossencofft wasn't done. He had a long list of credentials. He was an expert in genetics, he had six master's degrees, he'd genetically engineered his son, he spoke several languages and he was a professor at the University of New Mexico. Indeed, a "student" stopped by from time to time. Hossencofft was helping the young woman study to become a medical doctor.

Only once did Miller hear Hossencofft say anything negative about his soon-to-be ex-wife. It happened immediately after Demetri kissed a picture of Girly.

"Mama, Mama," the boy said.

"That's not your mama. Put that picture away," Hossencofft said.

Next he turned to Miller. "Somebody oughta put that bitch away."

Although he felt creeped out by Hossencofft, Miller maintained contact.

How can I leave if this kid's not eating? Miller thought.

William Henry Miller, known as Bill, was born February 26, 1950, in Jamaica, New York. He initially attended Kent State University, but found it to be too big.

Miller left Kent State the year before the infamous May 4, 1970, shootings on that campus; the Ohio National Guard fired on students protesting the Vietnam War. Four people were killed, nine injured. Miller later said his former roommate at KSU had been shot through the mouth in the melee.

By 1970, Miller had already discovered a smaller, quieter college. He found it in Las Vegas, New Mexico. Surrounded by forested mountains and fresh air, New Mexico Highlands

University offered the perfect setting for an outdoorsman in pursuit of higher learning.

Miller played for the football team and played some rugby, too. He studied world history and respected the oft-said quotation that to ignore history is to repeat it.

Miller had studied to be a history teacher, but he learned the pay scale was too low. He knew he could make more money with his hands. His talents included electrical work.

On December 13, 1976, Albuquerque police arrested Miller for grand larceny. His booking photo shows a rugged, bearded, twenty-six-year-old William Henry Miller in a T-shirt and overalls. His thick, dark hair appears combed across his head and wings out in thick, uplifting curls to each side of his face.

He was never convicted. Miller ultimately spent about twenty years working for the state's largest school district, Albuquerque Public Schools. He specialized in maintaining and repairing the district's air-conditioning and heating units.

By the late summer of 1999, Miller had a thickly lined face, thinning salt-and-pepper hair, a wife of twenty years and two teenage children, one girl and one boy.

The retired electrician took on odd jobs when and where he wanted. His wife, Nan, brought home a steady check. She was a schoolteacher. The Millers lived in a single-story home in a slightly older, middle-class neighborhood.

Miller drove a 1986 Ford F150 pickup truck; each family member drove a separate vehicle. The guys drove trucks.

Miller liked to hunt. Elk were a favorite target. Forty-eight-year-old John Buckles was Miller's hunting buddy and friend of twenty years. The two met while working together at the school district. In addition to sharing some occasional hunts, the pair also enjoyed bike riding together on Albuquerque area trails.

Buckles counted Miller as one of his best friends.

"Bill is one of the best human beings I think I know, personally. I would trust Bill with anything. I think he's a good family man. . . . I think Bill's a fine human being, I really do," Buckles said.

To many people in Albuquerque's Northeast Heights, Miller was a kindhearted, gentle giant, the kind of guy who could easily strike up a conversation with a stranger, and step right in and help wherever it might be needed. And he was known to be really good with kids. For years, Bill Miller had helped coach his daughter's soccer teams.

That public account of Miller was in sharp contrast with impressions shared by members of the UFO Group.

At the UFO club, everyone received an opportunity to talk about his or her topic of interest: cattle mutilations, aliens, UFOs, Black Hawk helicopters, parapsychology, etc.

Miller's thing was the looming threat of a government takeover, not a foreign government, either. Watch out, your rights and civil liberties are in jeopardy. Be prepared to fight.

Miller passed out literature on the government threat. No one in the group seemed to think Miller was actually a card-carrying member of any militia, not as far as anyone knew. He simply didn't trust the government.

Some thought he made some reasonable points. Look at the massacre at Waco.

The approach of Y2K only added fuel to Miller's fears. New Mexicans, especially, must be prepared to defend themselves, he warned. Hadn't anyone noticed the large number of military bases in New Mexico? Better be ready. Looks like the government is going to run roughshod over the "Land of Enchantment." Don't be surprised if New Mexico is the first test case for the government's takeover.

UFO Group member Alexis Holland never really liked Miller. Holland said she once told Miller about some financial difficulties in her life, and upon hearing it, Miller launched into a mysterious story. She says Miller said he'd previously lived outside of the country, then had a difficult time getting back in. He explained that once he did get in, he'd lived at YMCAs, made calls from phone booths, struggled to get a driver's license and a job.

Holland wondered if Miller had been involved in some "nefarious activities."

She'd also heard he was a family man. Holland didn't buy it.

According to Holland, the UFO Group finished its meeting one day and drifted across the street to the Page One bookstore for coffee and dessert. This was the way the group often ended the afternoon.

"He was creepy," Holland later said.

She said she continued to attend the UFO meetings, but made a point of not making eye contact with Miller. She stopped going to Page One with the group, too, although, she said, Miller kept asking her to go.

Miller's years in the UFO Group did produce friendships with several of its members, including Peter Eckberg, Rick Carlson, and Ron Wilkin.

Eckberg seemed to be Miller's closest friend. He helped publish a tiny newspaper called *The Free American* and hosted a no-budget, community-access television program by the same name.

While many of the UFO Group members had known Miller for years, few had ever met his wife.

"I know his wife's not aware of all his varied interests in the paranormal. . . . She's totally oblivious to his situation with Hossencofft and has no idea of what's going on at all, and neither do his children," Carlson said.

"The one thing that I definitely know is that he wants to move out of his house. . . . He's wanting to divorce his wife," Wilkin said in the fall of 1999. "He kept saying his wife would never believe half of what he talks about, and she's pretty much not in the know, so to speak. She doesn't get any of this at all. . . . And even if he told her, she wouldn't believe him, and just brushes him off."

It didn't take long for the Henning-Hossencofft-Miller clique to form, although some viewed Miller as a third leg. Miller, like Henning, often defended Hossencofft when group members suggested he was a fraud.

As the summer of 1999 snaked forward in the high desert, the trio spent a great deal of time together. In a dry and dusty riverbed called the Rio Puerco, Miller practiced target shooting with Hossencofft and Henning. He'd provided them with guns for their keeping.

Also in mid-August, Miller took Henning to visit his friends who lived in a remote area outside Magdalena. Henning and Miller spent the night.

And coincidence or not, something interesting happened that summer: Miller and Hossencofft put their homes up for sale. Henning prepared to put her town house on the market.

In explaining his desire to move, Miller told members of the UFO Group that he wanted out of New Mexico because of the potential government takeover. But he told his wife he wanted to move because some of his neighbors weren't taking good care of their homes and some loud dogs were a real bother.

Alexis Holland believed there were two Bill Millers: the public persona and the one lurking in shadows.

Ron Wilkin saw a bit of both. "He's not a bad person at all. He's really a neat guy. He just gets suckered into stuff, but he's definitely got his own thoughts about things. He's not easily swayed. But he has a flare for the important, or the secret, the black-ops-type thing. He's definitely motivated . . . to investigating it."

As August gave way to September, Wilkin invited Miller over to evaluate a power problem at his house.

Miller couldn't figure out what was wrong with the solar- and wind-powered home, but Wilkin later said the handyman made an outrageous comment. According to Wilkin, Miller shared that he'd been recruited by Hossencofft to "kill his ex-wife."

Wilkin said he asked Miller if he'd told anybody about the proposed hit. He said Miller told him no.

The response, Wilkin said, was "really bizarre."

It was on the first day or two of August 1999 that Steve Zachary appeared to be getting some great news on the telephone from his longtime friend Linda, who was now actually using the last name of Henning.

Henning told Zachary that she had met a remarkable doctor. Dr. Hossencofft's unique abilities could free Zachary of his brain tumor and multiple sclerosis. It sounded too good to be true.

"Linda, give me a break," Zachary told her.

Still, Henning was adamant. She wanted Zachary to come to New Mexico where Dr. Hossencofft could examine him and heal him.

"Send me his résumé," Zachary said.

When Zachary got a look at Hossencofft's seven-page curriculum vitae, he found it suspect from the start.

"It had a multitude of typographical errors. In my estimation, it looked copied from a book," Zachary said later.

He sent it to a couple of friends "with more degrees than a thermometer" to evaluate the résumé. "The friends said, 'No way.' "

Zachary, always direct and to the point, spoke to Henning on the phone and told her what he thought about Hossencofft. He told her the guy was a fraud, that Hossencofft probably didn't even have enough brains to fill the head of a pin.

"She went berserk and used language that I have never heard from her. All of a sudden, I had a torrential flow of faxes coming my way, warning me that the end of the world was coming . . . stuff about cryogenic containers, reptilians and robots attacking."

Zachary thought the faxes read like the movie *The Matrix*.

"You've compromised his position with the NSC, the NSA and the CIA," Henning told Zachary.

"He's not even with the Triple A!" Zachary replied.

"He's decided we're going to have to have you killed," Henning warned.

"She just kept on calling and yelling and threatening."

Zachary was beyond stunned. This was not the Linda he had known for the better part of fifteen years, the woman who rushed to the aid of spiders, birds and cats. This was not the sweet lady who helped care for a six-year-old girl.

This Linda seemed to be possessed.

Two weeks after an excited Henning ran out of the health club, owner Pat Nichols received a phone call from Hossencofft.

Hossencofft explained that he'd just been released from the hospital and that his house was for sale.

"My wife and I are looking to buy a house. Mind if we come take a look?" Nichols asked.

"No, please do, 'cause I need to sell it."

As Nichols and his wife approached the house on Moon Northeast, they immediately noticed Henning's car pulling into the driveway.

As the Nicholses approached the door, they could hear the loud laughter of Hossencofft and Henning coming from inside. When Nichols knocked, the laughter stopped.

A moment later, Hossencofft answered the door, appearing quite sick. The place was a mess, and it smelled like dirty diapers. Nichols noticed Henning's purse and keys right there inside the home. He wondered where Henning had gone, but he did not ask the question.

Hossencofft provided a tour of his home. Henning was nowhere to be seen.

Hossencofft played show-and-tell with some medical equipment. He held up a book on oxygen therapy, explaining that he'd been going down to Mexico for treatment because he couldn't get it in the United States.

At the end of the tour, the Nicholses sat on the couch. Demetri Hossencofft, who looked too old to be in diapers, sat on Mrs. Nichols's lap.

The child's diaper smelled soiled. His father smelled drunk.

Hossencofft said that he'd been trying to find someone to adopt Demetri. When the conversation turned to the value of the house, several red flags went up in the Nicholses' minds. Hossencofft explained that he owned it free and clear. He said it had $250,000 worth of furniture inside.

Pat Nichols gazed about the sparsely furnished home as if to ask, *What?*

Hossencofft pointed to a picture on the wall.

"That's a thirty-five-thousand-dollar picture," he said.

Nichols knew he could go down to the mall and buy it for $35.

During all of this, Demetri kept getting up and down from the couch, disappearing to another part of the house.

"Mommy, Mommy!" he'd say.

Hossencofft wasn't finished. "This Oriental rug is worth fifty thousand dollars. It's a hundred years old.

"That garage has ten thousand dollars' worth of curtains stored inside.

"This is a seventy-five-thousand-dollar vase. It's pure gold."

Nichols and his wife gave each other that knowing look; they both knew Hossencofft was lying to them. This was getting really weird.

"Well, we're going to go," Pat Nichols said.

As they walked out, Nichols wondered what had happened to Henning.

Then he thought he'd forgotten his sunglasses inside the house. When he went back inside, he ventured into the bathroom at the back of the house, thinking he'd left his sunglasses in that room.

He didn't find his sunglasses. He did find Henning.

"Hi, Pat" was the nonchalant, matter-of-fact remark.

"Hi, Linda," said Nichols, who then turned and walked out.

"Did you find 'em?" Hossencofft asked at the front door.

"No. I found Linda, though," Nichols said as he walked out the door.

26

Living alone and feeling hunted, Girly decided to prepare for the worst: hand-to-hand combat.

On June 26, 1999, the mild-mannered woman enrolled in karate classes. At first, Girly appeared timid. But in time, she embraced her karate lessons and became a devoted student; she was never late for class and often practiced at home.

Lead instructor Jesse Lucero respected Girly's determined effort. Instructor Barbara Flores, who'd survived years of domestic violence, empathized with Girly; she knew the fear.

At work, Girly continued to wear a friendly smile as co-workers began to notice the defined muscle emerging in her shoulders and legs. They playfully complimented her. They were impressed.

Girly had approached her karate lessons as she did everything else in life: head-on and with gusto.

She had also made her intention quite clear to her instructors. She'd said she wanted to learn how to protect herself against two attackers.

While Girly took up karate on that final weekend of June 1999, Bill Miller and Linda Henning traveled together to Pagosa Springs, Colorado.

The reason why is not clear.

July 8, 1999, was a day Girly had looked forward to. This was the day her estranged husband was to go on trial for violating his restraining order. Perhaps a judge would put Hossencofft away behind bars and she could rest a bit easier.

The trial was postponed. A new date was set: September 24, 1999.

27

Was Girly dead? Was she clinging to life somewhere and crying for help? Who had attacked her in her apartment? How did they get in? Was it someone she trusted? Where was she now? Where was her estranged husband?

A severe sense of urgency permeated the Hossencofft investigation as events seemed to unfold at a blinding speed.

Girly's bloody clothing was found near Magdalena; her identification turned up on a street a short distance from her apartment; Linda Henning had seemed a rather benign witness, but now she was avoiding police.

Police and prosecutors began working from 6:30 A.M. to midnight. An awareness that they were up against someone intelligent and evil took hold. Every lost second could give a killer an opportunity to do more harm, and to eliminate evidence.

Detective Fox spent hours constructing detailed search warrants, and then reviewing them on the telephone with ADA Spiers. Everything was searched: homes, vehicles, storage units, and safety-deposit boxes.

Strange findings began to emerge.

Hossencofft's divorce attorney had attempted to adopt his

son, Demetri. The divorce attorney's mother had attempted to buy his house.

Peculiar things were being said: Standing outside the grand jury room as Henning testified, Miller turned to Detective Pete Lescenski and asked if bloodhounds could find a body buried six feet underground.

Out of nowhere, Hossencofft started making phone calls. He called his divorce attorney, the adoption case worker, and Kari Wyeth, telling all of them that he knew they were talking to police. All three women felt threatened.

Hossencofft's calls were traced to the East Coast. On September 21, 1999, the FBI tracked him down in South Carolina and charged him with three counts of making telephone threats over state lines. It was enough to hold Hossencofft while investigators raced to take more severe charges to a grand jury.

Could Spiers and Fox prove that Hossencofft was responsible for Girly's disappearance?

Investigators discovered that Girly had a safe-deposit box. When they searched it, they made a discovery that more than opened their eyes.

28

Girly always tried to do what was right. She respected people, their boundaries and their privacy. Before fearing him, she respected her husband.

In between the respect and fear, there was suspicion.

Hossencofft had always told his wife to stay out of one room inside their home on Moon Northeast. She honored that request.

Until one day, date unknown, when Girly decided to venture inside the forbidden room. Perhaps it was when she learned that her husband had been having an affair; maybe it was during one of his many extended out-of-state trips.

Inside the banned area, Girly found a three-page written letter to her husband from an Albuquerque attorney. The letter revealed a horrible truth: Girly's entire marriage had been built on lies.

In the letter, Girly learned that a court had ordered her husband to stay away from another woman.

There was much more. The sensational sentences appeared one after the other:

> *"The truth about you . . ."*
> *"Your given name is Armand V. Chavez. . . ."*

"You have at least four different Social Security numbers. . . ."

"We also have evidence that you attempted to poison a woman. . . ."

"Impersonating a physician: Under the guise of 'research,' 'gene therapy,' and 'cancer eradication,' you have been drawing blood . . ."

The letter in her hands confirmed what she'd been feeling deep inside of herself. This was beyond deception. This was evil.

In the days that followed Girly's disappearance, Detective Lescenski went to the Bank of America, where he'd learned Girly had not only worked, she'd kept a safe-deposit box.

Inside the safe-deposit box, Lescenski discovered a copy of the three-page letter Girly had discovered in the forbidden room.

"Hossencofft." To Paul Spiers, the name seemed invented by someone desperate to seem important, someone who lacked stability. When he learned about the letter discovered in Girly's safe-deposit box, the prosecutor realized Hossencofft was not just a suspect. He was a con man.

29

Armand V. Chavez Jr. was born on March 5, 1965, in Houston, Texas. No doubt Yolanda and Armando Chavez Sr. loved their baby boy very much. But little Armando's world would not always be held together with the immediate affection that fills a delivery room.

According to Stanley Chavez, his half brother, Armando Jr.'s life changed drastically before he ever reached the age of ten. His parents not only split; Armando Jr. and his older sister, Susan, were soon leaving Texas with their father, destined to begin a new life just outside of Phoenix, Arizona, where their father remarried.

"To be . . . removed from your mother at six or eight years old, that's got to leave some kind of scar," Stanley Chavez remarked during a television interview at an Albuquerque park in January 2001. "I'm sure that may have some bearing [on] who he is."

Separating from family would eventually become a behavioral pattern in Armando's teenage and adult life. Still, family pictures taken in Arizona show a happy Armando Jr. The photos feature him with his older sister and two younger half brothers, Enrico and Stanley.

As the youngest child, Stanley benefited from his oldest brother's affection. In one photo, baby Stanley is sitting in his high chair as older brother Armando gazes at him with loving eyes.

That same dynamic appears in other photos featuring the two boys: baby Stanley looks at the camera while his older brother's caring eyes are fixed upon him, not the camera.

"He was one of the most compassionate people I knew growing up," Stanley Chavez said. "He was my older brother. He always looked out for me. Brothers fight. But he never fought with me. He was always at my side."

By the time he was sixteen years old, Armando Jr. had stopped using the *o* at the end of his name and simply went by Armand. He apparently felt he could do without his stepmother, too. According to Stanley, Armand moved out of his father's house, preferring to live at the home of a nearby friend.

"Families are not perfect, none is, but you try to stay together," Stanley offered. "But unfortunately, we didn't stay together, and maybe that has something to do (with how Armand turned out) as well. I can't help but feel somewhat responsible."

"How?" this author asked.

"Not keeping in contact with him. In fact, I told my dad last night [that] we should have never let him go."

Maybe a head injury had something to do with the way Armand "turned out," too.

Despite his small stature, Armand enjoyed competing in wrestling and football.

"He was an *amazing* football player. He won a presidential award in athletics when he was only in eighth grade from Monte Vista School," brother Stanley said.

As a football player at Girard Catholic High School, Armand suffered a head injury. Stanley Chavez said his brother was airlifted to St. Joseph's Hospital, where Armand remained for four days. Some people have said that Armand never seemed quite the same after the head injury. His personality seemed to change.

Did it?

"Maybe, I don't know; sometimes head injuries cause personality changes. Maybe that's what happened to him. Maybe," Stanley Chavez answered. "He was in the prime of his life, a high-school athlete. He was fit as can be. But I think that head injury, him being there for four days, had to be major."

Not even a bad head injury discouraged Armand from reaching his goal of going off to college.

On February 23, 1983, Girard Catholic High School's guidance director, Rita Simons, filled out a college entrance recommendation form on behalf of Armand "Christopher" Chavez.

Simons, who had known Chavez for 3½, years, wrote that Armand was a good student but that there was some instability in his family life and it was reflected somewhat in his grades.

The document included specific test scores and other insights into the measure of Armand Chavez's knowledge. He scored 460 on the verbal portion of the Scholastic Aptitude Test (SAT) and 380 on the math section.

In rating Armand's intellect, Simons wrote "average." Simons continued to chronicle relative mediocrity: Academic ability: average. Motivation: above average. Writing skills: average. Speech: above average.

Simons wrote that Chavez's primary interests were athletics and science and that he had an "unusual aptitude" for art. He received a "fairly strong" rating for both "academic promise" and for his "character and personal promise."

Upon graduating from Girard Catholic High, Armand Chavez could tell his friends that he was bound for Notre Dame. But he wasn't going east to South Bend, Indiana.

Notre Dame de Namur University (NDMU), formerly known as the College of Notre Dame, was a four-year college located on fifty acres in the city of Belmont on California's San Francisco Peninsula.

30

At the tender age of twenty, Armand Chavez married twenty-three-year-old Rosemary Guerrero. Guerrero worked as an accountant for a publishing firm. The couple exchanged wedding vows on February 23, 1986, at the Assemblies of God church in Gilroy, California. The marriage produced one child, a son.

Chavez had stated on his marriage certificate that he was a technician for an immunology laboratory. While he held a part-time job at San Mateo Hospital, he was still very much a college student. He had a hard time with his grades and was forgetful. His wife could see that he really wasn't very intelligent.

But in December 1987, Chavez did manage to graduate from the College of Notre Dame with a bachelor of science degree in chemistry.

The marriage had started out rather uneventfully, but strange behavior did emerge.

His wife witnessed a young man who grew depressed after his applications for medical school were rejected.

In the late 1980s, she found him in the bathtub taking his own blood.

From time to time, he'd used a name that sounded like Diazien Hossencofft, an effort, it seemed, to sound important.

Rosemary concluded that her husband didn't seem to like himself. Near the end of the marriage, Chavez made a remark so odd that his wife didn't take it seriously. If he ever killed anyone, he said, no one would ever find the body because he could use chemicals to eliminate it.

True to his history of brief relationships with women, Chavez's first marriage lasted less than three years, ending after Rosemary learned that he'd been unfaithful.

She'd discover he wouldn't be faithful about paying child support, either. Around 1992, Chavez called his ex-wife and asked her to take out a large life insurance policy and name him as the beneficiary, a request that made her recall his statement that he could get away with murder by not leaving a trace of the body.

Rosemary knew that her ex-husband had buttons that, when pressed, triggered intense anger.

One, not being accepted to medical school. Two, a lack of respect from anyone. And three, anyone who didn't think he was intelligent.

When ADA Spiers learned that Hossencofft had earned a degree in chemistry, he grew concerned that he may have used science to incapacitate or kill Girly. It also convinced him that he must use the police department's science people.

Already, some witnesses had said Hossencofft spoke of using chemicals to make Girly disappear. Spiers considered that outcome to be unlikely because it would have been a sloppy job that required a lot of chemicals—work.

Hossencofft hardly seemed like a guy interested in real work.

31

In 1988, Paula Young (an alias) still managed to enjoy some leisurely exercise despite suffering from severe depression.

Young's father, a wealthy hotel owner, had hired several people to shop, prepare meals and clean house for her.

One such person had been balancing her checkbook and serving her meals for more than two years. His name was Armand Chavez.

In May 1988, Young nearly died inside room 351 in the intensive care unit at San Francisco's Presbyterian Hospital. Doctors concluded that she had been poisoned with arsenic. Her heart, liver and kidneys were all damaged by the poison.

Sergeant Alfredo Matteoni of the San Francisco Police Department interviewed Young in her hospital room. The former model explained that she felt a severe burning sensation and believed it was connected to the dinner she had eaten the night before.

The diarrhea, the vomiting, it was all "thirty times worse" than anything she'd previously experienced. Young said she feared that her dinner of chicken and vegetables had been laced with poison—specifically, the squash. It had tasted sour . . . bitter.

"Who brought you the food the night before?" Matteoni asked.

"Armand," Young replied from her hospital bed.

Young's doctor determined that she had ingested a high-level dose of arsenic. Given Young's psychiatric history, Sergeant Matteoni more than considered the possibility that she had attempted suicide. Young was deeply offended by the policeman's conclusion and told him it was cruel.

Had Chavez said anything, in particular, when he served the meal of chicken and vegetables?

Young had no problem recalling Chavez's words of encouragement: "Eat your vegetables. . . . Are you eating your vegetables?"

She began to cry, insisting that someone had poisoned her. And she feared it had been Chavez.

"Why do you feel that it may be Armand that would do this thing to you—[for what] reasons?" asked the sergeant.

"For the fascination of watching it happen as a medical study. . . . I hope it's not Armand, you know. Because I really kind of love Armand."

Maybe Young hadn't attempted suicide, Matteoni considered. After interviewing Chavez and finding no arsenic in Young's home, Matteoni found no evidence that someone had poisoned Young. Charges were never filed against anyone.

32

In July 1989, Charles Grissom blazed an exciting trail for himself.

Grissom, who celebrated his thirtieth birthday that month, had just moved from the University of California at Berkeley to the University of Utah in Salt Lake City.

He looked forward to teaching biochemistry to graduate students in a laboratory setting, where the students could experiment with their newfound knowledge. Grissom had no idea that one of his students was destined to experiment on him and the entire class secretly. The student would test their faith in humanity. That student would move to Salt Lake City in one year.

In July 1990, twenty-five-year-old Armand Chavez walked into Assistant Professor Charles Grissom's biochemistry laboratory class. The Chavez kid seemed to have it all together. Not only did he have charisma, he'd already received personal acceptance to the University of Utah's College of Medicine. Likable, talkative and interesting—that was Armand Chavez.

But he brought a sad story with him, too. Classmates soon found themselves showering pity upon poor Armand, the student whose wife and son both had died in a horrible car crash. Worse yet, Chavez related, it happened as his wife was driving to pick him up at school back in Belmont, California.

Charles Grissom heard the story, too. "I had some suspicions. He didn't seem like an individual affected by the tragic loss of a loved one," Grissom later recalled.

If the story was true, surely it would have been written up in a newspaper.

The assistant professor settled in to do a bit of research at the university's Marriott Library. It shouldn't have been too difficult to find a news article because Chavez had told him when the accident had occurred. Grissom diligently searched the archives of the *San Jose Mercury News* but found no mention of the crash that killed the wife and young son of Armand Chavez.

When Grissom later traveled to Stanford University to help his wife prepare for a move from Palo Alto to Utah, he went to Stanford's library, too. Once again, he was unable to find any record of the fatal crash.

That wasn't the only odd thing about Chavez. As his fellow students became even more familiar with him, some of them allowed him to draw their blood.

"I can't remember for what, but I told him to knock it off," Grissom recalled.

Chavez had an interesting little habit, too, though not terribly unusual. After all, what student doesn't doodle on the fringes of his notebook paper from time to time? But Chavez always seemed to draw the same symbol, as if practicing. The symbol was nothing recognizable. It sort of resembled a lightning bolt morphed into a swastika.

Despite Chavez's peculiarities, it was his charisma that really stood out. Here was an interesting guy that you just enjoyed listening to.

On December 25, 1990, Chavez arrived at Grissom's home for an informal Christmas dinner. It was really a spur-of-the-moment thing. It was Christmas and people who didn't have any place to go should have a place to enjoy the holiday.

The small dinner included Grissom's mother and secretary.

Once again, Chavez had a story to tell. "He told me that he had taken a homeless man to the Village Inn for breakfast that morning," Grissom later said.

Grissom wondered if that story was true, too. He did determine one story was a lie. Chavez's wife and child never died in a car crash. And the professor suddenly had irrefutable proof, discovered in the most unexpected place.

Inside the lab was its least-read book, the *Radiation Procedures Protocol*. It's a bit like the label on a mattress; seldom read but required by law. If state inspectors came through the lab, they'd want to make sure the radiation notebook was available, up to date and in plain sight.

It was while flicking through the pages of the *Radiation Procedures Protocol* notebook that Grissom made a startling discovery. He found several letters from Chavez's ex-wife, Rosemary Guerrero, pleading for him to return home to California. One letter was written by Armand Chavez to Guerrero. In it, Chavez explained that he wouldn't be returning to her because he had a "calling" to pursue.

Grissom wasn't sure what that calling might be, but he had an immediate response to the surprise discovery. Grissom felt his mysterious student wanted him to find the letters.

"It was an interesting moment to realize that he wanted someone to find this . . . to know this [story about the fatal car crash] was a falsehood," Grissom said.

Were the letters Chavez's way of telling his professor, *I pulled the wool over your eyes?*

Grissom had to wonder.

Then it all ended. "He left one day," Grissom explained matter-of-factly, adding that it wouldn't be appropriate for him to discuss the reason why.

When it ended, though, Grissom realized that Chavez still had some books Grissom had loaned him, and keys to the lab.

Grissom still had Chavez's microscope, though, so he laid down the law in a phone call.

Bring me back the books and the keys, and you'll get your microscope back, Grissom had said.

Later that night, a student from another lab noticed something unusual inside the science building. A determined Chavez was trying to open the doors to Grissom's lab. Chavez was even using some sort of tool in an attempt to pry the doors open, but without success.

Before leaving work earlier that day, Grissom had fastened a half-inch steel padlock to the doors.

A day or two later, Chavez returned the books and keys. Grissom reciprocated by giving Chavez the microscope. A sticker on the bottom of the microscope read: PROPERTY OF COLLEGE OF NOTRE DAME. Chavez told Grissom that the good sisters at the college had given him the microscope.

Two weeks after Chavez left his lab, Grissom received an interesting phone call; a woman purporting to be with the campus police department asked if the professor was missing any lab equipment.

After Grissom explained that he wasn't missing anything, the woman shared that police had just impounded Chavez's white pickup truck after seizing lab equipment from it. Investigators were also getting a search warrant for Chavez's apartment.

Twelve years later, Charles Grissom still didn't know what that episode was all about.

School records and other sources, though, have revealed what reads like a rap sheet for Armand Chavez, and ultimately might explain his swift departure from the University of Utah:

- Falsified and manipulated his lab results
- Purloined stationery from a hospital in California and created a false letter of recommendation
- Falsified a federal grant application by listing himself as married to obtain more funding
- Took advantage of, lied to, and obtained money from at least two women

The University of Utah rescinded its acceptance of Chavez to its College of Medicine.

"He really accomplished very little ... nothing," said Grissom.

Grissom considered himself fortunate that he wasn't a victim, too.

"By the grace of God, I felt like I was a step ahead. In retrospect, I don't know why, I feel like I came out of it pretty cleanly."

In the fall of 1999, Assistant District Attorney Paul Spiers learned about Diazien Hossencofft's attempted con at the University of Utah.

Spiers considered the possibility that Hossencofft, stung by admonition, started using science as an instrument for retribution, a way to get back at the community that had rejected him.

33

Seventy-two-year-old Sunny Blake (an alias) seemed to have it all: a wonderful husband, tons of money and a beautiful home right on the second hole of a private golf course in Santa Fe, New Mexico. Blake was an heiress. Each month, $30,000 landed in her checking account.

Lots of Benjamins, but never enough men. While it outwardly appeared to be monogamous, the Blakes' marriage was actually an open one. In 1993, she placed a personal ad in the *Albuquerque Journal*.

"It basically said, 'Wealthy woman looking for lover,'" recalled Blake's son.

As a result of that newspaper ad, Blake met the most fascinating and unique gentleman she'd ever laid eyes on. His name was Dr. Diazien Hossencofft.

Hossencofft told her that he was a cutting-edge geneticist who had invented a serum that could eradicate her breast cancer *and* reverse her aging.

Blake put her health solely in his hands. Hossencofft regularly billed her for his services. One statement itemized forty-one charges Blake had received over six days, including:

- Genetic Separation: $243
- Polymer Decoding Sequencing: $262
- X-Ray Chrystallography: $173
- Radioactive Isotopes 32/,3/,17/,83/: $225
- DNA Decoding Sequencer: $123
- Cryogenic Containment Field: $215

Hossencofft had convinced Blake that since he'd taken the *original* youth serum, his blood now contained all of its healing and age-reversing properties. If she would only let him inject her with *his* blood, she'd be on her way toward youth and perfect health.

Blake let him do it. And paid him well.

In 1994, Rosemary Guerrero received a surprise phone call from her ex-husband, the man she'd known as Armand Chavez.

He wanted her to open bank accounts in her name in San Francisco. He'd put the money into the accounts, he said.

Guerrero didn't bite. Later, Chavez called her in a rage.

"If anybody ever asks about me, I'm dead," he said. "And I'll say the same thing about you and our son."

Sunny Blake's heart went out to her charismatic doctor.

Hossencofft had told her that his "daughter" had died in a car crash. However, he was going to use a strand of his dead child's hair to re-create her genetically in his laboratory.

Hossencofft would certainly need a house in which to raise the kid. Blake bought Hossencofft a two-story house in Albuquerque.

By summer 1995, Blake's cancer-stricken breast had grown several times its natural size. At her son's insistence, she agreed to be examined by an oncologist. That doctor's written diagnosis was everything Hossencofft's analysis was not, quick, to the point, far less expensive, and without much hope:

> *Sunny Blake has locally advanced breast cancer. I anticipate that she will survive six to eighteen months.*

Blake's son estimated that Hossencofft had conned his mother out of $25,000 a month for a total of nearly $500,000. He resolved to cut Hossencofft out of his mother's life and succeeded in becoming her court-appointed temporary guardian.

Against his mother's wishes, the son managed to get a restraining order that prevented Hossencofft from having any contact with his mother. Despondent, Blake rarely spoke to anyone again. She died at home in the early-morning hours of January 27, 1996, from complications related to her severe breast cancer.

In her final days, she had been miserable. Not just from the horrific pain, but from the absence of the hope she'd found in Hossencofft.

34

In the late 1980s and early '90s, Armand Chavez took to scribbling names. Among the various combinations of letters randomly jotted on blank sheets of paper were Yasien, Yiasien, and Diazine Chavez.

By July 17, 1992, he came up with a name he felt suited him best. On that date, Chavez filed a Petition to Change Name at the Second Judicial District Court in Albuquerque. The single-page document lent little insight into Chavez's reason for changing his name, only stating: ". . . he desires to change his name from ARMAND CHAVEZ to DIAZIEN HOSSENCOFFT and that it is in his best interests to so change his name."

While his motivation was destined for much speculation, Hossencofft eventually revealed that his new name reflected what he considered to be the "master races" of Japanese and German.

The name change became official on August 31, 1992. Four months later, Diazien Hossencofft proved to be a very busy man.

On December 28, 1992, he purchased the $7,500 wedding ring at Krugers in Albuquerque.

Three days later, on New Year's Eve, Hossencofft's fiancée arrived in Albuquerque from Malaysia. They were married eight days later.

On January 12, 1993, four days after her wedding, Girly Chew Hossencofft applied for permanent resident status.

That documentation included a letter dated December 29, 1992, with letterhead for a company named Alltech Environmental, Inc. The letter is addressed to the INS:

> *To whom it may concern:*
>
> *Please be advised that Diazen Hossencofft is a full time employee of Alltech Environmental, Inc. effective December 28, 1992.*
>
> *His position is Senior Chemist with a base salary of $30,000 per year plus a bonus upon the completion of our fiscal year.*
>
> *I am unable to go into the details regarding the long term contract for legal reasons. However, Alltech Environmental, Inc., is looking forward to working with Dr. Hossencofft.*
>
> *If you have any questions or concerns please feel free to contact me.*
> *Sincerely,*
> *Henry B. Ojeniji*
> *President*

Through much of January 1993, Girly continued to jump through all the hoops necessary to become a permanent resident: On the fourteenth, she was fingerprinted by the INS. On the fifteenth, she took the required physical exam.

A letter dated January 16, 1992, on Bank of America stationery, served as proof of Hossencofft's checking and savings accounts. It stated that he currently had nearly $6,000 in his checking account and more than $22,000 in his savings account.

The results of Girly's medical examination arrived January 18, 1993. The doctor had concluded that Girly was in good health, although she did have a reaction to the tuberculin skin test. However, Girly tested negative for TB.

While Girly was the picture of an excited new resident of the United States, her husband was the portrait of success: the well-dressed doctor always on the go. And Hossencofft already had a wonderful place to live: a two-story home in a pleasant Albuquerque neighborhood.

The downside was that his work often took him out of town. He initially had medical conferences and lectures to attend, and then as his career progressed, he traveled to perform heart and lung transplants.

In truth, Girly had no idea that her husband was an unemployed narcissist who fed off the trusting hearts of others. Sure, he had money, but he was conning it out of old people, primarily a woman named Sunny Blake.

Hossencofft was not licensed to practice medicine anywhere. He was not a doctor. It was all show.

Those out-of-town trips were actually adventures near and far. There were women to meet, women to date, women to sleep with and always women to con.

The getaway destinations were homes as close as Rio Rancho, and cruise ships in Alaska and the Caribbean. Other destinations included Hawaii and Canada.

While on a trip to Banff in Alberta, Canada, Hossencofft set his sights on a stunning prize: a conquest that would yield spoils beyond sex and money.

35

In the summer of 1995, twenty-five-year-old Dwayne Baker couldn't help but be impressed with the shiny, new blue Jaguar pulling into the parking lot of the IMAX Theater in Albuquerque's Old Town. When he approached the man who drove it, Baker had no idea he was about to initiate a chapter in his life that would play out like a sci-fi movie.

"What does a guy have to do to get a car like that?" Baker asked as he approached the driver.

"Get a good education," the driver said after turning around to view the stranger.

Baker, obviously impressed, kept asking questions. The Jag man, soaking up the fanfare, gladly indulged him.

Within minutes, Baker learned that the rich, classy guy with the Jag was a heart-and-lung-transplant surgeon named Dr. Diazien Hossencofft.

"Are there any employment opportunities with your company?" Baker asked.

"Why, yes, there are," came the response.

A week and a half after that initial meeting, Baker met Hossencofft for dinner. Hossencofft explained that he worked at an Albuquerque hospital, but he was about to give up being a doctor because he was going to be working for a company that used "alien technology" to manipulate human genes and chromosomes, ultimately extending life itself.

As the bond between Baker and Hossencofft tightened, the pair often went bowling together. Hossencofft began throwing around some tough talk at strangers who annoyed him: bowlers who were loud, people who were just having a good time.

More than once, these angry strangers approached the sharp-tongued, tough-talking Hossencofft. That's when the six-feet-two-inch and 190-pound Baker would stand up as if ready to intervene. And he was.

"You'll need to go through him," Hossencofft told anyone who took issue with his rude remarks.

Hossencofft suddenly had a bodyguard.

It was during this time, in the fall of 1995, that Hossencofft asked Baker to travel with him to Banff, in Alberta, Canada.

Officially, the visit to the ski resort town was a business trip. A new company in the tourism industry was seeking financial backing from investors. Hossencofft appeared to have the desired deep pockets.

Baker watched as Hossencofft listened to a pitch from a start-up company that hoped to lure tourists to Banff by offering them Harleys to ride and cabins to sleep in. The people making the pitch were obviously under the impression that Hossencofft was a very wealthy man who might invest in their venture.

"We'll think about," Hossencofft told them.

But that meeting had nothing to do with the real reason that Hossencofft went to Banff. The actual purpose for the trip would remain a dark secret for years to come.

36

Appearing to be straight out of medieval lore, the Banff Springs Hotel, built in 1888, still stood, 107 years later, much like a fortress overlooking Canada's Bow Valley.

The Scottish-style castle was still considered one of the finest hotels in the world. In the winter, the thick forest surrounding the castle bent beneath the weight of snow in a storybook setting amidst the northern Rocky Mountains. Inside the hotel were skating rinks, a theater, a bowling alley, fifteen restaurants and a few haunted tales. But a visit from Hossencofft would yield more than a simple ghost story.

In early 1995, twenty-eight-year-old Naoko Sato (an alias) was busy assisting an elderly woman at the Banff Springs Hotel's jewelry store when a young man entered the business. Charismatic and well dressed, Dr. Hossencofft explained that he specialized in traveling with elderly people on trips so that they would always have a physician nearby.

In short, the good doctor made one glowing impression on the beautiful Japanese jewelry store worker. In the weeks that followed, Hossencofft often sent Sato cards and letters from all over the United States, explaining that he was traveling with his patients.

In April 1995, Sato traveled to Albuquerque to spend time with Hossencofft. They joined nearly 20,000 people inside The Pit at the University of New Mexico for the Gathering of Nations Native American Indian Powwow.

Hossencofft also brought Sato to his home, which she noted was sparsely furnished; she saw a chair, a computer, a TV and not much else. Although she didn't get to tour the entire house, Sato saw no sign of another woman.

Hossencofft explained that it would be wise for them to stay at a hotel. Workers were coming and going at his home as they remodeled a bathroom.

Over the next three days at the hotel, Hossencofft and Sato became romantically involved.

Hossencofft returned to Banff to visit Sato on three occasions later that year. It was that final visit that would change her life—and the life of a woman she would never know—forever.

Dwayne Baker knew the deal. He wasn't supposed to say a word to anyone about the money Hossencofft kept inside a safe-deposit box, the faraway trips, anything to anyone about anything that he and Hossencofft did together.

Baker certainly knew the *real* objective of their trip to Banff in November 1995, and it had nothing to do with investing in any company. The mission was for Hossencofft to get Naoko Sato pregnant. "The doctor" had told Baker he wanted the mother of his child to be Japanese, not Malaysian. He wanted to have a "completely Japanese" child.

Hossencofft, Sato and Baker enjoyed several days together in Banff that November. Hossencofft and Sato spent the final day alone.

After returning to Japan in December 1995, Naoko Sato learned that she was pregnant. She informed Hossencofft that he was the father. He responded with phone calls and letters over the next several months.

It was during this time that Hossencofft informed Sato that their child would be inheriting a rare genetic disorder that affected all members of his family. His child would require lifelong medical care. Given the child's genetic problem and his ability to provide financially, Hossencofft argued that it would be necessary for Sato to bring him the child as soon as possible following its birth.

On August 8, 1996, in a hospital in Sakae-Cho, Sato gave birth to a son and named him Minoru Sato (an alias). She wasted no time getting a passport for her infant.

Pursuant to Hossencofft's instructions, Sato flew with her newborn from Japan to Mexico City to Ciudad Juárez. Her baby was only twenty-four or twenty-five days old.

For three days, Naoko Sato met with Hossencofft in a Juárez hotel. For three days she cried.

Prior to this rendezvous, Hossencofft had promised that he'd finally explain why he'd been so secretive during their relationship and why he could not marry her.

Yet he revealed nothing.

Still, Sato believed that her son might die from a rare medical condition if she kept him. In tears, Sato reluctantly handed her child over to Hossencofft. He told her not to try to contact him, because he would be leaving New Mexico soon.

Sato never spoke with Hossencofft again. And she never returned to Japan. She was too ashamed.

Somehow, Hossencofft and little Minoru Sato crossed the border from Mexico and into the United States. Father and son soon arrived at his house on Moon Northeast, where Hossencofft introduced the child to his wife. He told Girly that they were adopting the baby and called the child Demetri.

37

After an empty bar stool, the next best place for easily striking up a conversation with a willing stranger might be a hair salon. The stylist looks at you, touches you and even follows your instructions. And, paid to keep you happy, she's willing to engage in a conversation on your chosen subject during the washing, snipping and blowing.

It all added up to fertile hunting ground for a con man who fancied himself a ladies' man.

In the summer of 1996, hairstylist Kimberly Glasgow (an alias) found an interesting man in her chair at a Supercuts in Northeast Albuquerque. The guy had a sense of humor, seemed rather pleasant and sure knew how to throw around compliments. And to top it all off, he was a doctor. And single.

"He could charm a person. He could talk to you and look you in the eye," Glasgow recalled years later.

Not long after his first haircut, Dr. Diazien Hossencofft returned for another one. Glasgow had a steady customer.

And after two or three visits to her chair, Hossencofft and Glasgow had their first date. He seemed to enjoy wining and dining his new girlfriend, taking her to some of Albuquerque's finest restaurants.

But then the weirdness started. Glasgow was surprised to see her new boyfriend injecting himself with a needle, not just once in a while, but two or three times a day.

"He would inject himself on the pelvis, on his ankle and on his wrist," Glasgow remembered.

Hossencofft broached what surely must have been a difficult subject for him. He explained that the syringe contained morphine to help ease the pain of the disease that was slowly killing him, leukemia.

As months of increased familiarity advanced across the relationship, the good doctor's quirks and revelations continued to pop up like a jack-in-the-box.

Dating a doctor had its perks, however. When Glasgow's fourteen-year-old daughter, Samantha, needed a physical in order to compete in high-school sports, Dr. Hossencofft was more than willing to oblige.

"He told her to take her clothes off . . . but he didn't physically . . . he just looked at her," Glasgow later said.

Having worked late one night, Glasgow arrived home and received a report from her two boys that upset her terribly. Her sons, ages ten and twelve, explained that Hossencofft had taken their blood. When confronted by his girlfriend, Hossencofft coolly explained that he had a perfectly sound reason for taking blood from her sons. Because he was dying from leukemia, he desperately needed a bone marrow match. Her sons might save his life.

There were few boring moments with Hossencofft. He was full of surprises.

"Would you kill for me?" Hossencofft asked his girlfriend.

"Are you crazy? No!" Glasgow responded.

"You know, I could get rid of you."

"How are you going to get rid of me?" Glasgow asked.

"By putting some acid on your body. It would make you disappear," Hossencofft answered.

Glasgow simply decided to blow off her boyfriend's bizarre comment. But something happened in 1997 that Glasgow could not close her eyes to: a single event convinced her to terminate the relationship immediately.

Glasgow was at her job at Supercuts when a woman walked in, desperate to speak with her.

"She was real concerned, and she looked scared, and she was talking real fast," Glasgow said.

The hairstylist wasted little time and stepped outside. The visitor had just made the startling comment that she was married to Hossencofft.

Standing in that parking lot made the unexpected visitor feel like a deer in an open meadow during hunting season. She was an easy target. The women got into Glasgow's vehicle.

The stranger revealed that her name was Girly Hossencofft, but she seemed devoid of any anger concerning her husband's affair. Instead, fear was dripping from her every word, even her facial expressions.

"She told me that if he caught her talking to me at the time, he would kill her," Glasgow said.

It would be the first and only time that Glasgow would ever see Girly.

Kimberly Glasgow confronted Hossencofft and asked him if he was married. When he said no and that he wasn't attached to anyone, Glasgow decided to end it all, right there and then.

"So how did you find out I'm married?" Hossencofft ultimately asked, conceding that Glasgow had it right.

"Nobody told me. I just found out on my own," she told him.

But Hossencofft wouldn't let it go. With shrewd persistence, he kept asking his ex-girlfriend how she came to learn of his existing marriage.

Finally, hoping to get him off her back, she gave in just a little.

"Well, some lady called me over the phone and told me about it," Glasgow said.

"I have a feeling I know who it is," Hossencofft responded, as if pleased.

38

On August 4, 1998, Julie Kay McGuire turned fifty. She'd been married three times and had endured tremendous physical abuse in one of those marriages.

Divorced and hardworking—often sharing laughter that hid her inner pain—McGuire owned the Enchantment Lodge in Aztec, a northwestern New Mexico town in the "Four Corners" area, so named because the corners of four states—New Mexico, Arizona, Colorado and Utah—connect at a single point.

As the owner of her motel, McGuire worked long days and nights, wearing a variety of different hats. She checked in guests, cleaned rooms, did the laundry. Such was life as a small businessperson struggling to make it in a dusty, desert town.

But there were moments when business was slow and McGuire was done working. During these times, she often surfed the Internet. In the summer of 1998, McGuire posted an ad on an Internet dating service. It included a glamorous photograph. In it, McGuire's blond hair appeared full and thick as playful curls cascaded onto a red feathered boa.

Diazien Hossencofft found the ad and the photo—she

was what he deemed an easy target. The red boa might as well have been a bull's-eye.

On August 29, 1998, Hossencofft introduced himself to McGuire via e-mail. He wrote about his background, explaining that he had a B.S. in biochemistry from Tokyo University, a master's in "organo-metallic chemistry" from Stanford University, a master's in genetic engineering from San Francisco University and a M.D./Ph.D. from Cornell.

Regarding his upbringing, he wrote that one of his parents was Japanese, the other German, and that he still had a Japanese accent.

"On the phone often people mistaken my voice for a woman ha ha ha," he wrote. Hossencofft added that he owned a private laboratory that specialized in building chromosomes, often for the government. He said he flew planes and had even taken some helicopter-flying lessons.

It was the image of a successful, rich, well-rounded man of adventure. And he played humble.

"I imagine you have many suiters," he wrote to McGuire, misspelling "suitors."

Later that day, Hossencofft provided more information about himself in a second e-mail. It included a smiling photograph of him standing and wearing a kimono over a bright, collared dress shirt and tie. He held two books in his right hand and posed much like a model. He looked scholarly. He looked triumphant. His actual stature, though, was not of gladiator proportions.

In the e-mail, Hossencofft explained that he was five feet six inches tall and weighed 135 pounds. He said that he was born two months premature.

This e-mail seemed to deviate from the first. Having previously stated he was from Japan, his second e-mail said that he was born on a Swedish ship, the *Crasvinovia*.

As for his adult relationships, Hossencofft explained that he was once married, but that his wife had been killed by a drunk driver. To make matters worse, he felt responsible, sharing that he had convinced his wife to pick him up at the hospital where he was working in San Francisco. She was tired, but she still agreed to pick him up, "like a good wife."

The tragedy turned even worse, he wrote, when the ambulance brought his dying wife to his emergency room, where he operated and tried his best to keep her alive. Alas, he could not save her.

Hossencofft wrote that he was sorry to share such a sad tale, but "it is best to be honest about ones life."

The light in his life was a living testimony to his late wife; their son Demetri was now two years old, he said.

But there was more: "I do not like to argue nor do I have a temper."

No one could argue that there would be truth in his closing remark. "So as the circle of my life now touches the circle of your life we both may never be the same after here. . . ."

For the eleven days that followed his introduction on the Internet, Hossencofft and McGuire enjoyed chatting live on the computer, using the text-messaging service ICQ; Hossencofft used the handle "zymogentic," while McGuire went by "Foxybrat." The ICQ conversations took place almost daily.

Ultimately they delved deeper into the mystery that was Diazien Hossencofft.

On September 8, 1998, the instant messaging addressed his scientific research. He explained that he could manipulate human cells, and thereby make people younger. He warned the process is irreversible.

> *Foxybrat: You mean I could stay young forever. . . . I would love that . . . you see I never want to grow old.*

Hossencofft explained that the process was expensive and required commitment. He shared that a few movie actresses had had it done, but didn't say who.

Foxybrat: How old do you get
Zymogentic: you can not get younger than your
structural integrity of your bones.
Foxybrat: Well sweet I want to be 21 again. . . .

McGuire wrote that she was afraid of looking old. Hossencofft asked why.

Foxybrat: may be because I lost so much when I was
young and I just have always wished to stay young. . . .
When I was 14 I remember saying that I never wanted
to grow old. . . .

Hossencofft and McGuire arranged to meet each other at her home in Aztec. He would also bring Demetri.

The day before he drove to Aztec, the anticipation stirred as the two chatted on ICQ for two hours in the morning and for more than an hour at night.

The comments ranged from the mundane . . .

Foxybrat: We will have lots of fun . . . and so will
Demetri.

to the curious . . .

zymogentic: I would like to take a sample from you be-
fore we leave.

to the cuisine of good genetics. . . .

Foxybrat: I have lobster tails here all the time. . . .
zymogentic: that is great no wonder you are so pretty
oil of the lobster is very good genetic stabilizer.

On September 10, 1998, Hossencofft and his two-year-old son made the three-hour drive from Albuquerque to

Aztec. Over the next three days, McGuire got to know a man who appeared to have it all together.

As Demetri played with some toy cars McGuire provided, his father told wondrous stories. McGuire's son and daughter-in-law also listened while sitting at the kitchen table. Hossencofft explained that Demetri was one of twelve boys who had been genetically engineered by the National Security Agency (NSA); all twelve were created in a single month. His sperm had been used to fertilize the eggs of twelve different women. All of the kids were born at eight in the morning on August 8, 1996.

"How can you tell us that?" McGuire asked. This *was* supposedly top secret government intelligence coming from Hossencofft's mouth, after all.

"Nobody would believe you if you told them," Hossencofft responded. Everyone at the table laughed.

"How come Demetri's always saying, 'Girly'?" McGuire asked.

That was the name of the NSA experiment that produced the twelve kids, Project Girly, he explained.

McGuire immediately liked Demetri. But the things he said often sounded odd. From the beginning, the child called her "Mommy."

"He calls all women 'Mommy,'" Hossencofft explained.

Whenever she asked Demetri a question, the child repeated it. At first, that was funny. But McGuire began to notice the robotic inflection of the child's voice. The way he repeated questions and the way he said "Mommy," thought McGuire, all of it sounded as if he'd been programmed.

Hossencofft wanted to take his new girlfriend to a casino in nearby Colorado. McGuire's son and daughter-in-law agreed to look after Demetri. The drive to Colorado paved the way for some more interesting conversation.

During the drive, Hossencofft began to speak a lot about aliens. He explained that aliens actually lived on the dark side of the moon and that the space shuttle *Challenger* was headed that way when it exploded. The *Challenger* disaster, he said, was no accident.

Hossencofft claimed that aliens don't have feelings, but there are "good aliens" and "bad aliens." In fact, he revealed, he was half alien.

As the strange story unfolded in the car, McGuire was told that she had apparently been visited by aliens. Hossencofft told her that she had an implant in the bridge of her nose. The good aliens had put it there. The implant's shape resembled the strange symbol on Hossencofft's business card and, often, near his signature. It looked like some distorted swastika.

McGuire listened as Hossencofft told her that she was one of the "chosen ones." She would be allowed to leave the planet before the evil aliens attacked Earth's humans. When the time came, he said, she would be taken to a space station in Colorado Springs, where she would meet her mate.

The drive to the slots and blackjack tables would end with a bit of gambling. She had no idea just how high the stakes would eventually become.

Hossencofft's first trip to see McGuire lasted three days. And he had plans for poking her with needles, too.

In fact, he offered McGuire quite a deal. Because she was a special friend, he would give her his youth serum treatments at a bargain-basement price: 90 percent off. Instead of $32,000 per injection, he'd only charge her $3,200. Of course, the treatment required numerous injections over six years.

Before her new boyfriend returned to Albuquerque after a three-day visit, McGuire decided she'd like to give the youth serum a shot.

When Hossencofft returned in October 1998, he explained that he must first analyze her DNA. With that, he drew blood from her right arm. McGuire was impressed. He was very good at drawing blood.

He wasn't done. He said he needed to take what he called

a hormonal sample so that his lab workers could map out her DNA.

While McGuire wore her underwear, he placed a damp cloth over her eyes, explaining that many patients do not like to see the long needle he was about to use.

He said he needed to take the fluid from an area near the groin, below the navel and to the right, about an inch from the crease in her leg. McGuire didn't feel the needle and asked why. Hossencofft told her that it was because there were few nerve endings in the area he had penetrated. McGuire never saw the long needle, either.

In time, Hossencofft's random behavior made a deep impression.

Another bizarre moment came as they lay in bed together one night. McGuire was very tired and was about to doze off when Hossencofft started to whisper in her ear.

"Feel relaxed . . . feel relaxed . . . feel relaxed . . . ," he murmured over and over.

McGuire grew annoyed, then rolled over to look him in the eye. "What are you talking about?" she asked.

Hossencofft seemed startled. He'd apparently thought she was asleep.

He's trying to hypnotize me, McGuire thought.

The relationship that started hot and heavy for Julie McGuire in the summer of 1998 suddenly grew cold as the calendar reached mid-November. Their occasional e-mails and live chats on the Internet became the extent of their limited contact.

The relative silence from Hossencofft was suddenly broken in early January 1999. When Hossencofft returned to Aztec, he brought a grave sense of danger with him.

The NSA was out to kill him and Demetri, he explained.

Hossencofft told McGuire that the NSA had learned that he'd been sneaking off with youth serum and giving it to McGuire at a fraction of its value. That youth serum was worth $1.8 million, and the government wanted him to pay up or die. Hossencofft didn't have the money.

McGuire told him she felt responsible. She said she felt like it was all her fault. Or so she said. In truth, McGuire had shared Hossencofft's previous stories with a friend. The friend said he'd worked for the NSA and that none of Hossencofft's information made sense, especially his claim that he had a "level twenty-two" government security clearance. McGuire no longer believed Hossencofft had ever worked for the NSA, although she still believed he was a genetic scientist.

The frantic Hossencofft behaved dramatically different from the man she'd known. Suddenly his moods were up and down. Previously he always seemed to be so even-keeled and content. Never high, never low. In fact, McGuire had grown to think of him as an emotional flat-liner. That was all changing now.

With urgency, he also stated that the NSA was out to kill all twelve of the genetically engineered children because they were becoming too powerful. With their minds and bodies developing at such an accelerated rate, it was only a matter of time before the twelve children took over the world. That's why the NSA wanted them dead.

Hossencofft was so despondent he hit the bottle harder than ever. McGuire watched him drink a fifth of liquor in less than half a day. Sometimes he'd call at 3:30 in the morning and babble until he passed out. That angered her. She could always tell when he'd been drinking during their ICQ conversations—more babble.

At McGuire's home, Hossencofft disappeared into the bathroom for fifteen minutes or longer. On one particular occasion, that was a real nuisance because McGuire's bladder felt as if it were about to explode.

When Hossencofft finally came out of her bathroom, she rushed in to relieve herself.

"What were you doing in there for so long?" she asked.

Hossencofft explained that he had been giving himself an injection because he had a blood disorder.

McGuire found no needles, though, no sign of any evidence left behind.

Hossencofft did have a plan, though, a way out of danger. He asked McGuire if she could obtain two passports. He wanted them, he said, so he could flee to China. McGuire told him she'd ask around.

39

Judged by her glossy promotional photograph, Felissa Garcia Kelley was not just another divorce attorney. She had a face you'd remember: fair skin, big brown eyes that jumped out from between perfectly lined mascara, bright red lipstick. Her thick, shoulder-length, coffee-colored hair revealed a red tint beneath the studio lights. The woman was a knock-out.

Based on that photo, Kelley was a poised and competent divorce lawyer. Not bad for a former disc jockey and mother of three. And she was still only thirty-two years old. On February 5, 1999, she established a relationship with a client who would be far from ordinary, too. For on that day, Kelley agreed to represent Diazien Hossencofft. Strange occurrences soon unfolded.

On April 27, 1999, Hossencofft named Kelley as his secondary beneficiary in his will; Demetri was named the primary beneficiary.

Also in April, Kelley decided she wanted to adopt Demetri; she even secured an attorney to represent her in the matter. Kelley's moves took place against an interesting backdrop.

Girly had a $50,000 life insurance policy that named Demetri as the beneficiary.

There was more. On May 4, 1999, Kelley's mother-in-law wrote a check for $1,000 to Hossencofft as earnest money toward the purchase of his house.

What in the world was going on?

Julie McGuire had always loved trying to solve a mystery. As winter gave way to spring in 1999, she was beginning to feel a lot more like a detective and less like a girlfriend.

The promise of eternal youth was wearing thin. She would have ended all ties with Hossencofft—except for the boy. McGuire feared that Demetri might be in harm's way.

The NSA had laid down the law: Project Girly must be terminated, Hossencofft claimed.

Whenever Demetri was left with McGuire, Hossencofft always told her that she must never reveal the boy's location to anyone, especially not the police or Social Services. Trust no one. They could be NSA in disguise!

The strange story took another twist when Hossencofft told McGuire the NSA had sentenced him to death and had injected him with leukemia. He expressed his despair during an ICQ chat with McGuire on April 28, 1999: "I have not the strength to kill myself."

When Hossencofft and Demetri visited McGuire on May 1, 1999, McGuire thought the boy appeared sluggish, and more robotic than ever. He looked drugged, she thought.

Two days later, McGuire went to Albuquerque with a plate of food and visited Hossencofft at his home for the first time.

There was no routine arrival at his driveway. Just as she'd been told to do, McGuire parked her car at a health clinic just three blocks from his house. Because the NSA was staking out Hossencofft's home, he wanted to meet her at the clinic.

As planned, McGuire called Hossencofft from her cell phone after she arrived at the clinic. Later, Hossencofft arrived at the clinic. McGuire got into the back of his car and lay low to avoid NSA detection during the short car ride.

Hossencofft drove to his house, then straight into the garage. The brief trip was long enough for the crouching McGuire to consider that Hossencofft's wife may never have died in a car crash and that he may still might be married.

Inside the garage, Hossencofft promptly went to an electronic panel and began punching several buttons, explaining the NSA had the place wired but he knew how to scramble their code. To McGuire, that electronic panel sure looked a lot like the control box for the garage doors.

Suddenly it was time to learn hand signals. To further minimize NSA detection, Hossencofft explained that McGuire must use sign language while inside his home. To answer yes to a question, hold up your hand, she was told.

This guy has to be totally out of his mind if he thinks I really believe this bullshit, McGuire thought.

The inside of Hossencofft's house made quite an impression on McGuire: the beautiful white carpeting, white sofa, expensive curtains, the gorgeous artwork. The possessions were valuable. McGuire relished the thought of owning such beautiful things.

The house was clean, although a bedroom at the back of the house was full of boxes. Hossencofft's bed was beautiful. The mattress was so high off the floor that small steps were nearby so that one could get to it.

A television set was beyond the end of the bed. A bookshelf was filled with a collection of movies and TV shows, including *Death Becomes Her, Stargate* (the movie), *Stargate* (the entire TV series) and *The Pretender.*

During this visit to Hossencofft's home, a man and woman stopped by briefly. They appeared to be a realtor and a buyer. They handed Hossencofft a check. McGuire watched

Hossencofft put the check into a blue bank bag. She noticed something else in that bag: diamonds.

Demetri was not at the house. Hossencofft explained that his son was across the street at a neighbor's home.

There would be no sex between McGuire and Hossencofft on this visit. He was hitting the bottle hard. His libido had softened. The sex had been tapering off, anyway. That was okay with McGuire, who thought Hossencofft made love like a boy. And there was another odd thing about their lovemaking. Whenever he had an orgasm, he never made a sound, not even a whimper.

Still, McGuire didn't dare cut him off entirely. She wanted to protect Demetri from his father. And although she suspected Hossencofft was playing her for money, she sensed he had another motive. What was he really up to?

After returning home to Aztec that same day, McGuire began chatting with Hossencofft on the Internet. "Use your instincts and remember that things are not always as they seem," he wrote to her.

It was a direct reminder that she must not trust anyone.

Seven days later, McGuire returned to Albuquerque for her second visit. This adventure would be more interesting than the first.

It began with the drill: she drove to the clinic and hid in the back of his car while it made a beeline for his garage, as if it were the Bat Cave.

During this visit, McGuire was in for several surprises. Inside her boyfriend's bathroom, she found blood all over the counter and inside the bathtub. There were needles everywhere. . . . They had blood in them. The caps were left off the tips. Blood-soaked gauze was all over the counter, in the sink and in the tub.

The sight turned McGuire's stomach and confirmed her suspicions. In their past encounters, she noticed bruised track marks up and down his arms. And he had a hole, a bit larger than a quarter, inside the bend of his right arm.

Hossencofft had dismissed the track marks by saying that he'd been withdrawing his own vital fluid because it contained the blood by-products that were needed for the twelve genetically engineered children.

During this second visit to his house, she also found him sucking on inhalers. Empty inhalers were found in the bathroom and living room. He had a box of them in the kitchen.

And there was liquor. He was drinking a lot. McGuire, Hossencofft and Demetri went to see a movie. Instead of *Toy Story 2* or *A Bug's Life,* they saw some flick about a prostitute who tried to clean up her act and leave the streets behind her. Her pimp ordered her to stay. When she refused to honor her pimp's wishes, she was killed.

That sparked a disturbing after-movie conversation.

Women are to honor and obey men. They are to be *shadows,* Hossencofft declared.

"No man's ever going to tell me what to do!" McGuire told him.

As Hossencofft drifted into inebriation, he told McGuire that he had done some very dark things in his life. "If you only knew," he said.

McGuire played along and kept him talking.

Hossencofft pulled out a thirty-inch weapon and told McGuire it was a samurai sword. He had killed those who failed to honor him, he said.

"Women?" McGuire asked.

Yes, women, too.

He next showed McGuire three guns, including a nine-millimeter. He seemed empowered. He was downright scary.

Octopus must be eaten the day it's bought. Any older and it isn't fresh, Hossencofft explained as he chopped up bits of the raw sea creature and presented it beside exquisite rolls of white rice and shrimp wrapped in seaweed.

Hossencofft was a killer cook.

While her boyfriend prepared their after-movie dinner, McGuire drifted into his nearby computer room, where she noticed some papers with the name Girly on them. Not wanting to get caught snooping around, she left the room and returned to the kitchen.

After dining on the succulent raw octopus and shrimp and rice, McGuire and Hossencofft cleaned the dishes. A moment later, the doorbell rang. A young woman had come to visit Hossencofft. Hossencofft introduced the visitor as Francine Olmstead, a medical doctor.

"This is Julie, Demetri's baby-sitter," Hossencofft told Olmstead.

He then asked McGuire to take Demetri to the next room, where the boy could play with some toys. From the nearby room, McGuire noticed Olmstead handing Hossencofft a small piece of paper, which appeared to be a prescription.

Olmstead's visit was a brief one.

Hossencofft next did as he often did; he sat at the computer. Hossencofft assumed because McGuire wasn't wearing her bifocals, she couldn't read what he was typing. McGuire noticed he was chatting online with another woman. Soon a second woman began chatting with him, too.

"It's just some guy I know," Hossencofft lied.

McGuire noticed that one woman called Hossencofft "love" and "honey" in her instant messages.

She's as intimate with him as I am, McGuire thought.

McGuire was catching on now. Her boyfriend was trolling for other women on the Internet.

McGuire's anger was about to intensify.

He was writing to another woman about the youth serum. The cost? $3,200!

McGuire was never given a ninety percent discount. Inside, she was fuming, but she managed to keep calm. By the time he went to bed that night, Hossencofft was already smashed and still reaching for more alcohol.

He reached for McGuire, too. While his hands showed

their eagerness, McGuire could see the rest of him was too drunk to perform, not that she welcomed his advances. Besides, someone interrupted.

"Don't touch Mommy!" said Demetri.

The nearly three-year-old boy crawled between his father and McGuire, who could have hugged the child.

Hossencofft settled for another drink. A moment later, he passed out.

A movie continued to play in the VCR: *Alien*.

As McGuire began to leave Hossencofft's home on May 11, 1999, Demetri became hysterical; he screamed and cried for her to stay.

As she drove away alone, McGuire thought of the little boy. She had never seen a child so upset and frightened.

40

A spontaneous, middle-of-the-night meeting would prove to be McGuire's final visit to Hossencofft's home.

During a phone conversation, Hossencofft said he was extremely sick due to the leukemia. McGuire agreed to come immediately and take Demetri until Hossencofft felt better. She left her home in Aztec at 10:30 P.M. on June 15, 1999, and arrived in Albuquerque at 1:30 A.M. the following day.

This time, however, she was told to drive straight to his home. Hossencofft explained that the NSA hadn't been around lately. But just in case, he would remove his vehicle from the garage so she could hide her car inside.

After a few hours' sleep, McGuire buckled Demetri into her car shortly before nine o'clock that morning and prepared to take him to her Four Corners home. The little boy was tickled pink.

Demetri never hugged his father good-bye or even looked his way.

"Wave to Daddy," McGuire said as she began to pull out of the driveway.

"No," replied the child.

At that moment, McGuire knew something was very wrong.

While caring for Demetri, McGuire noticed disturbing marks on the boy's body, including greenish bruises on his temples.

"Daddy pinch," Demetri explained.

McGuire considered familiar sites on the boy's body in a new light. The boy's rectum was swollen. His father had always said it was because Demetri had fallen on it. His uncircumcised penis was not only very unclean, as she had often seen it, it had a red rash on it now.

McGuire called the state's Department of Social Services and reported the disturbing marks and swelling on Demetri's body.

But because Demetri lived in Albuquerque, and not the Aztec area, Social Services took down the information over the telephone and referred the case to its Albuquerque area office.

McGuire wasn't done. She also took her concerns to a friend in local law enforcement, who decided to run a background check on Hossencofft—something he really wasn't authorized to do without an official reason.

The results of the background check amazed McGuire: Hossencofft was married to a woman named Girly and was going through a divorce. He had been charged with domestic violence. He was born in Houston, Texas, and was known as Armand Chavez until changing his name in 1992.

Rather than run, McGuire engaged in a game of cat and mouse with the man she no longer loved but feared. The next surprise came quickly.

When McGuire returned home after speaking with her friend in law enforcement that day, she gave Demetri a bath. She was surprised when the boy complained of pain between his toes. McGuire took a closer look and discovered what appeared to be small holes between each toe. They looked like track marks.

McGuire wondered if Hossencofft had been injecting something into his son to make him fall asleep, thus allowing Hossencofft to slip away while Demetri slept unattended. When she called Hossencofft and confronted him, he provided another lame story, claiming that Demetri had been playing with a pushpin and had made a game of pricking himself between the toes.

McGuire was both frustrated and concerned. From the beginning, Demetri was never one to reveal anything. He always answered questions by repeating them. The exchanges between McGuire and the boy typically went this way:

"Do you hurt?"

"Do I hurt?"

"Does this hurt?"

"Does this hurt?"

McGuire consulted with a friend in Oklahoma, a psychologist.

"Julie, stop asking him questions. He's not going to answer you because D has programmed him, and he's done it very well," the friend told McGuire over the telephone. "Here's what I want you to do: Get him a teddy bear and tell him, 'This is your friend. He's been really hurt. His mommy and daddy have hurt him, but he's with me now. Demetri, will you take care of him? He's a little boy just as you are.'"

McGuire wasted no time and did exactly as her friend advised. Sure enough, Demetri began talking to the teddy bear.

"No more hurt," he said over and over. "We safe."

McGuire felt as if it were all coming out, that Demetri was confirming what she'd suspected, the boy had been abused.

McGuire noticed something else interesting about Demetri's behavior in the following weeks and months. Whenever his father was nearby, the boy refused to talk to his teddy bear.

41

It's not that they were about to accost Diazien Hossencofft, but the guy's act was wearing thin on the members of the UFO Group. Sure, he tried to be very convincing there, like when he declared that aliens were going to poison the water supply in two months. He acted out the scenario wonderfully.

But no one was buying what he was selling, except Linda Henning.

Each Thursday, Hossencofft continued to press the issue, while insisting that he was a ten-thousand-year-old alien dying of leukemia. Group members locked in on his mannerisms. This obvious paragon of deception never looked anyone in the eye when he spoke. Typically, he looked down with his hand near his mouth.

People wanted proof of his expertise: if you're a doctor, show us your credentials!

"I don't have any ID with me," he replied every time, week after week.

Since Hossencofft also claimed that he could predict the future, members of the UFO Group asked him to foretell something that would happen the next day or the following week. He never did.

"You guys just don't understand. You don't get it," Henning told them.

Group member Alexis Holland had always liked and admired Henning, but Henning also seemed easily manipulated. Some of the group's members speculated that Henning had been drugged or was under the spell of some sort of mind control. Her personality had drastically changed after meeting Hossencofft.

There was also a buzz going around the UFO meetings that Hossencofft concocted the story about aliens planning to poison the groundwater so that Henning would want to flee from New Mexico for an out-of-state vortex. Of course, she would want to sell her town house. Rumor had it that Hossencofft planned on using her money to buy a plane.

Rick Carlson asked Bill Miller if there was any truth to that rumor. Miller said nothing was going to come of it.

Carlson heard a lot more about the vortexes and aliens during visits to Henning's town house. She'd asked him if he would come over to repair the skylights because she was going to put the house on the market.

While Carlson did the handiwork, Hossencofft and his son were often visiting Henning. On one occasion, Demetri wore a kimono as he sat on the bed watching cartoons. During another visit, Carlson observed Demetri playing dice on a table. *What a wonderful and happy kid,* Carlson thought.

With Hossencofft nearby, Henning told Carlson that Demetri had been conceived in a petri dish. Carlson wanted to bust out laughing, but he managed to keep a straight face because he could see that Henning and Hossencofft were serious. He also wondered where the story might go next.

What became clear was that Henning and Hossencofft planned to leave Albuquerque soon because they were among "the chosen few" who would survive the alien attack.

On July 16, 1999, Hossencofft's intention to move was more evident than ever when he put the Tierra Madre real estate company's For Sale sign in his front yard.

That same day, Felissa Garcia Kelley moved to withdraw as Hossencofft's divorce attorney. Due to the attorney-client privilege, the reason for Kelley's decision was unknown. But the outcome was not—motion denied.

By summer 1999, twenty-nine-year-old Dwayne Baker had worked hard to put his life back together. It had been nearly three years since he'd left New Mexico and what had become a living nightmare.

Baker now worked for Highland Dairy in Wichita, Kansas, when he took a six-day vacation near the end of July. He looked forward to visiting friends and relatives and made the seven-hundred-mile drive from Wichita to Albuquerque on a Saturday.

After visiting his father and a friend, Baker began thinking about the elderly neighbors he had enjoyed knowing years earlier in Northeast Albuquerque.

On Tuesday, he went to see the tough, tell-it-like-it-is Kari Wyeth. With the staccato delivery of a machine gun, Wyeth delivered the latest headlines concerning the "fella" living on Moon Northeast: "Whacked-out"; "Flipped his lid"; "Not the same person."

As Baker left Wyeth's home that day, she offered some parting advice: "Just don't go over there. He's totally flipped. You don't know what he's capable of," she said.

Baker didn't go far. He ventured around the next block to Delamar Avenue to see if his old friend Pedro Tirado was home. He was pleased to find the old man taking out the trash. All that Tirado wanted to talk about, though, was Hossencofft. He gave a report similar to Wyeth's, explaining that Girly had been beaten and Hossencofft was a changed and violent man.

The reports from Wyeth and Tirado stayed with Baker that day. He resolved that he'd go and get a firsthand look. Besides, Baker had driven his truck from Wichita. If Hossencofft still had Baker's furniture and computer, perhaps he could get it back.

Yes, he'd go and see Hossencofft the next day.

"Come on in! Are you hungry? I've got some food."

Baker was surprised to get such a warm greeting from the guy he'd betrayed nearly three years earlier, especially after everything Wyeth and Tirado had told him.

Hossencofft wasted no time and launched into a story about the latest exciting development at Hossencofft Industries; the Biogenics Reactor had just been manufactured by a company in Pennsylvania.

Not only did Hossencofft act as if he and Baker had last parted on good terms, he wasted no time slinging the same old lies. Baker pretended to believe the story about the Biogenics Reactor; the incentive was right in front of him.

While almost everything in the house was packed in moving boxes, a few items were not, including Baker's computer and furniture.

He stayed for dinner that night and returned to visit the following day, still hoping to get his possessions. But Hossencofft wanted something done first.

As the topic of conversation turned increasingly to Girly, Hossencofft's anger started to pierce the pleasantries. Girly was getting his mother's jewelry and 50 percent of the equity in the home in the divorce settlement, he said. That was so unfair.

He reminded Baker about the large amount of money he'd shown him in a safe-deposit box more than three years earlier. Baker remembered.

Hossencofft told Baker that he wasn't married to Girly at that time. Girly shouldn't get any of that money. Would

Baker agree to come to his divorce attorney's office and sign a statement that he'd seen the cash prior to the marriage?

Baker said he would, prompting Hossencofft to call his attorney immediately and set an appointment for the end of the week. When Baker arrived at Hossencofft's house the following day, Hossencofft continued to speak disparagingly about his estranged wife. Baker continued to play along.

"I can't believe she's doing that to you."

Baker just wanted to get out the door, load his furniture into his truck and leave.

Hossencofft asked if Kari Wyeth or Pedro Tirado had mentioned where Girly lived.

"No," Baker replied.

Hossencofft showed Baker the temporary restraining order against him. Several lines were blacked out so as not to reveal Girly's address.

"Does she always drive the BMW? Too bad you didn't buy it for me," Baker said.

Hossencofft countered with a surprising remark: if the BMW wound up destroyed, it wouldn't bother him.

"What are you talking about?" Baker asked.

"She doesn't have insurance. The less she gets out of this divorce, the happier I'm going to be," he said.

He asked Baker if he'd tail Girly home from work, explaining that he knew that Girly lived in the Northeast Heights because he had seen her driving through the nearby intersection of Moon and Comanche a few times.

"Fine. I'm sure I can find where she is."

Years later, Baker said he had no intention of following Girly. He said he simply wanted his furniture and computer and was telling Hossencofft what he wanted to hear.

Hossencofft wasn't done. "Do you know how to destroy a car?" he asked.

"What do you want me to do?"

"Just bust a window, throw some gas in and light it. There's no insurance. She'll lose the car."

"I'm sure I can find out where she lives," Baker said.

He was careful never to say he'd blow up the car.

Near the end of the workweek, Baker and Hossencofft waited in the lobby at Kelley's law office as her secretary typed out a statement for Baker to sign.

"Did you follow Girly?" Hossencofft wanted to know.

"No." Baker explained that he'd spent the night with a girlfriend.

After signing the paperwork, Baker asked Hossencofft if he could borrow his Isuzu Rodeo. He had a dinner date with his girlfriend that night, and he'd really like to take her out in the SUV rather than his old pickup.

Hossencofft handed Baker the keys to the Isuzu, and he also gave him his hotel discount card.

And he kept pressing Baker to follow Girly home. He seemed to be getting antsy. Baker told him not to worry about it.

After going out to dinner, Baker and his girlfriend ended up crashing at his dad's house and slept in until nearly noon. Before returning the Isuzu to Hossencofft, Baker stopped by to say hello to a friend early that afternoon. Finally he filled the Isuzu up with gas and returned it to Hossencofft around 2:30 P.M.

Hossencofft was pissed. Baker hadn't even called to say where he was.

"You're not going to find out where she lives, are you?" Hossencofft asked.

"I don't have time."

"Okay. Well, at least we got the thing done with the attorney," Hossencofft said, realizing that he still relied on Baker coming back to testify in court regarding the statement he'd signed.

It turned out to be the final time Baker would see Hossencofft in person. He returned to Kansas with his computer and furniture. That was all he wanted.

"I don't care for him. I'd love to see him burn."

42

The computer chats between Hossencofft and Julie McGuire ran fast and furious between May and June 1999.

On May 9, 1999, Hossencofft wrote that he had endured an extremely emotional and heated afternoon at his house.

The NSA had come to take his son away for a few hours, he wrote.

> *"He will always be MY SON!!!!! I just wanted them to know I will never give up my son never!!!!!!!!!!"*

After the day Julie McGuire detected her boyfriend chatting on the computer with other women, McGuire decided she'd throw lies right back at him. She'd tell him everything he wanted to hear, and more. Her goal was to hold his interest while trying to find a way to protect Demetri from any harm.

Although she believed Hossencofft was a lying cheat, McGuire still believed he was a geneticist and held the key to a fountain of youth.

A May 23, 1999, ICQ chat propelled the stories of Hossencofft's declining health and the looming threat of the

NSA's taking Demetri away forever. It provoked strong words of allegiance from McGuire.

> *Foxybrat: you know that I would lay my life on the line for the both of you.*

By this time, Hossencofft had also hatched a new plan for McGuire to meet him in Seattle, where they could marry and live in secret with Demetri. Of course, that would take money. And McGuire still had her motel on the market.

Later, the ICQ briefly turned to sex.

McGuire e-mailed Hossencofft a picture of her buttocks. He liked that very much. He had a thing for anal sex.

> *zymogentic: you always know how to make me happy =)*

McGuire didn't like anal sex, and only halfheartedly tried to accommodate him once, although the effort stopped short because of some tearing.

> *Foxybrat: please don't feel bad I am OK . . . I just felt bad because I could not do it*
> *zymogentic: it is ok I just never asked you again*
> *Foxybrat: I am so sorry*
> *zymogentic: do not be it is an asian thing*
> *Foxybrat: I did not know that*
> *zymogentic: it brings two people together as one. . . .*

That McGuire had learned on May 10 that Hossencofft chatted with other women on the computer turned out to be a prelude to a hoax. In June, she was locked and loaded with powerful information after her friend in law enforcement ran a background check on Hossencofft.

Like a cat playfully pawing at a dying sparrow, McGuire played with Hossencofft's deceit in subsequent ICQ chats.

The stage was set on June 23, 1999, when Demetri played

in the pool at McGuire's motel. While enjoying the water, he told McGuire something that certainly got her attention: His mommy's name was Girly. That night, McGuire shared the story with Hossencofft during another ICQ session.

> *Foxybrat: He talks about Girly all the time*
> *zymogentic: the power puff Girls??*
> *Foxybrat: NO . . . He says that Girly is his mommy. . . .*
> *zymogentic: No His mothers name was Naoko Demetri calls all women, "Mommy." He calls you his mother too and especially when you're not around*
> *Foxybrat: I would not know that. . . . Maybe Girly does not know where he is. . . . Did you divorce her yet*
> *zymogentic: long time ago*
> *Foxybrat: how about if you tell me the truth about everything now*
> *zymogentic: I am telling you the truth*
> *Foxybrat: well lets see you were born in Texas March 5 1965*
> *zymogentic: and*
> *Foxybrat: well what else would you like me to tell you I have only asked for the truth*
> *zymogentic: you can tell me anything you want. . . . I will not deny anything you have my son youu wish not to help me with him now??*
> *Foxybrat: well you were arrested in January 1998 for aggervated assult of a family member*
> *zymogentic: yes I know*
> *Foxybrat: I love Demetri but I want you to tell me the whole truth about everything now . . . no more lies*
> *zymogentic: than let's talk on the telephone*

But the phone conversation didn't happen. It continued on for another half hour on the computer. In that time, Hossencofft apologized for not being up front about his pending divorce. He said that speaking about Girly was difficult because she had rejected him and his son.

zymogentic: All I ever wanted was a child and a wife that wanted us. . . .

Always the victim, Hossencofft promised to be truthful with McGuire from that point forward.

Foxybrat: We have cleared the air now and that is good.

The ICQ conversations became rare after that night in June. Their final chat took place during the early evening of August 26, 1999. It flip-flopped from sex to concern for the child.

Foxybrat: so how is Demetri doing
zymogentic: he is gone now
Foxybrat: he is with his new family?. . . . my heart is with you.

43

The Four Corners area is not simply a collection of small western towns and villages. It is also home to the nation's largest Native American reservation.

The Navajo Nation's twenty-six thousand square miles include stark, windswept plains, lava tubes and volcanic boulders, red earth, lakes, meadows and snowcapped mountains; and all of it fell quiet beneath the most magnificent of starlit nights as the aroma of burning piñon or alligator juniper drifts upon the fall desert air.

Serenity wraps around the soul as if it were a warmed blanket from Mother Earth, interrupted only by the early-evening and early-morning yips and howls of coyotes that pass by as they hunt.

Enchantment Lodge owner Julie McGuire enjoyed a mystery. But unlike mystery writer Tony Hillerman's Navajo crime-solving lawmen, McGuire's thriller was nonfiction. The danger was quite real.

McGuire desperately wanted to find a home for Demetri. She loved the boy. If left with no alternative, she would adopt him. But McGuire was now a fifty-one-year-old single grandmother. She felt Demetri deserved to be raised by a mother and a father, a couple with more life in front of them than behind.

She found one.

McGuire had previously introduced Demetri to a husband and wife from nearby Farmington, New Mexico. The couple already had a little girl and longed for a boy. After hearing that the boy's father was dying and that his mother had rejected him, the couple decided to adopt Demetri.

On August 6, 1999, excitement ruled the day as members of the Farmington family drove to Albuquerque to rescue a child. Hossencofft said that he had all of the necessary paperwork for the adoption and that his lawyer had approved it.

He wanted to make sure Demetri's new parents took a very special photograph with them, a picture his son could treasure for the rest of his life. It was a family picture of Demetri, Hossencofft and an Asian woman. But the woman's picture had been superimposed onto the image, as if someone had used a computer to cut her picture out of one photo and paste it into the father-and-son shot.

The woman, Hossencofft explained, was Demetri's "real mother."

Moments later, Demetri's new life began with his adoptive family. It lasted only one day. The Farmington couple did a sudden about-face, deciding that adopting Demetri was a bad idea.

On August 7, 1999, they delivered the boy and a disturbing story to Julie McGuire. Demetri, they said, attacked their one-year-old daughter, slamming her against the wall and physically hurting her.

McGuire was horrified. Was he copying his father?

She kept her thoughts to herself and agreed to take Demetri from the couple, telling the man and woman not to worry. She'd take care of everything.

The following day, Demetri's third birthday, McGuire threw a little party for him and called his father to report that the adoption had failed. Hossencofft became enraged.

"Now, D, just settle down, and we'll get this handled," McGuire told him.

"Put the kid on a bus!" he told her.

"No, I will not do that. Let me see what I can do from my end, maybe Social Services can help us."

McGuire called the Department of Social Services, but she didn't get very far. McGuire was told that if the state took the child, he'd go into a safe house; and that would automatically prompt a state investigation into the child's present care.

McGuire had no intention of turning the boy over to a safe house; he would *really* feel abandoned, she thought.

Hossencofft finally said that he had a solution, explaining that he presently had a nurse caring for him and that the nurse would come to Aztec to get the boy. But it didn't play out that way.

On August 10, 1999, McGuire looked outside her motel office and noticed a pickup truck as it pulled in front and parked. The driver stayed in the vehicle, while the passenger struggled to get out. He looked quite ill and limped badly.

"Here comes your dad," McGuire called out to Demetri.

McGuire met Hossencofft at the door. He said he was in great pain and had difficulty walking because he had an IV in his leg. McGuire had a hard time believing it, but he did make the predicament look so genuine.

"You got a cigarette?" Hossencofft asked before returning to the truck.

Puffing and limping, Hossencofft went back to the truck and asked the driver for some help. Demetri's toys and clothes were in the motel, and Hossencofft needed help getting them and loading them into the truck.

The driver, a much bigger man than the diminutive Hossencofft, walked as far as the office entryway, but he never went inside the motel.

"This is my friend Bill," Hossencofft told McGuire.

With Demetri now back in Albuquerque with his father, McGuire was hardly relieved. She still feared for the boy's safety and made a point to keep tabs on Hossencofft.

About a week after the failed adoption attempt, McGuire spoke with Hossencofft on the telephone. Once again, he was fuming. As usual, his rage was directed at Girly. She wanted everything, he said. If she had her way, he'd be left with nothing!

Hossencofft said Girly was a total bitch, a monster who wanted him to die so that she could have every last penny.

But he made his stories about his malevolent wife sound so believable. And McGuire did believe. Hoping to decompress Hossencofft's rage, McGuire made an off-the-wall comment.

"Too bad you're not like most men. Most men would have had her knocked off," she said.

McGuire had been physically abused in a prior relationship. She knew the type.

Hossencofft and McGuire laughed briefly. Finally Hossencofft said something that McGuire would never forget.

"She'll never spend a dime of that money."

McGuire paused. She had never heard him sound more serious. "What do you mean by that?" she finally asked.

"Well, I shouldn't get you involved."

"I've come this far. I'm here for you, and only you."

"Yes. I know I can trust you. There are some people that have already met Girly. As soon as she signs the papers, they're going to take her . . . and she's never going to be seen again."

"So? What does that mean?"

"No one's ever going to see her again because she's not going to ever be found. She's never going to be seen by anyone ever again."

"So, you mean that she's going to be killed?"

"Dissected is the better word for it."

"You mean cut into pieces?" McGuire asked, her voice rising in disbelief. "D, you're going to get caught."

"No way. My telling you this isn't even going to make any difference. I have no motive to kill her. I've paid for her, given her everything, I'm dying. I have no money. All my assets have been frozen all this time."

"How are you going to pay for it?"

"You know the blue bag?"

"Yeah," McGuire said as she remembered the diamonds she had seen in his blue bag. "Aren't you afraid of what you're doing?"

"She deserves it."

As she witnessed the apparent decay of Hossencofft's world, Kari Wyeth cared because fate had placed a child in his universe. Hossencofft's personality appeared to change after Girly had moved out. He seemed bitter and filled with resentment.

"Girly just left me and Demetri," he told Wyeth.

On many occasions, he'd stressed the abandonment theme by stating that he had no idea where Girly even lived.

Wyeth witnessed a man who claimed to have nothing in his home but crackers and water. His story had so moved some local Jehovah's Witnesses, they raised $90 and bought him groceries.

That angered Wyeth. She knew he had a freezer filled with food in the garage. He was just too damn lazy to cook it, she thought. Plus, he fed off everybody's pity.

In the cold, early months of 1999, Hossencofft refused to turn on the heat in his home. When temperatures finally climbed into the eighties and nineties in May, he did not use his swamp cooler. He was too poor to afford any of it, he said.

And then there was a smell. Wyeth noticed soiled diapers throughout the home.

Wyeth had never hesitated to tell people what she thought. Certainly, she'd grown skeptical of Hossencofft's tiring claim that he was dying. When he tried to tell it yet again, she ultimately put him in his place.

"Well, why don't you die and let us go on with our lives?"

After years of knowing Hossencofft, Wyeth realized she really didn't know him at all. She'd finally decided that he was a compulsive liar. Heck, he lied about stuff he didn't even need to lie about. He just couldn't help it. And he was so shameless and reckless with his deceit, giving neighbors different explanations for the circumstances in his life.

By the time Demetri landed in the nearly daily care of Wyeth, he was 2½ years old. For the next six months, she'd get to study the child closely.

Wyeth noticed that the young boy's hands closely resembled Hossencofft's. She grew convinced that Hossencofft had told her the truth at least once. She concluded he was Demetri's biological father.

There were heart-wrenching moments, too, especially those first weeks after Girly moved out. Demetri often called for his mommy.

"She is not your mother," Hossencofft said.

One time, Hossencofft grabbed a picture from the wall and held it before his son. It featured an Asian woman's face.

"This is your mother" he told the child.

But the woman in the picture was a stranger to the boy.

In the months that followed Girly's departure, Wyeth often looked across the street and saw Demetri with his face pressed against the living room's bay window in the late afternoon. Looking out toward the street, the boy cried as he waited for his mommy to come home.

She never would.

44

In the middle of August 1999, Linda Henning and Bill Miller traveled together to Magdalena. The two-hour drive from Albuquerque was capped off with the twenty-mile excursion into the rough terrain and heavily rutted Forest Road 123 that led to the isolated home of Miller's friends, Geneva Liddon and Randy Bell. Miller and Henning spent the night at the Liddon-Bell home before returning to Albuquerque.

It was also during the middle of August that Miller provided guns to Henning and Hossencofft. The trio traveled to the desert area west of Albuquerque known as the Rio Puerco and practiced taking aim at targets.

What, if anything, did the guns, target practice and trip to Magdalena have to do with the fate of Girly Chew Hossencofft? Was it all merely circumstantial?

On August 20, Henning's typical banking pattern suddenly shifted. Normally, she made deposits for her employer at specific Bank of America branches in the Albuquerque area. But on August 20, she made a deposit of $514.73 at the uptown branch, where Girly Chew Hossencofft worked as a teller.

Coincidence?

Six days later, Henning returned to make another deposit at the Bank of America uptown branch. Henning later said that she never noticed the name on the teller's large name-plate: Girly Hossencofft. The same unusual last name belonged to her lover.

Forty-five-year-old Vonda Cheshire had never worked an adoption case quite like the Hossencoffts'. Originally, Hossencofft had produced a New Mexico birth certificate that stated that he and Girly were the biological parents of three-year-old Demetri. That was odd, though, because Hossencofft could not produce any medical records proving that Girly had ever been pregnant. The child's medical records dated back to about one month of age, but nothing earlier.

When pressed for an explanation, Hossencofft had explained that he was the boy's biological father and admitted that Girly was not the blood mother. He said that the biological mother was an Asian woman who had simply provided an egg. Hossencofft said he fertilized the egg and grew it into a child in a laboratory.

Cheshire already knew that the Hossencoffts were in the midst of a bitter divorce, but now the case had turned from strained to fantastic. Cheshire learned that Hossencofft had told people that he was dying from leukemia. That information stuck with her because a medical examination required for the adoption revealed that Hossencofft did not have leukemia or any other serious illness.

Where did Demetri really come from?

Had he been kidnapped as a baby?

Cheshire's concern for the child led her to the FBI. On August 23, she spoke with Special Agent John Schum and reported the stories surrounding the Hossencofft adoption case.

Three days later, a fearful Girly succumbed to Hossencofft's pressure and agreed to sign papers relinquishing her parental rights. While regretful about the decision, she hoped it would save her life.

Despite her modest salary, Girly had even agreed to pay Hossencofft $100 a month in child support. To help ends meet, she had taken a second job on August 24 and went to work for Software Etc. in the Winrock Center Mall.

On August 26, the same day Girly surrendered her rights to Demetri, McGuire made a breakthrough in her efforts to play detective with her mysterious Internet lover.

In a recent phone conversation, Hossencofft had already told McGuire that once Girly finally signed the relinquishment papers, she would fall prey to trusted people and would ultimately be dissected. Hossencofft had also told McGuire that he had tipped his hand to his divorce attorney, but he said that he did not reveal the plan. He said he only told Kelley that Girly would never see a dime of the divorce settlement.

During their August 26 computer chat, Hossencofft told McGuire that his attorney asked what he had planned for Girly.

As usual, Hossencofft's remark came after a bit of sex talk. And, once again, he typed as if he were drunk.

> *zymogentic: miss your naked body =)*
> *Foxybrat: I miss you also. . . .well did she go to court?*
> *zymogentic: yes she went to court all things going*
> *as schedule and my attory asked again about her*
> *but I said it is better you know nothing*

45

Girly had a reason to celebrate on August 27, 1999. It was her thirty-sixth birthday.

Unbeknownst to her, the day was also marked with another festive occasion. That morning, Hossencofft and his two friends took three-year-old Demetri fishing in Northwest Albuquerque. It was intended to be an opportunity for Hossencofft, Henning and Miller to say farewell to the boy. Hossencofft was scheduled to hand his son over to an adoptive family later in the day.

The fishing at Shady Lakes was always good for kids. The privately owned lakes were actually the size of small ponds and were constantly stocked with an abundance of fish.

Before leaving Shady Lakes that morning, Hossencofft, Henning and Miller posed with Demetri in a group photo. It looked like a wholesome scene from Walton's Mountain.

During the short time Vonda Cheshire came to know Hossencofft, she witnessed a strange man's tortured world. He was going through a bitter divorce. He struggled with a drinking problem. And he said he was "dying" of leukemia.

On August 27, 1999, Demetri's adoptive parents arrived at the Hossencofft house around noon to sign the final paperwork and to take the boy home with them. Demetri's clothes and toys were all packed and ready to go.

Inside the home, most of Hossencofft's belongings were also packed in moving boxes.

That afternoon, Hossencofft's cries of agony and torment took center stage. He appeared to be severely grief-stricken about handing over his son.

Shortly after leaving Hossencofft's home, Cheshire was so concerned about his mental state that she decided to return. Hossencofft remained distraught. He made quite a production of showing Cheshire a gun and bullets.

Cheshire recognized that the weapon was a revolver. Her husband owned one, too.

"Do you intend to kill yourself?" she asked.

Hossencofft didn't say yes. But he didn't say no, either.

But, at last, he did calm down a bit.

"Promise me that you'll call me if you start thinking about killing yourself," Cheshire said.

But Hossencofft wouldn't promise anything. He had only one thing left to say: "You can go now."

Cheshire couldn't let it go. Hossencofft might have been preparing to kill himself. After leaving his house, she called 911. After hearing her account of the events that afternoon, the operator dispatched an officer to the house.

Several times a day, each day of the year, Albuquerque police are asked to check on the safety of citizens who haven't been seen or heard from in recent days and weeks.

There is a tendency to call these welfare checks "routine." But, as officers of the law are often quick to point out, there is nothing "routine" about their work.

Hossencofft, though, assured Sergeant Ade that he was okay and that there was nothing to worry about.

Still concerned that Hossencofft might have some suicidal tendencies, Sergeant Ade asked him whether he had any guns. Hossencofft said he had three firearms. The veteran lawman skillfully suggested that it might not be a bad idea for a friend or neighbor to look after the firearms while Hossencofft dealt with his grief. Hossencofft agreed with Sergeant Ade and immediately asked his neighbor John Deyber to hold onto the guns for a while. Deyber agreed.

Satisfied that a wise step had been taken, Sergeant Ade began to walk away from Hossencofft's house when he turned to ask a final question. "By the way, where's your wife?"

"She's dead," Hossencofft lied.

Her troubling encounter with Hossencofft earlier in the day remained on the mind of Cheshire that night. While dining at an Albuquerque restaurant, she decided to share her concerns with her husband. She knew that sharing specific case information wasn't ethical, but something in Cheshire was now telling her that she should be concerned about her safety.

As Cheshire finished up her story with details of the gun, the bullets and her call to 911, a chilling voice with a disapproving tone emerged from just over her shoulder.

"You shouldn't be telling such stories."

It was Hossencofft sitting in the booth directly behind her. He was dining with Henning.

46

Girly spent part of her birthday at the FBI's headquarters in Albuquerque. Special Agent John Schum contacted her after learning about Vonda Cheshire's concern that Demetri Hossencofft may have been kidnapped as an infant.

Girly voluntarily came downtown to give him a statement; the information revealed new insight into her history with Hossencofft. According to FBI records, Girly said that she met her husband through *Pen Pal* magazine, eight or nine years earlier. She explained that she had corresponded with several men throughout the world, including the United States, and had even traveled to the United States from Malaysia to meet some of them.

Eventually she corresponded with the man who called himself Armand Christopher Chavez. He lived in Salt Lake City at the time and said that he was a doctor. He told her he was half Japanese and half German and that he had been raised by a rich grandfather in Switzerland.

Girly said that she first visited Chavez after he moved to Albuquerque. By that time, though, he was using the name Diazien Hossencofft. He had said that was his real name and that Armando Christopher Chavez was an alias he used to perform secret work on behalf of the national defense.

Later, she returned to marry him.

As Girly continued to speak with Special Agent Schum, her story soon shed new light on Demetri.

Girly explained that Diazien had wanted a child, but she was devastated to learn that she could not get pregnant. Her husband said that they would adopt, and eventually he said that he would conceive a child with another woman. He said he had narrowed his prospects to two women. Girly, he promised, would be able to raise the child as her own.

She said it was late August or early September 1996 when Hossencofft brought the baby boy home. Hossencofft explained that the mother was Asian and that he had obtained sole custody through a legal adoption. Her husband never told her anything more about the biological mother.

Girly explained that she had agreed to raise the child as her own. She also said that it wasn't uncommon for her husband to travel out of town for three to seven days. He called these excursions "business trips."

In time, she learned that he was corresponding with numerous women throughout the United States and Canada. It started when she began receiving phone calls. Mysterious women wanted to know if Hossencofft was home, and they were always surprised when Girly answered the phone. Many of the women told her they were engaged to Hossencofft.

One woman was no longer enchanted with him. She told Girly that he had stolen passports from her and her daughter.

More evidence of Hossencofft's playing around arrived on Demetri's birthdays. The child always received gifts and cards in the mail from unfamiliar women. Girly was hurt as Hossencofft often told Demetri to call these women "Mama."

As Girly continued to unravel some of her husband's mysterious history, she explained that he had converted one of the bedrooms in their house into an office. He'd kept it locked and she was never given a key. The room was off limits.

Occasionally he mistakenly left the door unlocked. Girly had dared to venture inside and made more troubling discoveries, including romantic messages from women on his computer and papers dated 1995 that indicated, among other things, that he'd been impersonating a doctor and had provided medical treatment to a woman in Santa Fe.

Girly said that she eventually questioned Hossencofft about the other women, but that he had responded with anger and remained secretive. In time, he had become physically abusive. One time, she said, Hossencofft hit and choked her, and she fled to a neighbor's house. That episode had prompted her to move out of the house and get a restraining order.

Girly told Special Agent Schum that she was in the midst of a heated divorce and that she had moved into an apartment.

"Does he know where you live?"

"I don't think so."

47

During the third week of August 1999, sixty-four-year-old Kheng Chew and his wife, sixty-three-year-old Margaret Chew, carefully put together a care package for their only daughter, their beloved Girly, who lived half a world away.

Beginning with five Oriental cookbooks, Mr. Chew carefully placed the items into the cardboard box destined for his daughter's home in Albuquerque.

The care was coupled with concern. As any older parent knows, the worry over a child's welfare never stops. For Kheng and Margaret Chew, that anxiety increased the day Girly became engaged to the man who called himself Dr. Diazien Hossencofft.

From the beginning, the Hossencofft gentleman seemed out of the ordinary. It was difficult to know what to believe, their daughter's reassurances or a parent's instinct.

Kheng Chew added one packet of curry powder and some dried curry leaves to the care package.

He remembered the letters that had come from Hossencofft seven years earlier, just months before Girly left Penang for a life in the United States. In a letter dated April 20, 1992, Hossencofft launched into the delicate task of explaining why he'd never asked Girly's parents for permission to marry their daughter:

> *I ask you and your wife's forgiveness in anything that your daughter and I have done which might have upset the harmony in your lives to this point as this was not my intention. I want to apologize to you also for not asking your permission to get married.*

That three-page letter appeared to have been produced with great care. Entirely typewritten in italics, Hossencofft's story looked pleasant on paper. It was also steeped with impressive claims. Hossencofft wrote that his "point of origin" was Zurich, Switzerland, and that he worked for the United States government's space program, specifically, NASA's National Defense Systems.

Back in the spring of 1992, that letter had done nothing to make Kheng and Margaret Chew feel better about their daughter's plan to marry Hossencofft. Mr. Chew had said as much in a written reply.

Hossencofft wasted no time responding to the letter from his fiancée's father. Hossencofft's second letter was handwritten, almost sloppy. It appeared to be a casual effort:

> *Dear Mr. and Mrs. Chew,*
> *I received your letter today . . . I was very sorry to know that you were upset with your daughters and my choice to get married without your permission . . . Both Girly and I really love one another very much.*
> *Fondly,*
> *Diazien Hossencofft*
> *18-5-92*

Mr. Chew placed some red skirt material beside the cookbooks, curry powder and dried leaves. There was something else, though, to be added before sealing up the box and sending it on its way to the United States: four audiotapes of Buddhist chanting to Kuan Yin, the goddess of mercy.

The package was mailed in short order, but Girly would never receive it.

48

For Kari Wyeth, the morning of Wednesday, September 8, 1999, started out with a pleasant word from a neighbor. Hossencofft called to ask if she'd like any of the food in his freezer. He was about to move, and it would be a shame to see good food go to waste.

The freezer was full. As Wyeth went about the task of putting the food into the grocery bags she'd brought with her, the movers arrived to pack Hossencofft's furniture and other possessions.

Wyeth carried the bags of food back to her house, then returned to retrieve some more. As she left the kitchen a second time, a woman was at the door and wasted no time making an impression.

"Are you Marilyn?" the woman asked.

Wyeth detected an unmistakable tone of hate.

"No, I'm Kari."

"Well, just what are you doing in this house?" the woman asked.

"I don't know. Why don't you ask D? He may tell you. Then again, he may not."

Wyeth had seen that woman before. She'd noticed her visiting Hossencofft's home in recent weeks. Sometimes she'd drive a Cadillac, sometimes a liver-colored Honda. The ugly encounter wasn't the lingering impression at Hossencofft's home that day. When Wyeth had walked out of Hossencofft's garage, she glanced inside his white Isuzu SUV. The tailgate was open and she noticed a shovel inside. The notion seemed odd to Wyeth; she'd never known him to undertake manual labor.

Ten-and-a-half hours after her rude encounter across the street, Wyeth heard her doorbell ring. It was Hossencofft, wearing a long-sleeved polo shirt with broad navy-blue and yellow stripes. He held a gallon of milk.

After putting the milk into Wyeth's refrigerator, Hossencofft went to the den to say farewell to Gary Wyeth. Mr. Wyeth, unable to move or talk, maintained eye contact and listened.

Before returning home that night, Hossencofft stated that he still had a lot of work to do before the move. Thursday was going to be a very busy day, he said.

49

Much has been written about fear, especially the intuition that something bad is about to happen while everything appears to be okay. Does the human mind possess some intrinsic mechanism that senses approaching danger?

If such an instinct does exist, it had certainly kicked into overdrive for Girly on September 8, 1999. The sense that she was about to be attacked was so grave, she decided to call the FBI and speak with Special Agent John Schum.

On the telephone with Schum, Girly stressed that she feared for her life. She felt desperate. She reminded him that Hossencofft had beaten her in the past.

"He's capable of anything," she told him.

Schum considered reasons that could prompt an immediate arrest. Had Hossencofft made any recent threats?

"No," Girly told him.

Had he been stalking her?

"No."

Without any threats or stalking, he had no grounds for an

arrest, he explained. Schum added that Girly should contact him if Hossencofft did start to threaten or stalk her. And if she felt "immediate fear for her life," then she should call 911.

50

By the early fall of 1999, forty-one-year-old Terrie Gruen had enjoyed working with Girly for the past two years. Gruen was especially impressed with Girly's work ethic; she outworked everyone.

For several weeks, Gruen and Girly rushed to the break room at the Bank of America for a quick glance at the *Albuquerque Journal*'s stocks section; each had options in Bank of America stock. The two women had vowed not to sell until the stock hit $85 a share. Day after day, the stock inched closer to their magic number.

"Don't sell, don't sell," they kept telling each other, trying to maintain their resolve and not give into the temptation to sell before the stock hit $85.

One morning, they opened the paper and discovered the stock had plummeted. The two women laughed.

"That's what we get for being greedy," Girly said.

Gruen agreed.

Once a month, the pair enjoyed going to Furr's Cafeteria for lunch, usually around payday. Their coworker Jesse Grove often joined them. As the trio made their way down the buffet line, Girly always got the same thing: fish, mushrooms and some dessert to satisfy her sweet tooth.

On September 9, 1999, Girly was leading all employees in the latest contest to see who could get the most number of referrals. But the contest required that all of the applications for the prospective bank members be entered into the computer by the end of the workday.

True to form, Girly had accumulated a large number of referrals that day.

"There's no going home until all of those applications are entered into the computer," Girly told Gruen at the end of the workday.

The two did their little "happy dance" while sharing a laugh, then set about the task of entering the data into the computer.

"See ya tomorrow," Girly said as the two finally left the bank.

But tomorrow never came.

51

On September 9, 1999, around 4:00 P.M., Hossencofft went to the Winrock Center in Northeast Albuquerque and ventured inside a specialty store called The World of Knives. Inside, he found a variety of swords. Once, he had told Julie McGuire he owned a samurai sword, a warrior's weapon of honor. That, however, was not the type of sword he purchased that afternoon. Instead, he bought a ninja sword, the weapon of an assassin.

Ron Wilkin had just picked his wife up from work when they decided to stop by the Page One bookstore in Northeast Albuquerque shortly after 4:00 P.M.

While reading his favorite car and travel magazines at the back of the store, he heard a familiar voice say hello. It was Bill Miller.

"I want you to meet Dr. D," Miller told him.

Wilkin had long heard the stories of Diazien Hossencofft, and based on the bizarre accounts from people in the UFO Group, Wilkin never had a desire to meet the guy. But because Miller obviously wanted to make the introduction, he agreed.

Wilkin followed Miller to the coffee shop inside the front of the bookstore and found Dr. D with Linda Henning.

Hossencofft appeared to be sick and offered little eye contact. Henning explained that he had leukemia.

Wilkin reached out to shake Hossencofft's hand and found it disturbing. A man who believed he could always detect some sort of energy from people, Wilkin felt nothing positive or negative about Hossencofft's grip. It was simply dead.

The conversation soon launched into familiar topics from the UFO Group. Although Wilkin had not been to a meeting for several months, his friend Rick Carlson had kept him up to date on the increasingly odd behavior from Henning. Wilkin still had no idea just how drastically the woman had changed. Until now.

Henning looked disheveled; her hair appeared to have been through a whirlwind; her clothes looked messy. Her speech was scattered. She seemed jumpy. It was a drastic departure from the beautiful, professional businesswoman whom he had known at the UFO meetings earlier that year.

Henning dwelled on her favorite topics: reptilian aliens and newly revamped freeway overpasses. The aliens were among us and the overpasses featured symbols taken from their unique language. Wilkin listened and watched as the strange gave way to the bizarre.

Henning, holding a walkie-talkie, drifted from the coffee shop to other nearby parts of the bookstore.

"Where are you?" Hossencofft demanded to know as he spoke into a second handheld radio.

The scene played out repeatedly every few minutes.

What a weird couple. They seem like two little puppies together.

The frenetic Henning told Wilkin about her lovemaking

with Hossencofft. The sex was so energized and incredibly intense, she said, that the duo transformed into lionlike creatures.

Henning used a finger to pull back her lip as if to reveal the fangs that she said actually protruded during the frenzied climax.

This is not the woman I used to know. It's as if she's undergone some sort of shock treatments, Wilkin thought.

Hossencofft had walked a short distance away from the coffee shop and was barely out Henning's line of sight when he demanded to know her whereabouts again.

"Look, pal, we're over here. We're just talking. So just relax," Wilkin told him.

Hossencofft's anger at Henning, his determination to control the woman, annoyed Wilkin.

The more he saw of Hossencofft, the less Wilkin cared for him. The man seemed sneaky and sounded like Truman Capote.

Wilkin noted Miller's enthrallment with Hossencofft. *Bill's treating him like the next Messiah.*

While everyone was seated in the coffee shop, Hossencofft, Henning and Miller spoke about their urgent quest to get out of New Mexico as soon as possible. Wilkin and his wife listened as Miller talked about the looming martial law he felt would surely unfold once Y2K arrived. Hossencofft, too, spoke about the trio's attempt to get out of Albuquerque. They wanted to get to South Carolina, and they had been trying to find a travel trailer or recreational vehicle to drive there.

The big hang-up for the speedy retreat to South Carolina, Wilkin learned, had been Henning's town house. There was no way she was going to be able to sell it right away. It just didn't make sense that she'd be able to leave immediately.

Wilkin thought that Hossencofft, Henning and Miller all seemed nervous and agitated.

Eventually Hossencofft and Henning got up from the

table to get a sandwich. Seconds later, the first words out of Miller's mouth were the kind you never forget: Miller said that he and Henning had been recruited to kill Hossencofft's ex-wife. Both Wilkin and his wife heard it.

It was the same revelation that Miller had made a few weeks earlier at Wilkin's home. Back then, Miller had seemed relieved to get it off his chest. This time, however, it seemed that Hossencofft's hold over Miller was more intense and that the deed was fast approaching.

Wilkin was surprised that Miller still hadn't reported the plot to the police.

"You've got to do something about it now, Bill. You're a direct link to this. If it comes from me, it's only hearsay."

Wilkin thought he noticed a funny look in Miller's eyes. They looked glazed over.

This guy's serious, Wilkin thought.

It seemed Miller was in a state of disbelief and wanted out of something that was going too far.

"Bill, you really need to do something. This is just nuts," Wilkin added.

Having just entered her referrals into the computer and said good-bye to Terrie Gruen, Girly left work and set out for her post office box.

Having a PO box was smart. It made tracking her down more difficult.

Girly inserted a long white envelope into the slot for outgoing mail. It was the letter she'd written earlier in the week to her parents in Malaysia.

Upon returning home, Girly wondered why she hadn't received her phone bill yet. At 7:03 P.M., she called the phone company to ask why.

A few minutes later, Girly's telephone rang. Ernie Johnson was making her regular evening phone call.

But there was no answer.

Johnson called repeatedly that evening.

Girly must be working late at the mall . . . or maybe she's gone to see a movie.

Having convinced herself of a logical explanation for her unanswered calls, Johnson went to bed around 10:00 P.M.

52

Scattered clouds stretched across an early-evening Albuquerque sky as a slight breeze swept through the Northeast Heights. It was right around 7:00 P.M. on September 9, 1999. Daylight still clung to the Albuquerque area, but dusk was drawing near.

Moments earlier, a brief rain shower left behind the sweet scent of moist desert air.

"It smells so good outside, let's sit here on the front porch for a few minutes before you leave," Kari Wyeth said to her friend, fifty-nine-year-old Florence "Flo" Pugh.

Pugh agreed that it was a great idea and joined Wyeth on the bench near the front porch.

The tranquil moment was interrupted by a car coming up Moon Street from the south, not at a high rate of speed, but with apparent urgency.

The two women immediately recognized the Honda. It belonged to the caretaker who was looking after Hossencofft. She had been coming to his house for the past several weeks.

The Honda cut crosswise into Hossencofft's driveway. The brakes slammed, the car parked at an angle.

"Oh, Kari, he has company, a black man," remarked Pugh, who happened to be African American.

But Wyeth recognized the lone man who'd emerged from the Honda. She knew that walk, the hair, the height.

"Oh, no, that's not a black man. That's him."

Sure enough, it was Hossencofft in a dark green, short-sleeved shirt and shorts. But his entire body was painted black: his face, his legs, his arms—everything in sight.

Pugh was stunned. The man was charcoal black. But as she continued to study him, she could see it truly was Hossencofft.

"Why, he's blacker than I am," she said.

The two women laughed. Hossencofft did not appear to notice them. In seconds, though, Hossencofft's odd appearance troubled Wyeth and Pugh.

The car had arrived quickly. Hossencofft walked at a deliberate pace and with his head down as he made his way to the front door.

"Let's get in the house. Something's wrong," Wyeth said.

Sitting in the living room, the two women stared out the window toward Hossencofft's house across the street. He was turning the lights on inside his home.

Wyeth looked at the clock on her wall. The time was 7:20 P.M. She started to get a sick feeling.

Less than five minutes after he entered his house, Hossencofft emerged and got back into the Honda. He backed out of the driveway, punched the accelerator and sped away northward on Moon Street, the tires squealing.

The two women were now frightened by what they had just witnessed.

Whoever had painted Hossencofft had done a damn good job. It was as if he wanted to be camouflaged.

Later that night, Wyeth awoke from a frightening dream. In it, she encountered Hossencofft in her hallway. He was dressed all in white. In fact, he sort of looked like the Stay Puff Marshmallow Man. It sounded funny to say that later. But in her dream, the sight of Hossencofft terrorized her.

Flo Pugh awoke in the middle of that same night. It was about 3:00 A.M. on September 10, 1999, when she thought she heard the unmistakable voice of a woman screaming.

"Help me! Help me! Help me!"

Shaken by the cries for help, Pugh got out of bed and looked outside her front door. There was nothing. She peered outside her bedroom window: still, nothing.

Finally she decided it must have been her imagination.

53

"Welcome to Albuquerque."

The words awoke thirty-three-year-old Sherry Clinton (an alias) in her seat aboard the Delta Airlines flight.

At last, she'd finally made it to Albuquerque.

Nothing was going to spoil Clinton's excitement. She was about to meet her fiancé in person for the first time.

Dr. Diazien Hossencofft probably wouldn't be at the airport, though. He'd said he'd be busy moving that night. No problem. She had a cousin in Albuquerque who could pick her up.

Clinton had no idea that her fiancé was making love to a woman in a Northeast Albuquerque town house at that moment.

Before she'd left her home in South Carolina, Clinton made sure that Hossencofft knew she'd be staying at the Marriott Residence Inn. At 2:07 A.M., Clinton checked in to room 123. She was impressed with the studio suite. It seemed more like an apartment.

As she went to bed, she decided to leave her door unlocked, her concern for safety outweighed by fanciful machinations that her fiancé might arrive at any moment.

Simultaneously exhausted and aching for the man she'd only known through the Internet, Clinton drifted to sleep.

Around 4:00 A.M., Clinton was suddenly frightened and wide awake in the dark.

Right there in front of her, just inches away from her, was a man's face. It scared her shitless.

The man told her to calm down. Everything was okay.

It was Diazien! Clinton's fear subsided to relief.

"Don't you ever scare me like that again," Clinton said.

"You left the door open. That was stupid," Hossencofft said. "Why did you leave the door open?"

"For you."

Behaving like lovebirds, the two spent the next few minutes becoming better acquainted before Hossencofft explained that he must leave. There was still some business he had to attend to, including some last-minute packing. Clinton agreed to wait for him at the hotel.

With the woman from South Carolina tucked away at a hotel, Hossencofft attended to other affairs.

At 10:30 A.M. on Friday, September 10, 1999, Hossencofft and Henning showed up late for a scheduled appointment at American RV in Albuquerque. Salesman Tim Rich had initially met the couple two days earlier. They had made it clear to Rich that they were interested in buying an RV that could be shielded from satellite tracking. And the bigger the water-storage capacity, the better.

Rich had shown Hossencofft an RV and pointed out that there was plenty of space beneath a bed for an extra water tank.

"You could probably hide a body in there," Hossencofft remarked.

On Friday morning, the pair attempted to hammer out a deal for an RV, but to no avail.

Buying lunch was much easier. Henning and Hossencofft dined at the Tomato Café and enjoyed the buffet.

As usual, Henning picked up the tab.

Several hours later, around 6:00 P.M., Kari Wyeth noticed Hossencofft driving away from the house on Moon Street.

About an hour later, Clinton and the man of her dreams were in his Isuzu Rodeo bound for marital bliss in South Carolina.

It would be the unforgettable journey of a lifetime.

54

Hossencofft, Spiers mused.

From the beginning, the name sounded like a lie to Assistant District Attorney Paul Spiers.

On an instinctive level, the name alone was enough to tell the ADA to check out Hossencofft's background. And Spiers already knew that Girly's estranged husband had left town while his house remained on the market.

It hadn't taken long for his suspicion to deepen. Spiers spoke with Girly's divorce attorneys, Bryan Fox and Traci Wolf, and learned that Hossencofft's lawyer had been seeking an unusual stipulation: Girly could not go to the FBI and reveal Hossencofft's true background.

It wasn't the first time investigators would hear about the FBI, either. Doyle Monk, Hossencofft's cellmate in the Torrance County Detention Center, later told investigators Hossencofft had confided in him.

Monk said that Hossencofft had told him that Girly had planned to go to the FBI on September 13, 1999, just four days after she had disappeared.

Had Hossencofft feared that Girly would expose him?

The FBI certainly already had an interest in Hossencofft

prior to September 1999. On August 27, 1999, the adoption caseworker, Vonda Cheshire, expressed trepidation when she told Special Agent John Schum that she felt Demetri might have been kidnapped.

Yes, when it came to Hossencofft, the prosecutor got bad vibes from the beginning. But the introduction provided by the initial weeks of Girly's investigation would pale when compared to the sinister revelations in the months, and years, to come.

55

Ron Wilkin had long believed that he had a gift, a spiritual connection to the hereafter. Perhaps it was because he'd apparently been there and back. Wilkin told people that he'd had two near-death experiences.

Wilkin also felt he had other links to the spirit world. Using a pendulum, he believed he could reveal the unknown. Having just met Hossencofft on the late afternoon of September 9, Wilkin wanted to know what the pendulum might reveal about the man.

"Either Hossencofft had killed somebody, or he was about to. And the pendulum reacted so strong, I didn't really even get to finish my thought or my question," Wilkin told police officers.

Wilkin said that while the pendulum had told him something frightening, a more significant moment occurred the following day. He said it started to unfold as he drove on Montgomery near Minato's restaurant. His wife was with him. He couldn't stop thinking about events related to his encounter with Hossencofft, Henning and Miller at the bookstore the evening before.

Because he had met Hossencofft, Wilkin believed he could use that connection to reach Girly in another realm.

If you want to tell me something, then tell me.

Wilkin said that's when he felt a massive wave of energy come toward him, causing the hair on his arms and the back of his neck to stand like never before. It was at that moment, Wilkin told detectives, that a woman's voice cried out from *the other side.* She was in great trauma.

Wilkin said he sensed tremendous pain and tears swelled in his eyes as he drove. He said he nearly wrecked his car, and then he pulled over to the side of the road, still sensing sheer terror. He told the detectives that something that felt like static electricity gripped his body as he sat in his parked car. There were visions of violence and rage.

Wilkin told detectives that the woman's spirit appeared before his eyes and shook him. *She's shown me her murder.*

Before driving on, Wilkin said, he told his wife that Hossencofft's estranged wife had been killed with a blunt object.

Wilkin told the detectives that he was so moved by his vision that he called two people later that same day: Bill Miller and Rick Carlson. He said he left a message on Miller's answering machine imploring him to call police. Wilkin said Miller never returned his call.

He said he also called Carlson and told him about the spiritual revelation.

"She's gone, buddy. He whacked her."

He asked Carlson to call the police, too.

Near the end of his interview with detectives, Wilkin urged them to search the foothills behind Henning's home. The pendulum and Girly's spirit had both indicated that the foothills were important, he said.

"I would definitely look for some tarps. I would look for something that the body would have been carried in," he told police.

"Where did you get the tarp from?" Detective Fox asked.

"From her (Girly's *spirit*) . . . Apparently she'd been carried in one or some sort of a bag or some sort of large-type tarp."

Had Wilkin really tapped into the spirit world? Or was the information merely suggested by the recent news coverage of Girly's disappearance?

Sunday morning, September 12, 1999, turned out to be a day Steve Zachary would never forget. Henning called, frantic.

The police wouldn't let her inside her town house because they were searching it. She said her friend Michael Harvey was standing beside her and was allowing her to use his cell phone to call Zachary.

That was a shock. Zachary knew that Harvey was a former boyfriend who had remained a close friend. Where was that Hossencofft character that Henning had obsessed over?

"Police just don't show up at your house, Linda. Are you late on some parking or speeding tickets?"

"It must be because of my views about the government. Several of us in the UFO Group are being followed," she said.

"What, did you penetrate Los Alamos or something? Area fifty-one?" Zachary asked.

Henning's call was a surprise. Zachary hadn't heard from her for 2½ weeks. And back then, she was bombarding him with a torrential blast of angry faxes and screaming phone calls. It had all been a response to his conclusion that Hossencofft was a fraud.

The ensuing silent treatment had been a bit of a relief. But Zachary had remained troubled by the extreme change in Henning's personality.

"Let me call Richard," he said.

Richard G. Sherman was a prominent Los Angeles attorney. He was sleeping when Zachary's call woke him at 7:30 A.M. Pacific time.

Zachary explained that police had taken over Henning's home and she needed help right away.

"Linda?" Sherman said with surprise.

Sherman and his wife had come to know Zachary and Henning in the 1980s. They had traveled in the same social circles and enjoyed the same restaurants.

"You know Linda, Richard. She's like Barbra Streisand in *The Way We Were,* always on a soapbox for some cause: cruelty to animals, children, the environment. This time, it's UFOs."

"What did she tell you?"

"It's something to do with the UFO club. She says the cops are following her and a few others. Maybe Gort has landed at Linda's house."

The two men laughed at Zachary's reference to the robot in the 1951 sci-fi classic, *The Day the Earth Stood Still.*

"Steve, it's Sunday morning. It's seven-thirty. I gotta hear this bullshit?"

"Hey, she's in New Mexico. What can I say?"

Sherman agreed to make a call for his longtime friend.

A moment later, Sherman was speaking with Henning. He asked her to put a police officer on the line. The officer explained that police had a legal search warrant and that Henning was not under arrest.

Later that day, police interviewed Henning and videotaped the interrogation. On camera, Henning stated that she was Hossencofft's caretaker; the relationship was professional. Heck, she really didn't even know how to pronounce the man's name. That's why she'd settled on calling him D.

Police wondered if Henning had been somehow victimized by Hossencofft. She seemed like a kind, unsuspecting woman who may have somehow figured into Hossencofft's web of deceit.

Although he knew that her recent behavior did not warrant such loyalty, Zachary resolved to stand by Henning. He hadn't forgotten the months she had spent looking after him a decade earlier, when multiple sclerosis had first gripped his body.

At that time, he was bedridden. He had no control over bladder or bowel. But she stood beside him and cleaned up all of his messes. Now that was loyalty.

A friend through thick and thin, Zachary began to send Henning money via Western Union and AmEx Grams.

As investigators finished up their search at Henning's home, two patrol officers responded to a routine burglary call more than fourteen miles away on Marquette Avenue Northwest, the law office of Felissa Garcia Kelley, Hossencofft's divorce attorney. Among the items reported stolen was a Smith & Wesson .38 Chief's Special revolver.

Kelley's landlady made the call to police at 2:20 P.M. Although it was a Sunday, the landlady said she had gone to the building located near downtown Albuquerque to do some work. She said that as she arrived, she discovered that someone had kicked in the back door to Kelley's office.

The landlady told police that Kelley had recently wanted some extra protection, so she loaned Kelley her revolver and its pouch.

Upon her arrival, Kelley told police that other items were missing from her office, too, including a stereo, some CDs, and a bottle of tequila. Kelly said that she had a likely suspect in mind: her brother. She told police that he was a heroin addict and had recently visited her office. He had seemed to be looking around her office, as if casing it, she said.

Sherry Clinton and Hossencofft had left Albuquerque on September 10, 1999, and headed for South Carolina. The confinement of the SUV meant it didn't take long for Clinton to witness her fiancé's erratic temper, moments never exposed within their cyber courtship. Inside the SUV, Clinton often witnessed Hossencofft injecting himself in his arms. He said the needles contained his medicine, morphine.

As the miles passed, Clinton noticed the track marks on Hossencofft's arms, and that if he didn't take his morphine, his body shook uncontrollably.

It was frightening.

She was so relieved after he took that medicine. He always calmed down nicely. He could think. And he obviously had a lot on his mind. Clinton also noticed a horrid hole in the bend of Hossencofft's arm. It penetrated beneath the skin toward underlying tissue. He said that the hole was an injury he'd suffered while he was exposed to radiation in a lab accident earlier in the year.

Clinton learned that Hossencofft had another medicine, too, a white powder. She often watched him put it under his tongue for immediate effect.

Clinton finally had the man of her dreams, but she had no doubt he was going to die soon. He was so ill. But a little time on earth with her soul mate would be better than no time at all.

It was destined to be a very bad time.

Hossencofft suddenly vomited blood, a lot. The convulsions of heaving, red puke set into motion the mad scramble for napkins from the most recently visited drive-through restaurants.

The lab accident caused the fits of blood coughing, too, he claimed. Still, despite his crumbling health, the injections, the eating of white powder, the driving and spewing of blood, he spent a lot of time talking on Clinton's cell phone.

During countless calls in the SUV, Clinton heard Hossencofft rattle off a lot of names, too many for her to remember. Besides, she had other things on her mind: a wedding, the move into a new house, her prince's less-than-charming health and one hell of a storm.

Hurricane Floyd was closing in on South Carolina.

Still, one thing annoyed Clinton. Over and over during their cross-country trip, she answered her phone and listened to the same woman's voice asking for D.

"Why does she call you D?"

"Everybody calls me D."

"It sounds really personal to me," she told him.

"Well, she's an inside informant. So, she's been telling me some important information."

Hossencofft said that people were dropping like flies back in Albuquerque.

"What are you talking about?" Clinton asked.

Hossencofft said several of his fellow researchers were coming up dead. He said he was afraid, because he could be next.

Were these people all contaminated in the lab accident, she wondered. Or was someone tracking these people down and killing them?

Clinton decided that she didn't want to know the details. A chain-smoker, she reached for another one of her Austin cigarettes.

On Monday, September 13, 1999, the final moments of an ordinary lunch hour were about to become unforgettable for Vonda Cheshire.

As she drove back to work at the Triad Adoption Agency, her cell phone rang. It was Hossencofft on the line. He said he was with his friend Bill Miller and that they were driving through Tennessee on their way to South Carolina Memorial Hospital for some preliminary leukemia treatment. He'd eventually be going to Juárez, Mexico, for some ozone treatment. Soon *powerful* anger crept into Hossencofft's voice.

"I know that you've been talking to John Schum."

The sparks of his anger accelerated into a full rage.

"I'm watching you, and I know what you are doing. You better be careful."

It felt like a threat.

Before hanging up, Hossencofft promised that he'd call again.

Kari Wyeth's phone rang around 10:30 A.M. on Tuesday, September 14, 1999. But no greeting came from the caller, only a purposeful statement.

"I understand you called the police and told 'em I was dressed in black. I was *not* dressed in black."

Wyeth was startled. It took a brief moment for the mysterious voice to connect with her brain. She realized that the caller was Hossencofft. *Is he still in town?*

Wyeth chose her words carefully. "I did not call the police."

Wyeth gently hung up the phone and reached for the business card she kept nearby. Detective Michael Hughes had left it when he had stopped by a few days earlier. The person who answered the phone at APD explained that Hughes was very busy at that moment.

"I don't care how busy he is! You get him on the phone right now," Wyeth ordered.

Within seconds, Hughes was on the line. Wyeth was practically hysterical as she told him about the call she'd just received from Hossencofft.

"How did he know that I told you guys anything?" she asked.

In a calm voice, Hughes told Wyeth that he wanted her to do something right away: hang up the telephone, then pick it up again and dial *69, which could reveal the number from which Hossencofft had called. Wyeth wasted no time and did exactly as Hughes had suggested. A moment later, she called him back.

It had worked. Wyeth read aloud the ten-digit phone number she'd just written down. It began with an 843 area code.

"Now we know where he's at," Hughes told her.

The number came back to South Carolina.

That was a bit of a relief to Wyeth. But stress clung to her. The woman had already been caring for a paralyzed husband for a decade. She already had enough anxiety in her life. And now she felt threatened by Hossencofft. He was apparently across country, but somehow he was watching her.

She felt vulnerable.

Fourteen days had passed since Julie McGuire had heard from Hossencofft when the phone rang at her Enchantment Lodge around 1:30 P.M. on Monday, September 13, 1999. The caller was a woman with Social Services in Albuquerque.

"Do you have Demetri?" asked the social worker.

"No, he's with his father or with a foster family."

"Well, Demetri's missing, and his mother's presumed dead. The Albuquerque Police Department will be calling you soon."

McGuire felt panic-stricken. She'd never thought he'd do it. D was all talk. Everything else he said was a lie.

Girly's dead?

At about 2:45 P.M. that same day, Detective Fox called McGuire and wanted to know how she had come to know Hossencofft.

"I met him on the Internet. He contacted me after he saw my ad on *American Singles.*"

McGuire was relieved to learn that Demetri was, in fact, with his adoptive family. He was okay. Fox made arrangements for the Aztec Police Department to keep a twenty-four-hour watch on McGuire. McGuire was told it was precautionary, just in case Hossencofft showed up. For the next several days, a police officer escorted McGuire to work each morning and home each night.

Special Agent John Schum had already received reports of Hossencofft's threatening phone calls to Cheshire and Wyeth when a third report came on September 17, 1999.

The female caller was extremely frightened.

It was Felissa Garcia Kelley, Hossencofft's divorce attorney. Kelley explained that Hossencofft had just finished screaming at her during a twenty-minute phone conversation. He'd sounded more agitated than ever before.

Hossencofft had said that he believed his son had been dissected. He demanded proof that the boy was alive and well. And then he gave her an ultimatum: he said that within sixteen hours there had better be convincing evidence on the Internet that Demetri was okay or "you're all going to die."

Kelley had no doubt whom he was threatening: herself, Schum and Cheshire. Kelley added that during his tirade on the phone, Hossencofft also said that he would destroy the planet.

Finally she also wanted Schum to know that someone had recently stolen a gun and a bottle of tequila from her law office.

After Kelley's phone call, Schum prepared an arrest warrant charging Hossencofft with three counts of transmitting in interstate or foreign commerce a communication containing threats to injure a person. A federal judge signed the warrant that same evening.

56

Jeff Zevely went the extra mile to keep his finger on the pulse of Albuquerque's violent crimes. Each workday, the twenty-nine-year-old reporter from Channel 7 called the police substations throughout Albuquerque to speak with the sergeants in charge.

Crime was Zevely's beat. And he was good at it, often lunching with cops around town and getting the inside scoop. In September 1999, Zevely learned from his sources at APD's northeast substation that a local woman had recently disappeared.

Right from the start, the cops told Zevely the missing woman's estranged husband had likely murdered his wife.

Zevely recognized the sharp, and wide, distinction that existed between "missing" and "murdered."

"Well, what makes you think this is murder?" the reporter asked his source.

"First of all, this guy is really weird. He's going around town telling people that he's a doctor and he's scamming them."

That wasn't enough for Zevely to buy the murder theory. He pressed the cops, asking for more information. His source shared that when police had entered Girly's apartment, they'd instantly been struck by the overwhelming smell of bleach. The source added that investigators had performed a presumptive test for blood by spraying luminol on the carpet inside Girly's apartment. The lights were turned off, and a blue light was used to detect any chemical reaction between the luminol and possible blood.

"I was told, 'The whole place lit up like a Christmas tree,' " Zevely said. "From that moment on, they thought she'd lost so much blood that she was probably dead. From that very second, they thought murder."

Zevely visited the Valle Grande apartment complex and noticed Girly's BMW parked outside apartment 53-D. The car's windshield was shattered. He also visited Hossencofft's house on Moon Street and discovered Detective Fox removing items from the trash can. Fox seemed uncomfortable to learn that a reporter was already onto the story.

As Zevely looked on from the street, he could see the detective removing glass containers from the trash. They appeared to be filled with blood. Zevely, whose father was a chemist, noticed that the narrow glass tubes appeared to be vials with rubber stoppers pressed into their ends.

Everything the reporter had seen and heard supported the possibility that a murder had taken place. But he struggled when trying to decide whether he should use the "M" word in his story of the missing woman. By the time the ten o'clock news began that Tuesday night, he had reached his decision.

More than four years later, Zevely easily recalled his exact words: "An Albuquerque woman is missing and may be murdered. I'm Jeff Zevely. It's a story you'll only see on seven."

Zevely had broken a solid story. He was hardly unfamiliar with crime and mayhem, and he had had several other exclusive murder stories in the past.

But this one would be different. Earlier that year, during the summertime, Zevely and his father had visited the Bank of America branch at the intersection of Montgomery and

Girly Chew with her brother Eric and parents Chew Shing Kheng and Margaret Chew. This photograph was taken April 29, 1967.
(Photo courtesy of Kheng and Margaret Chew)

Girly Chew celebrates her tenth birthday on August 27, 1973.
(Photo courtesy of Kheng and Margaret Chew)

Girly Chew *(left)* and Susan Oh, her best friend in Malaysia. The two worked together at the Bank of Hong Kong in Penang and enjoyed taking vacations together in the United States. This photograph was taken December 26, 1992.
(Photo courtesy of Kheng and Margaret Chew)

Girly Chew enjoys Christmas Day, 1992, at home in Malaysia.
(Photo courtesy of Kheng and Margaret Chew)

Girly Chew enjoys posing with her first Malaysian-made car.
(Photo courtesy of Kheng and Margaret Chew)

Diazien and Girly Chew Hossencofft at the home of Ernestine Johnson on Christmas Day. *(Photos courtesy of John and Ernestine Johnson)*

Girly and Demetri Hossencofft are all dressed up for trick-or-treating. Friends say Diazien Hossencofft designed and made the costumes seen here. *(Photo courtesy of John and Ernestine Johnson)*

Girly Chew Hossencofft with her close friend Ernestine "Ernie" Johnson on a visit to Taos, New Mexico. After Girly filed for divorce, Johnson typically spoke with her on the phone every night to make sure that she was okay. *(Photo courtesy of John and Ernestine Johnson)*

This photo of Julie McGuire appeared on the Internet dating service American Singles in 1999. Diazien Hossencofft responded to McGuire's ad. *(Photo courtesy of Julie McGuire)*

A statue of Kwan Yin, the Buddhist goddess of mercy, as Girly left it in her apartment. Girly often prayed to Kwan Yin while listening to a cassette tape of Buddhist chanting. *(Mark Horner photo)*

Attorney Bryan Fox represented Girly Chew Hossencofft in her divorce. "She really tried to stay focused on the future," Fox said on October 25, 1999. *(Mark Horner photo)*

Forensic scientist Catherine Dickey conducted one of the largest DNA investigations in the history of New Mexico. She is holding a court exhibit that demonstrates that Linda Henning's blood was located inside Girly Chew Hossencofft's apartment.
(Mark Horner photo)

Forensic scientist Catherine Dickey is seated next to the AVI 310 Genetic Analyzer in the Metropolitan Forensic Science Center's Polymerase Chain Reaction room. Dickey used the machine to determine that Linda Henning's blood was found inside Girly Chew Hossencofft's apartment.
(Mark Horner photo)

Friday, January 14, 2000: Diazien Hossencofft leaves court following his arraignment on murder, kidnapping, and other charges connected to his estranged wife's death. During the arraignment, Hossencofft winked at Deputy District Attorney Julie Altwies. "I thought it was revolting," Altwies said immediately following the court appearance. (Mark Horner photo)

Diazien Hossencofft stands inside an elevator, waiting to return to jail following a court appearance on Monday, July 17, 2000. (Mark Horner photo)

After failing to reveal the location of his wife's body in a plea bargain, the jail parking lot seemed to become yet another stage for Diazien Hossencofft. His eyes were still locked on the TV cameras as KOB-TV photographer Mike Andersen shouted, "Who *does* know where the body (of Girly Chew Hossencofft) is located?" Hossencofft laughed out loud. *(Photo courtesy of KOB-TV)*

January 14, 2000: Diazien Hossencofft's attorney Ron Koch speaks with the media following his client's arraignment in Bernalillo County District Court in Albuquerque. Mr. Koch died of cancer on December 19, 2000. He was forty-nine. *(Mark Horner photo)*

Linda Henning leaving court on April 24, 2000. *(Mark Horner photo)*

Linda Henning speaks with her attorney's private investigator, Dave Pfeffer, on September 26, 2002. *(Mark Horner photo)*

It is October 25, 2002, and the verdict is in. Attorney Gary Mitchell drops his head and Linda Henning remains stoic as the jury announces it has found her guilty of kidnapping and murdering Girly Chew Hossencofft. *(Photo courtesy of KOB-TV/Court TV)*

The remote area where Girly Chew Hossencofft's bloodstained clothing was located. It seemed possible that the killer or killers might have emerged from a nearby dirt road that leads into the Cat Mountain Ranch. A high profile search unfolded six days later and the area beyond this sign was suddenly off limits. *(Mark Horner photo)*

Searchers are briefed at the command post near Magdalena, New Mexico before setting out to look for the remains of Girly Chew Hossencofft on June 24, 2000. *(Mark Horner photo)*

Law enforcement officers address the media as a massive search is about to get underway near Magdalena on June 24, 2000. Facing the camera and holding the microphone is Albuquerque Police Department detective John Walsh. To the left of Walsh is Deputy District Attorney Julie Altwies. *(Mark Horner photo)*

William "Bill" Miller (left) is handcuffed as he is taken into the Bernalillo County Detention Center on Monday, February 12, 2001. At the time of his arrest, Miller was charged with first degree murder, conspiracy to commit first degree murder, kidnapping, conspiracy to commit kidnapping, harboring a felon, tampering with evidence, and other crimes in the Girly Chew Hossencofft case. *(Mark Horner photo)*

William "Bill" Miller *(center)* appears in court with attorney Timothy Padilla *(left)* during a "show cause" hearing July 17, 2000. Miller confirmed that he recorded a phone conversation with Linda Henning in October, 1999. He stated that he made the recording in Padilla's law office. Padilla told District Court Judge Richard Knowles on Monday that he simply lost the tape. Miller told the court that he never touched the tape, but simply pressed the buttons on the recording machine. Pictured at right is the late Ron Koch, who represented Diazien Hossencofft. *(Mark Horner photo)*

Assistant District Attorney Paul Spiers is questioned by the media immediately following Diazien Hossencofft's January 14, 2000 arraignment on murder, kidnapping, and other charges in Albuquerque. *(Mark Horner photo)*

June 25, 2000: After a daylong search of a mine shaft fails to produce the remains of Girly Chew Hossencofft, investigators look for signs of any soft ground before nightfall. *From left to right:* DEA Agent Mike Marshall and ADAs Jack Burkhead and Paul Spiers dig with hopes of finding the remains of Girly Hossencofft. *(Mark Horner photo)*

Andrew Chew minutes after his arrival at the Albuquerque Sunport on November 12, 1999.
(Mark Horner photo)

Andrew Chew is pictured at the home of the Pedro and Luz Tirado in November, 1999. Chew said that he came to the United States for "clearance," the beginning of the process of getting his missing sister's estate in order.
(Mark Horner photo)

October, 2002: During a private moment in the courtroom, Andrew Chew videotaped evidence in the Linda Henning murder trial so that he could show it to his parents and brother upon his return to Malaysia.
(Mark Horner photo)

This graffiti certainly captured the attention of investigators when they searched a dry river bed, called the Rio Puerco, for the body of Girly Chew Hossencofft. The painting depicts a man or alien pointing a gun at a woman who is on her knees. Bill Miller took Diazien Hossencofft and Linda Henning target shooting in this area prior to Girly's murder. There is no proof that this drawing is connected to the case in any way.
(Mark Horner photo)

Wyoming in Northeast Albuquerque. The attractive teller had been polite, professional and engaging.

As he walked away from the teller's window, Zevely's father—who was somewhat of a conservative cowboy—passed along some advice to his son.

"Now, that's the kind of woman you need, son. A woman who'll cook for you, keep the house clean and take good care of you."

Several months later, Zevely realized he'd just reported on that woman's disappearance.

"It was the first time I'd met a murder victim," he said.

Within minutes of Channel 7's broadcast, phones started ringing off the hook in Northeast Albuquerque as alarmed members of the UFO Group called one another.

Channel 7's report really seemed to confirm everything members of the UFO Group had feared.

Rick Carlson was stunned. Ron Wilkin had told him four days earlier that he felt Hossencofft's wife had been killed; the pendulum had told him so. And Wilkin had said a vision of Girly told him to search the foothills near Henning's home.

Carlson decided to call the FBI and told Special Agent John Schum what he knew about Hossencofft. He also expressed concern for Henning's safety.

After seeing the story on television about Girly's disappearance, UFO Group member Ann Stone performed her own pendulum reading and told Carlson that Girly was buried in the foothills near Henning's home. It was the same thing Wilkin had said.

Carlson decided to call the Albuquerque Police Department. Investigators on the Hossencofft case were not available, but he was able to speak with another detective.

"This guy was a guest of a lady that was coming to our luncheon group every week; then we all felt this guy was a con man, a scammer and a gigolo and that everything he said was a bunch of BS. And then, all of this came out Tuesday night, and several people in our luncheon group feel real strong that . . . they may have buried a body not far from this guy's girlfriend that he was living with that had come to our lunch group . . . and we would like to have the police search this area. . . . This may sound kooky or strange, but we've been right about everything else."

Carlson said two people had come to him on separate occasions and said they believed Girly's body was in the foothills near Henning's home.

"Yeah, and both of these people did not know that either had communicated this to me, and it's my moral and civic duty to call this in and have this followed up on in case it turns out to be right."

But Carlson had information beyond Hossencofft and Henning that also captured the interest of police. On September 20, 1999, he met with Detectives Fox and Bylotas, and much of their conversation ultimately focused on Bill Miller.

Carlson had known Miller for about two years. Their contacts were usually limited to the once-a-week UFO Group meetings. That's what made Miller's request, three weeks earlier, unusual.

"He asked me to join him for a cocktail at the sports bar one Sunday night. We talked for a couple hours concerning this situation," Carlson said. "He kept telling me that he wanted to get away from the situation, that Linda was calling him constantly on his pager and his phone, and complaining and crying about this and about that with Hossencofft."

He said Miller never provided specifics about what had distressed Henning.

"She was just real unhappy and upset at times, and then other times she'd call and everything was fine. The personality seemed to bounce back and forth from what Bill was telling me."

Carlson said that as he and Miller drank, Miller kept coming back to his desire to break free of Henning and Hossencofft.

"Bill had told me on numerous times that he wanted to get out of this, didn't want to spend time with him, that he was going away. But he always kept going back to the situation with Hossencofft and Linda."

"Would he say, specifically, what he wanted to get away from?" Detective Fox asked.

"No. He said he was tired of it, that he knew a lot more than he could talk about to anybody.

"I told him, 'Bill, if you know a lot of things that you don't want to talk about, then don't tell me anything. Don't bring it up, 'cause I don't want to be involved if there's something going on that's illegal.' And we let it go at that. But apparently he's talked to other people in the lunch group and told them the same thing, that he knew more than he could talk about."

Carlson said he'd seen Miller only once since that meeting in the sports bar. It was at a UFO Group weekly meeting in early September.

Carlson said he had spoken to Miller, though, minutes after the story of Girly's disappearance broke on Channel 7 Tuesday night.

"My phone started ringing off the wall from people that were in the luncheon group that were familiar with this. I called Bill Miller when this happened and asked him if he'd seen the report, and he said, 'No.' He said, 'Rick, keep quiet about it. Don't say anything. Shut up. Don't have any involvement with this at all.' And we let it go at that. And the next morning, he left town for two days, supposedly to go hunting."

"Do you know what he went hunting for?" Detective Bylotas asked.

"Supposedly for elk. And supposedly, at this time, it's only bow-and-arrow season."

"Is he a bow hunter?"

"I don't know. . . . Bill did call another member of our luncheon group when he got back. She asked him how things were going, and he lied to her over the phone. And she told him, 'Bill, this is all bullshit. You're not telling me the truth.' "

"What did she mean by that?" Bylotas asked.

"Well, [she] knew of Bill Miller's spending considerable time with Henning and with Hossencofft. And he came on to her as if nothing had changed, nothing was going on, everything was hunky-dory. And she told him that, flat out, that he was lying to her. . . . And she told me, she said, 'Rick, I think Bill has involvement in this case.' And she's known him for many years."

Carlson told the detectives that Miller had called him a second time, just hours earlier. The call did nothing to erase the uneasy feeling that Miller might be uncomfortably close to the murder.

"He called me this morning on my cell phone . . . and he said, 'I understand you've been visited by the FBI already.' And I said, 'No, that's not correct. I've spoken with them 'cause I was concerned about Linda Henning's well-being . . . and that's all that's happened. Bill, I would not be surprised, since : have worked at her residence, that they do come and visit me. I would not be surprised if they come and visit you.' He said, 'Well, let's get together and have a drink sometime this week.' I said, 'Fine.' And that was the end of our conversation."

"Do you think this is a possible way of [Miller] obtaining information about our interview?" Detective Bylotas asked.

"I'm sure it is. I would expect him to ask some leading questions. Possibly that he and Linda both want to know. It would not surprise me at all."

57

The traced phone calls had made it easy to locate Hossencofft. In a rather uneventful moment on September 22, 1999, the FBI in South Carolina moved in and arrested him, charging Hossencofft with three counts of making threatening phone calls across state lines.

Detective Fox and other members of the APD were in South Carolina the following day and searched the home rented by Hossencofft and Sherry Clinton.

In one bedroom, detectives found the 9-millimeter Taurus that had come from Bill Miller. In the master bedroom, they found three nine-millimeter Winchester Luger bullets. That bedroom also included a variety of medications and chemicals: one bottle of magnesium sulfate, one bottle of heparin, one bottle of Inhepar, two Flanax pills, a needle, and a glass vial. Under Clinton's bed, investigators found a lot of empty vodka bottles. She collected them, she explained.

The search of the home in South Carolina also turned up two vials of blood, a vial of brown powder, Girly's address book and a photocopy of her Malaysian identification.

Inside a bedroom, police found sticks of charcoal and immediately remembered Kari Wyeth and Flo Pugh telling them that they had seen Hossencofft painted in black the evening Girly disappeared.

The living room proved to be a gold mine for investigators. They found a steam cleaner there.

On a day shortly after Girly's disappearance, a woman showed up on the front doorstep of the house on Moon Street. She was obviously disappointed that no one would answer the door.

She told John Deyber, the man living next door, that she had met Hossencofft on the Internet and that she had recently stopped hearing from him. It was all so sudden. She needed to make sure he was okay. She had driven up all the way from her home in El Paso to do so.

Deyber began to explain that Hossencofft had recently moved and that he had been going through a divorce and that Girly Chew Hossencofft had disappeared and was feared dead.

As Deyber told the story, he could see the blood draining from the woman's face.

58

To ADA Paul Spiers, the woman sitting before the grand jury on September 27, 1999, seemed to have it together. Beautiful and sharply dressed, Linda Henning appeared like a Madison Avenue saleswoman. She drove a fashionable Honda and regularly dined at Scalo Northern Italian Grill on Albuquerque's historic Nob Hill, home to one of the best martinis in town.

Henning was supposed to be the best available witness, one who could possibly shed light on Girly's fate. But hours of testimony would soon unravel that hope. When the prosecutor asked Henning questions ultimately aimed at finding Girly, Henning refused to provide direct answers, preferring to reply with unprovoked and bizarre claims of government officials who were allegedly implicated in pedophile and sex slave rings.

"Her eccentric horse started poking its neck out, and eventually came out of the corral entirely," Spiers said later.

Members of the grand jury began looking at one another as Henning served up one weird accusation after another. Spiers found her answers to questions regarding Girly's safety and fate to be increasingly dismissive. Slowly a cloud of suspicion began to form over the witness.

Spiers began to wonder about Henning's relationship to the case. Perhaps she'd even played a role in the crime.

Soon a central question became the theme of every question asked by everyone: "Don't you want us to find Girly?"

As the voltage of that question amplified, Henning's dismissive retorts accelerated into tones of mockery. Spiers found it maddening, questioning Henning and meeting roadblock after roadblock.

"In her eyes, everyone else is just a store clerk . . . a mortal," he said.

What had happened to Girly? Henning clearly was trying to avoid any possible answer to the question.

As Henning's testimony stretched over the course of the day, other witnesses waited outside the grand jury room, just in case their names were called. Bill Miller was one of them.

Spiers knew next to nothing about Miller. But he was hearing about him from Henning inside the grand jury room. During her testimony, Henning mentioned that a man named Bill Miller had a crush on her.

"Why?" Spiers asked.

"Why don't you ask him?" Henning replied.

"I plan to."

For Detective Pete Lescenski, the hours of relative boredom outside the grand jury room were shattered with one question from Miller, who probably thought a little conversation would help pass the time.

"Could one of those bloodhounds, or tracking dogs, find a body if it were buried six feet underground?" Miller asked.

The question came out of nowhere. And it hardly seemed like a bright thing to ask a detective investigating a murder case with a missing victim.

At the end of a long day on the witness stand, Henning finally emerged from the district courthouse.

But she didn't leave alone that evening. Miller was at her side.

Spiers felt Miller wanted to know everything Henning had told the grand jury.

"It was a pantomime of two people trying to get their stories straight," he said.

59

One event in the summer of 1947 has forever linked New Mexico to the world of UFOs and aliens: the Roswell Incident, or Roswell Crash.

Impassioned debates about what actually crashed outside of Roswell continue today. However, another sensational New Mexico story concerning extraterrestrials emerged fifty-two years after the Roswell Incident, within the investigation into the mysterious disappearance of Girly Chew Hossencofft.

The alien story that emerges in the Hossencofft investigation is a story based on the teachings of a former British Broadcasting Corporation (BBC) reporter named David Icke.

Henning claimed to have met Hossencofft on June 20, 1999, when Icke presented his lecture at the University of New Mexico's Continuing Education Center. A canceled check proved that Henning paid to attend the Icke event, although there was no known proof that Hossencofft also attended.

In the weeks that followed Girly's disappearance, it became known that the suspects had an interest in Icke and that one of his documentaries occasionally aired on the Albuquerque cable-access television station, Channel 27.

It was the fall of 1999 when the author of this book arranged to meet Geraldine Amato at a tiny Mexican fast-food place near downtown Albuquerque. Amato had hosted a cable-access program for years and was also a fixture at Albuquerque's city council meetings, usually sitting in the audience right behind the microphone, eagerly waiting for her turn to weigh in on the latest issue before the city. Amato often spoke out against the establishment. Everything from City Hall to the White House was rampant with lies, deception and abuse of power, she believed. Amato wanted widespread change "before it's too late."

In its "Best of Burque" edition, the *Weekly Alibi* newspaper placed Amato second in its "Best Local Crackpot" category.

But it was on that fall day in 1999 that Amato graciously agreed to meet for lunch at that cheap Mexican restaurant. She shared that the copy of the Icke videotape that she occasionally played on her cable-access program belonged to a Northeast Albuquerque man who belonged to the UFO Group.

The house looked like a typical middle-class American home . . . from the outside. Once inside, though, the decor had an overwhelming theme of patriotism and seemed to speak of a threat to the country. A huge American flag stretched across one wall. Posters for underground movies, like *The Clinton Chronicles*, were posted, too.

The man who lived at the house fingered through a large collection of home recordings before he finally pulled out a VHS tape with a white sticker slapped on its side noting the two programs on it, REVELATIONS OF A MOTHER GODDESS and INTERNET: NETWORK FOR THE MARK?

As the author of this book left the house with tape in hand, a dark-colored, shiny car pulled up directly in front. A man wearing a black suit got out of the car and walked toward the house.

He made a beeline for the front door.

Later, the author learned he was an investigator with the district attorney's office pursuing his own copy of "Revelations of a Mother Goddess."

Born April 29, 1952, David Icke grew up in the working-class city of Leicester, England. He pursued a career in journalism and climbed to the top in England, becoming a television presenter, or host, for the prestigious BBC. Disturbed by the world's injustices, he later forged a political path and became a national spokesperson for the Green Party of Britain.

By the late 1980s, Icke had become disenchanted with both television and politics. What happened next was a defining moment in his life. According to his Web site, a mysterious *voice* started speaking to Icke, and on March 29, 1990, the voice led him to a psychic who revealed his true purpose in life.

Icke would later write on his Web site that, through the psychic, the voice told him: "[Icke] is a healer who is here to heal the earth, and he will be world famous. He will face enormous opposition, but we will always be there to protect him."

"Revelations of a Mother Goddess" begins with images of London's financial district. The camera keeps going back to slow-motion shots of men in black suits who are carrying briefcases and, presumably, about to walk into work.

Immediately the video seems to ask, *What is really going on here?*

Standing outdoors, amidst a constant swirl of cars, double-decker buses and pedestrians, Icke begins providing the answer.

Icke is good-looking, with a thick gray mullet parted down the middle. He's simultaneously charming and haunting.

He explains that he is not only standing in the epicenter of the worldwide financial system, but the center of a global web of secret societies that control the planet today. These societies, according to Icke, come from "a series of inter-breeding bloodlines, which you can trace back to the ancient Middle, and Near East, thousands and thousands of years ago. And the staggering truth is that these bloodlines, under different names, have increasingly controlled the planet. . . ."

Icke says that his video was about to introduce some "staggering, stunning and, I'm the first to say, bizarre information. The bizarre just happens to be true."

The intended highlight of this video is an interview with a woman named Arizona Wilder, who claims that she'd witnessed some of the world's most famous people take part in the darkest satanic rituals imaginable.

Icke first launches into his crash course on the reptilian agenda. He possesses the smoothness of a seasoned television journalist, which he is. Comfortably and expressively ad-libbing his way around London's financial district, he is walking and talking for twenty minutes at a time before a single edit to another location occurs in his tour of London.

"All of these apparently different companies, banks, insurance companies, political parties . . . actually at the top of their pyramids, interlock and are controlled by the same few people. About thirteen families run the world, and offshoots of these bloodlines under different names."

Standing outside the Mansion House, England's center of government, Icke shares that Arizona Wilder has witnessed satanic rituals "at the highest level" just inside its doors.

Once most everyone leaves the Mansion House at the end of the day, Icke says, the real business begins: human sacrifice, satanic ritual, blood drinking.

In his video, Icke states that London's Tavistock Institute has actually become the world center for global mind control and conspires with other institutions around the world, including California's Stanford University. He explains that the thirteen bloodlines of shape-shifting reptilians achieve mind control by taking newborn children and systematically traumatizing them for the first several years of their lives; this abuse results in multiple personality disorders or, "to be more accurate," DID, Disassociate Identity Disorder.

We're next told that Arizona Wilder was subjected to mind control since her birth. Her "teacher"? None other than Nazi Germany's "Angel of Death," Dr. Josef Mengele.

Icke also notes that dragons and reptiles are depicted throughout London, in a variety of statues, coats of arms and within other symbols.

"There's a reason that dragons appear everywhere. And that, of course, is the world's biggest secret."

Icke claims that in his research for his book *The World's Biggest Secret*, he came across a "stream" of people who all shared a similar story: "That they have seen, to their astonishment and amazement, they've seen key people in positions of power just de-manifest from a human physical form and become, before their eyes, a reptile, reptilian figure."

According to Icke, reptilians from outer space arrived on Earth about four thousand years ago and live all around us, except we can't see most of them. That's because, he explains, they live in a fourth dimension. However, many of these reptilians, Icke adds, decided long ago to interbreed with humans, but will only do so with the purest bloodlines: blond-haired, blue-eyed Aryans. The resulting offspring, Icke says, are the unique breed of "shape-shifters" that morph back and forth from human to reptile form.

It is these shape-shifting aliens that actually rule the governments of the Western world, according to Icke. And they're all intent on creating a New World Order.

But these shape-shifters have a temporary problem. Icke explains that they presently need to drink human blood in order to hold their human appearance and maintain the veil of deceit before the entire world. The shape-shifters first terrorize their human victims before digging in for the kill and relishing the resulting "starfire," which is the serotonin, melatonin and adrenaline secretions produced by, respectively, the pituitary, pineal and adrenaline glands.

But the ultimate starfire, Icke reveals, is menstrual blood, "for it is rich with these glandular secretions."

Icke finally seems to be coming to his own climax and appears to be concluding his meticulous introduction to Arizona Wilder's interview.

Standing outside Buckingham Palace, Icke claims it is the location where Arizona Wilder witnessed England's Royal Family in lustful moments of blood drinking and shape-shifting.

Icke concludes, "Across the millennium in years is 'crunch time' in this whole agenda, crunch time for the human race. This is the time when the network of interbreeding blood-lines wants to bring in its global, fascist structure of a world government to which nation-states would be administered to in units of a world central bank and a world currency, a currency that wouldn't be cash."

This future, he claims, will also bring a single-world army: NATO.

60

She looked like a woman you'd expect to see on a bottle of Ivory Snow dishwashing liquid. However, there is nothing perky about Arizona Wilder, no glint in her eye. Not a single smile in more than an hour of the David Icke documentary "Revelations of a Mother Goddess."

Wearing a conservative, white-collared blouse, her hair dyed darker than its natural blond, Wilder sits at the far end of a couch. At the opposite end of the couch sits Icke.

When asked a question about her past and the world she supposedly lives in, Arizona Wilder has no trouble giving a slow, methodical, often wandering reply.

She tells Icke that she was "bred for ritual abuse" and that from the time she was a baby, that abuse included electro-shock and other trauma. Wilder says that during her childhood her programmer threatened that if she passed urine, she'd have to drink it, and if she defecated, she'd have to eat it. She says she did both.

The soft-spoken woman with the downcast eyes explains that the entire trauma was aimed at overloading her senses, forcing her to compartmentalize her memories, so that they could be turned off and on like a switch. This would cause the multiple personalities that her master wanted.

Her programmer had a name, too: Dr. Green. But that wasn't his real name, she explained. His real name was Josef Mengele, the Nazi's "Angel of Death."

Icke asks Wilder about the reptilians that she calls the "Illuminati" and the human sacrifices she said she'd watch them perform. He asks of the importance of the blood that falls in line with something the Nazis called "virile power" and what he said the Hindus called "serpent power."

"Yes," Wilder responds.

"The blood has something in it. It has secretions from the pituitary gland and from the pineal gland, and it has a very strong drug in it that . . . keeps them from going crazy. It's like heroin or like endorphins, and it's much stronger. But what they need for it to be secreted in the blood, is they need terrorization of their victims before they are killed. . . . Or if a young woman is beginning to menstruate, they need the menstrual blood, and they have to terrorize [her] to get this to come out and be secreted in the blood."

She is talking about the "most desired" blood, starfire.

Wilder says that once terror has a firm grip on the victim, the Illuminati waste no time moving in. "[The reptilian] is staring into the eyes of this person, and they're held. It's a hypnotic gaze these reptilians have, and it holds the victim in an absolute trance, in a trance of terror. And then they are killed at that point as they are staring into their eyes."

Arizona Wilder claims that once engaged in the orgasmic frenzy of blood and flesh, none of the Illuminati can hold their human form; instead, they convulse back and forth between human and reptilian shape.

"It's like an animalistic excitement of the kill, and they, oftentimes, will just rip into the victim and eviscerate them and start eating the flesh of this person, too.

"I believe there is a time coming that, because of what

I've been told, when [the Illuminati] are not going to bother having to hold a human [form] . . . and they want that time to come. It's almost here."

Icke asks if that time is relevant to an approaching New World Order. "Is that [New World Order] coming in because people are going to see the reptilians and there has to be control of the people at that time?" he asks.

Wilder replies, "Yes.

"I had someone telling me, who was ex-Army Intelligence [and] ex-CIA, that I was being monitored by the National Security Agency. . . ."

Where did the Illuminati come from? How long have they been here?

Wilder explains that thousands of years ago the blue-eyed, blond-haired Aryans lived on their native planet, Mars. That is, until the reptilians arrived with a desire to breed with them.

According to Wilder, the Aryans—or more accurately, Martians—sought refuge on the Moon. But the reptilians eventually followed and executed a lunar attack.

Wilder explains that six thousand years ago, the Aryans left the Moon and escaped the wrath of the reptilians by coming to Earth. But after two thousand years of freedom, the reptilians came here, too. Wilder said the reptilians wasted no time going underground and taking control of our world's governments and religions.

After watching Icke's video, a viewer had to wonder what—if anything—this dark material had to do with Girly's disappearance—and murder.

61

For 2 million years, lava and ash burst from the place the Navajos called Turquoise Mountain. On at least one occasion, a tremendous explosion blew away the mountain's entire top.

The white man eventually named the mountain Mount Taylor, after the Mexican War hero Zachary Taylor, who went on to become the twelfth president of the United States.

Navajo legend upheld that this "Sacred Mountain of the South" was fastened from the sky to the earth with a great flint knife, decorated with turquoise, rain, animals and a dark mist.

The Navajos' Turquoise Mountain was also home of enemy gods or monsters. In Diné, the Navajo language, the word for "monster" literally translates to *that which gets in the way of a successful life*.

Forty-eight-year-old John Buckles was a bit surprised to see his best friend, Bill Miller, join him at his campsite on Mount Taylor on September 23, 1999. He'd known Miller might join him sometime during his seven-day hunt. But it was raining, not the most attractive day to seek out a friend hunting elk on a mountain more than seventy miles from Miller's home.

Miller and Buckles had a long-standing friendship forged in hunting. They loved the woods. When they met about twenty years earlier, they discovered their mutual interest and began bow hunting together.

In September 1999, Buckles had a permit to hunt elk beginning on the twentieth. He arrived on the eighteenth, though, so that he could spend a couple of days scouting the area.

Miller joined him for the final two days of the hunt. He could be useful. Elk are big, heavy animals, and removing their entrails goes a lot faster when two men do the job.

From the moment he arrived, Miller seemed to be consumed with Girly's disappearance. Buckles knew Miller had begun worrying about the case about a week earlier. Miller even brought along two articles about the case, which he'd clipped from newspapers.

For two days in the wilderness, Miller worried about the case and spoke about it so extensively that it was difficult for Buckles to digest all of the information. Miller talked of his relationships with Hossencofft and Henning. He had spent a lot of time with them. He'd sold a nine-millimeter Taurus to Hossencofft. He even gave him ammunition. He also sold a twenty-two-caliber Beretta and a shotgun to Henning.

Miller feared that his involvement with Hossencofft and Henning would drag him deep into the case.

When police interviewed Buckles seven weeks later, he attempted to make it clear that Miller was an innocent man. Miller had only tried to help a little boy, Demetri. That's how Miller became entangled with this mess.

"Bill loves children. He always has. Bill's initial interest was in this kid."

The police interview with Buckles stretched beyond four hours. And his comments about the boy, like many others, seemed rehearsed. The interview took place inside a glass room on the second floor of the district attorney's office. It was the very room where investigators had interviewed Miller in September. And Buckles was sounding a lot like Miller.

"I think Bill's involvement was, he met this individual (Hossencofft) through Linda, tried to help this guy out and—and then when . . . his wife showed up missing, he was, I guess, at the wrong place more than once at the wrong time. . . . And I think he—he truly regrets it."

Although detectives suspected Buckles's comments were contrived, they pressed to learn everything Miller had told Buckles on and off the mountain.

"I think Bill mentioned that either Linda mentioned to him or this guy (Hossencofft) did personally that the guy (Hossencofft) was God, seven hundred years old or much, much older than he appeared to be. That sticks out in my mind."

Investigators wanted to know if Miller had mentioned anything about the discovery of deer hair inside Girly's apartment.

"In Linda's apartment? Girly's? I think he did. Yeah. I think he did touch on that."

"Can we discuss that a little bit? Can you open up a little bit?" asked ADA Paul Spiers.

Buckles sighed, then answered the question with more detail. "He mentioned that there had been deer hair found, and he was asked about it because he is a hunter. They wanted to know what he knew about it. That's what I know about that. . . . I may have wondered, 'How did it get there?' And he wondered the same thing."

Something Buckles had told investigators about Miller at the beginning of the interview stayed with Spiers.

"*I think he's a good family man. He cares for his family, for the most part.*"

About an hour later, Spiers redirected the questioning back to that remark.

"You said he cared for his family, 'for the most part.' "

"Yeah."

"What does 'for the most part' mean?"

"Well, for instance, he doesn't tell his wife everything. Most husbands don't. He loves his children. He's a good father, and he's not a perfect husband. He's got his faults like everybody else."

"Does that include him telling you that he had slept and had sex with Linda Henning?" Spiers asked.

"The what?"

"You describe him as not being a perfect husband. Part of your description—does that include knowing, because he told you, that he had had sex with Linda Henning?"

"Yes, he did tell me that. He's not perfect."

It didn't add up to Spiers. Moments earlier, Buckles had said he'd told investigators everything he knew about Miller's comments about Hossencofft and Henning. Why would he leave out important information about Miller's sexual history with a primary suspect?

"I don't know. I probably at the time didn't [think] it's important. Perhaps to protect him. I knew you guys knew about this."

" 'Cause he told us," Spiers said.

"Yeah. I guess I waited to be asked."

"But did you ever have a discussion with him about preparing yourself with kinds of questions and things that we'd be interested in knowing from you?"

"Slightly. Yeah."

That's what bothered Spiers. Buckles sounded as if Miller had prepped him for the interview. The investigators eventually asked Buckles the bare-bones questions.

"Did anyone in this case, including Bill Miller, ever speak to you about being recruited to kill Girly Hossencofft?" Detective Lescenski asked.

"No."

"We understand you were recruited to kill her."

"I think I would remember that."

Spiers jumped in and aimed to make a point.

"Let's go through a few other things here. Since you know Bill better than any of us here, you could probably give us the best idea and answer."

"Okay."

"Bill's married."

"Um-hm."

"Married long enough to have two children."

"Yes."

"He likes soccer and he watches his daughter's games."

"Um-hm."

"He likes the outdoors, like you do."

"Um-hm."

"And I understand that his son does."

"Yeah."

"And yet, you go through and study this summer, summer of 1999, and what he's doing. He's spending almost all of his free time—and, indeed, even some of his work time—with Diazien Hossencofft, Linda Henning."

"Uh."

"And maybe the kid, Demetri, but not so much. And he's fishing with them," Spiers said.

"That's right. He did go fishing with them once to Shady Lakes. Yeah."

"You said that Miller really liked the kid, Hossencofft's kid."

"Uh-huh."

"Why, at his age in life, with his own kids, is he so interested in somebody's kid, somebody who you have described as being something of a kook?"

"Mr. Hossencofft?" Buckles asked.

"Yeah. And also, Linda Henning, you have described as being somebody who's off your radar chart."

"Well, yeah."

"So, you've got the question. So . . . why don't you run with it and see what your answer is?"

"Well, your question is why did Bill show such an interest in this kid?"

"Right."

"He loves children. Bill's coached children for years."

"The kid was not of coachable age," Spiers retorted.

"I know. But I have a little nephew. He's eight years old. Bill has known him since he was born. Bill is crazy about this kid. He loves children. He truly does. And he loves to get children involved in sports. He took this kid fishing, for Christ's sake. That's my answer."

"When was the last time you went fishing with a three-year-old?"

"Oh, it must have been my nephew."

Spiers seemed intent on making a point. Buckles was selling the notion that Miller's continued contact with Hossencofft solely stemmed from his concern for the child. Yet, he didn't spend a lot of time with the kid. Furthermore, Buckles said Miller was a family man, but he seemed to have spent a lot of his time with Hossencofft and Henning in the summer of 1999.

The investigators pressed Buckles harder for more specific information about his conversations with Miller.

"When was the last time you spoke with Bill?" Spiers asked.

"I think it was yesterday," Buckles said.

Spiers asked Buckles whether Miller had ever spoken to him about an abandoned house near Magdalena. The prosecutor told Buckles that Miller had made the house sound very important to them, and insisted that Hossencofft was always talking about it.

"I think Bill showed an interest, a year and a half ago, in buying that . . . and I think that that house may have sparked his interest as a potential fixer-upper," Buckles said.

"Let's just get serious," Spiers responded.

"That's what I think about it."

"Let's just get serious for a second, okay?"

"Yeah. Okay."

"When we talk about fixer-uppers, there's some belief that the house is actually going to be one you can live in, right?"

"Yes."

"This house that he was talking about . . . [looked] like an air strike had hit it."

"Oh, really?"

"Yeah," Spiers said.

Spiers next asked Buckles if Miller had ever said he'd been asked to kill Girly.

No, Buckles replied.

Once again, Buckles's response didn't seem to add up. Miller had already told investigators that Hossencofft attempted to recruit him to kill Girly. Two witnesses said Miller told them the same thing. Yet, he never mentioned it to Buckles, his close, if not best, friend.

Miller had also told police that Hossencofft wanted him to get a high-powered rifle. Did Miller ever mention anything about that to Buckles?

"A high-powered rifle? Absolutely nothing," Buckles insisted.

Buckles said he didn't recall Miller saying anything about the rifle or any talk of killing Girly. Not on Mount Taylor and not on a subsequent hunt at Apache Creek, an area west of Magdalena and the Very Large Array (VLA) telescope.

The investigators wanted to know what Miller had said during his most recent hunting trip with Buckles, the one down to Apache Creek.

Buckles said that Miller was focused on an upcoming day, explaining that if he wasn't indicted by that date, he could finally breathe a sigh of relief.

"So why is he so concerned about being indicted if he didn't do anything wrong? He knows that he can't be indicted," Detective Fox asked.

"People get indicted for not doing anything wrong," Buckles replied.

"They do?"

"Hundreds of people. Yes."

"Like who?"

"I'm sure somebody gets railroaded and indicted, and bang, there you are, doing ten years in Santa Fe or some federal prison somewhere," Buckles said.

"Yeah. But the point is, if he knows he didn't do anything wrong, then he's got nothing to be worried about," Fox replied.

"No, it doesn't mean that. . . . You can be as innocent as Jesus Christ and you can still get charged and indicted and sentenced, for certain."

The investigators felt that Buckles was holding something back.

"What other things do you need to tell us? If you're saving up here, you're stalling us," Spiers said.

"I'm not."

"Then you're measuring. . . . You're thinking, *what do we know? Who did we learn it from? Who said this?* So that you can coordinate your answer."

"That's what *you* think."

"But we already know. That's exactly right. So, you need to get on the right side of this."

"I'm trying."

" 'Cause you need to do it earlier than later. Because later means you're putting yourself in the hopper," Spiers warned.

"Okay, all right, all right. Bill thought, possibly, that his phone was tapped. . . . He's always felt that way, though, even before this [case] occurred."

Big deal. Investigators wanted juicier nuggets and tipped their hand with the hopes of landing one.

"Let me give you a heads-up on something else," Lescenski said.

"Okay."

"The bloody clothing . . . it was found in Magdalena."

"At this house that we were talking about?"

"I'm just going to tell you it was found in Magdalena."

Buckles said, "This is going to seem odd to you, but Bill did tell me, and I just remembered, I swear to God. Bill said that they had found the bloody clothing. 'Cause we were in Apache Creek, between Apache Creek and Magdalena. He told me that a week ago, perhaps."

"And you forgot that!" Lescenski exclaimed.

"I did. I remember it now."

"Mr. Buckles, let me tell you something," Spiers said.

"I know, that looks bad—"

"It's not hard to remember things like that. And I'm going to tell you something. It's looking worse for you. Here's your subpoena. We'll just give it to you right now. I'll sign it. I'm going to personally serve you with your subpoena to testify before the grand jury."

"Okay. All right."

"You'll be read the elements of perjury, okay?"

"You thought I perjured myself?"

"I'm just telling you that."

Buckles told the investigators that it was hard to answer their questions.

"It's not hard," Spiers said.

"It is for me."

"No it's not. It's not hard to do. What's difficult about it is figuring out how you're going to cover for a friend. That's what's difficult," Spiers said.

Investigators hadn't grilled Buckles simply because of his close relationship to Miller. They had uncovered evidence with his name on it.

September 24, 1999, passed without any major development in the investigation into Girly's disappearance.

Hossencofft had been charged earlier in the year with

three counts of violating a restraining order after allegedly calling Girly's workplace. By September 24, Girly had been missing for two weeks. There would be no trial.

On September 27, 1999, Albuquerque police executed a search warrant on Miller's home on Candlelight Northeast. They also searched his truck.

Detective Nick Gonzales made an interesting discovery inside Miller's fireplace: a partially burned business card belonging to Linda Henning.

Inside Miller's Ford F150, investigators found several neatly clipped newspaper articles about Girly's disappearance. A notebook found in the truck was an even more disturbing discovery. Miller had written about a reptilian gutting a menstruating woman. His notes stated that the evisceration was necessary because "the pituitary gland and pineal gland has strong drug in it—like heroin endorphins. Need terrorization for it to be put in blood."

They were nearly the exact words spoken by Arizona Wilder, the "Mother Goddess," in David Icke's video.

62

By the time police interviewed Bill Miller on September 27, 1999, he knew that the investigators had learned that he had a safe-deposit box at Western Bank, not his usual bank. It had recently been sealed as evidence. Police had yet to open it. They hoped Miller would sign a consent form allowing them to search the box.

Investigators learned that Miller had first opened a checking account at Western Bank two days before Girly's disappearance. He'd also used a Colorado address.

Miller returned to the bank two days later, September 9, 1999, to apply for a safe-deposit box. Bank employee Candice Skinner would not forget that day.

She waited on Miller as he held a medium-size bag. She noticed that as soon as a uniformed police officer entered the bank, Miller became very agitated and looked around nervously. He asked her to hurry up.

While the police officer still stood nearby, Skinner asked Miller if he'd like to put the items that were in his bag into his safe-deposit box. Miller declined, stating that he had to go. He didn't even wait for his change or a receipt. He seemed angry as he left, telling Skinner that she could keep the change.

Miller returned to the bank in the days ahead. During one of these visits, Skinner noticed that he'd arrived with the same medium-size bag and placed it into his safe-deposit box.

Early in the September 27 police interview, Miller brought up the subject and offered an explanation: "See, I have my house up for sale, and I'm looking at moving to Colorado. So, when I filled out the form, they wanted my mailing address. . . . So, I said, 'Well, I should have my house sold pretty soon.' That's why I put down Janet and I gave 'em my post office box. Janet is a friend of mine."

Miller voluntarily told the investigators what was inside the safe-deposit box. "I had cash, and I have coins in there. The cash, I sold some stocks last year, Lucent and AT&T stock. I got cash for it. I paid the taxes on it."

Miller said he wanted to cooperate with police and move on with his life. He'd consent to having his home and truck searched, but not his safe-deposit box. He'd told them what was inside, and he feared losing it.

Couldn't police just take his word, do their other searches and move on? It was not fun being scrutinized in a murder investigation.

"I'm a good, upstanding citizen, and I've coached kids for fifteen years in soccer. I'm a licensed schoolteacher. I almost got my master's in history. And I like kids."

"Right," responded Spiers.

"I got a daughter that's a senior in El Dorado High School, and I've got a son at TVI (Technical Vocational Institute). My wife's a teacher. And now all of a sudden, the whole community's gonna be buzzing, 'Hey, what is Bill Miller up to with this search and all?'"

"Well, let's worry less about the community and worry more about Girly Hossencofft," Spiers responded, then asked, "How can you explain that you're getting the safe-deposit box on the very day that Girly Hossencofft disappears and Hossencofft leaves for South Carolina?" Spiers asked.

"I don't know. I can't remember the day I got it. Is that when I got it?"

"Well, actually . . . it really is."

"I guess it's a coincidence."

"And how would you explain why a bank officer . . . observes you're going in there with something in your hand and notices that you're very rattled?"

"Yeah, I—I don't—"

"And emotionally unsettled. How do you account for that?"

"I don't think I was. . . . It wasn't the case."

Without Miller's signed consent, police knew they'd have to get a warrant to search his safe-deposit box.

Miller did somewhat agree to let investigators take a sample of his DNA. He allowed them to take a saliva sample, but did not let them take two other standards: hair from the head and pubic hair.

At the end of the interview, police offered Miller a ride home. Miller couldn't drive his truck home because police had seized it so that it could be searched.

Miller declined the invitation for a ride home, explaining that he'd prefer to take the bus. He arrived home as police searched his house. Investigators noticed that a friend had given Miller the ride home: John Buckles.

On September 29, 1999, Miller appeared before the grand jury. His testimony closely resembled the statements he had made in the glass room at the DA's office two days earlier.

Miller had a story and was sticking to it. And while he told it to the grand jury, police searched his home a second time, while Nan Miller looked on.

The reason for the second search was simple. Two days earlier, Detective Nick Gonzales had forgotten to collect a roll of duct tape that police had found inside Miller's Road

Runner slide camper, which was parked alongside the driveway. In an effort to keep everything aboveboard and by the book, police returned with a search warrant to get the duct tape. During that second search, investigators also rummaged through a garbage can outside Miller's home. In the trash, they found a receipt in Miller's name for a storage unit at Storage USA on Montgomery Boulevard.

Investigators searched the storage unit the following day. But first, there was another search already unfolding on September 29.

When police searched safe-deposit box number 45 at 1:05 P.M., September 29, 1999, they seized its contents and listed the items of the search warrant's inventory return: $10,350 in United States currency separated into four packets and wrapped in tinfoil, eighty silver-dollar coins, twenty-six $20 gold pieces, forty-two silver dollars, thirty-six small gold coins, eighty-five small Mexican coins, twenty-five gold Krugerrands, eight silver quarters and one blue Crown Royal bag.

The coins were valued at $12,479.

Miller had also listed a contact person when he applied for the safe-deposit box. He had written down the name of John Buckles.

At 4:00 P.M., September 30, 1999, police searched storage unit number L57 at Storage USA, the space rented by Bill Miller. It was empty.

"Why is your name associated with that box?" Detective Pete Lescenski asked Buckles during their marathon interview of November 8, 1999.

"It is?" Buckles responded.

"Yes. Your address, too."

"I had no idea."

Buckles expressed shock when he was told that Miller, whom he had just spoken with a day earlier, had listed him as the contact person.

"Why wouldn't his wife's name be on there?" Spiers asked.

"Ask him. I am."

Spiers told Buckles that Miller had opened the safe-deposit box on the same day Girly disappeared.

"The very day she disappeared?" Buckles asked.

"Right."

The investigators showed Buckles paperwork from Western Bank that stated Buckles had visited the safe-deposit box and taken items out of it. Buckles said he couldn't remember going to the box or taking anything out of it.

Spiers had a hard time believing him.

63

On October 8, 1999, ADA Paul Spiers and Detectives Fox and Lescenski felt a growing sense of anticipation as the miles rolled by beneath the unmarked Chevy Corsica that they were traveling in. They looked forward to seeing this out-of-the-way place called Magdalena, and the very spot where the tarp and Girly's bloodstained panties, blouse and other effects were discovered.

The 120-mile drive allowed plenty of time for the three investigators to discuss the case. Distancing themselves from Albuquerque and passing through the towns of Los Lunas, Belen and Socorro seemed to make them feel closer to the full force of the violence that had met Girly. The case felt less clinical, more personal.

Spiers abandoned his private contemplations as the Corsica pulled up to a dirt road nine miles northwest of Magdalena. The investigators saw the woman they had planned to meet at the beginning of Forest Road 123.

Just as she had agreed to do, sixty-six-year-old Geneva Liddon went to the prearranged meeting spot so that she could guide investigators into the area they wanted to see.

Liddon and her boyfriend, Randy Bell, lived together in a remote area seven miles up Forest Road 123, near La Jara Peak. Their friend Bill Miller had visited them in recent weeks. Miller reportedly liked to spend time at the abandoned home just two miles short of the Liddon-Bell place.

After the obligatory introductions, Liddon got behind the wheel of her Subaru Ranger and began to escort the investigators toward the abandoned home. The men from Albuquerque soon discovered that negotiating the dirt road was no Sunday drive. The dusty path crossed several sandy-bottomed arroyos. If a monsoon kicked in, the Corsica might get stuck and swept away by running water.

Spiers, Fox and Lescenski started feeling a bit out of their element. This was four-wheel territory, definitely not a place for a Chevy Corsica.

Suddenly Liddon's Subaru Ranger accelerated, prompting the concern from the investigators to do the same. Now eating Liddon's dust, they struggled to keep up while wondering aloud if they were driving straight into an ambush. Liddon and Bell were Miller's friends, after all. Miller was a man believed to be antigovernment and pro-militia.

Detective Fox reached for his police radio and called out for dispatch. No answer. He next attempted to make a call on his cell phone, but there was no cell service here. This was no-man's-land.

The lawmen made a quick inventory of the weapons and ammunition inside the car. As they finally approached the abandoned house, and with dust still hanging in the air from Liddon's arrival, the investigators could see her waiting for them.

All was quiet. There was no ambush, no trouble, at all. Just the old house where investigators believed Miller liked to spend time.

* * *

The first search for Girly's body that made headlines unfolded on the morning of October 13, 1999. Numerous investigators—on foot, horseback and from the air—searched the foothills less than a mile from Henning's town house. The four-hour search yielded nothing.

64

Linda Henning, the woman Detective Fox initially feared had become a second victim, was living beneath an extremely dark cloud of suspicion by mid-October. Her blood had already been found on the carpeting from Girly's apartment—a place she'd said she'd never been. Girly was a woman she claimed to have never met.

In October, the Albuquerque Police Department had her under twenty-four-hour surveillance. Using members of its Repeat Offenders Project Enforcement (ROPE) team and Gang Unit, APD had as many as eighteen detectives staking out Henning at one time. And she kept them busy.

At 6:30 P.M. on October 12, detectives installed electronic eavesdropping equipment inside Henning's town house. The wiretap allowed them to document numerous phone calls to and from a variety of people, including Michael Harvey, attorney Darryl Cordle (as required by law, investigators "minimized"—or turned down the volume—when Henning began speaking to her attorney) and several people responding to her newspaper ad. Henning had put her long-prized Barbie and Gene dolls up for sale.

For two weeks, police kept a nearly constant eye on Henning.

To be sure, there were mundane moments: visits to Walgreens, Smith's grocery store and Furr's Cafeteria. But there were many interesting things said and places visited.

At 10:01 A.M. on October 13, Henning's garage door opened and she emerged driving her 1992 four-door copper Cadillac. After several errands, she met Harvey at Garduño's Mexican restaurant in the Winrock Center. Two undercover detectives followed them inside and sat at a nearby table separated only by an aisle.

The noise in the busy restaurant made it impossible to overhear what Henning and Harvey were saying, but the detectives noticed that Henning appeared to be upset.

After lunch with Harvey, Henning drove home alone.

At 4:00 P.M., she went to the Sheraton Hotel. Once again, a detective followed her inside. Henning was on a pay phone across from the hotel's Regal Room. The detective sat down at a nearby table and reached for something to write on, a U.S. West phone book.

The undercover detective carefully eavesdropped by jotting down spurts of Henning's words, notes concerning her behavior and the time of day in military terms:

1603 hours
"... *neighbor saw shovel.*"
1610 hours
HENNING BECAME VERY UPSET AT THIS POINT.
"... *whole thing is a set-up.*"
"*Felissa ... she tried to put both of us away.*"
1613 hours
"*Steve ... pull out of present situation ... don't want you subpoenaed down here. ...*"
1623 hours
"*People are disappearing ... you, they know are a big threat.*"
1631 hours
CONVERSATION ENDS

At 6:22 P.M., Henning drove to the used-car dealership where he worked. Thirty-four minutes later, she got into a red Porsche with Harvey and sped away, causing investigators to lose sight of the car.

But police staking out Henning's home were looking on as the Porsche arrived at the town house at 7:45 P.M. When Harvey left that night, police tailed him, too. It didn't last long. Harvey ran a red light. When police stopped the Porsche, they found a nine-millimeter Smith & Wesson inside. Harvey told them that it belonged to Henning and she'd asked him to hide it for her.

Less than thirty minutes later, Henning left her home driving the Honda. She headed to Candlelight Northeast, where she abruptly stopped and turned off her lights. Bill Miller lived on Candlelight, but this location was seventy blocks from his home. About twenty seconds after her sudden stop, Henning turned her headlights on and returned home.

Police aimed to remain patient. The grand jury investigating Girly's disappearance continued to deliberate. Investigators planned on arresting Henning if, and when, the grand jury indicted her.

On October 14, Henning stopped by the used-car dealership in the morning, ran errands and saw a movie.

At 1:04 P.M., she stopped for lunch at the Hilton Hotel. Wearing a denim jacket, denim pants, a purple shirt, off-white shoes without socks, and her hair pulled back, Henning stopped at a long bank of pay phones before entering the hotel's restaurant. An undercover officer stood just around the corner and listened as Henning spoke on a pay phone, but the detective could only make out fragments of Henning's conversation.

"You just need to take care of this for me."

Hoping to hear Henning better, the detective circled around the hotel's hallway and took a position at the pay phone immediately beside Henning.

Henning hung up the phone. Seconds later, it rang.

She answered the call and spoke in very low tones. But as she appeared to become anxious and irritated, Henning raised her voice. She said something about a helicopter flying over her house for two hours.

She became very excited and spoke in words that were loud enough to be clearly heard. "How do you think it makes me feel to know that I had a role in the death, or impending death, of a small child? That child loved me."

Henning hung up the phone.

The following day, October 15, she spent much of her time on her home phone. She paged Steve Zachary several times. From New York, he always returned her pages promptly.

"I should have flown you out last night," Zachary told her.

Henning also called the DA's office.

"Call off the dogs," she said.

At 3:11 P.M., Henning drove to Pagers Plus. She apparently hoped that a pager with voice mail would allow her to have undetected communications. It did not.

Police soon had a court order allowing them to use a "clone" pager. It received every page and voice mail that Henning's pager received.

While Henning stayed busy, she rarely worked at either Atlas Resources or 21st Century. She was about to lose both jobs.

At 6:21 P.M. on October 15, Henning went jogging. She'd only been running for four minutes when police approached her and told her it would be a good idea for her to return home. She did, and found Detectives Fox and Lescenski waiting for her. They had a warrant authorizing them to search Henning's town house.

As police began their search, Henning explained that she had an appointment that she had to keep. She then drove away.

As Detectives Fox and Lescenski searched Henning's home, it seemed as if cats were everywhere. They wanted to take hair samples from the cats to see if they matched any of the cat hairs found in Girly's apartment, on the tarp found near Magdalena or inside the steam cleaner found in South Carolina.

Catching the last of six cats wasn't easy. The feline ran upstairs and into a bedroom. Lescenski and Fox weren't far behind. One of the detectives crouched to look under the bed, while the other stood by. Right then, they realized they'd found something curious, and it wasn't the cat.

A gray tarp was spread out like a sheet on top of the bed. Police had never seen it during their prior searches at Henning's home. And with fresh creases still crisscrossing it, the tarp appeared as if it had just been purchased and removed from its wrapping. It appeared to be identical to the tarp found near Magdalena.

The detectives seized the tarp and collected hairs from each cat.

If driving away from her town house had led Henning to believe that she had escaped the watchful eye of the police, she was wrong. At 8:30 P.M., investigators tailed Henning's Honda Accord to a home in Rio Rancho. Fifteen minutes later, Henning and another woman emerged from the house. Henning got behind the wheel of her Honda, while the other woman got into a Chevrolet Cavalier. Henning followed the Chevy to the parking lot of a nearby restaurant, where she parked her car and climbed into the other woman's car.

Police followed the Chevy for several miles before it finally parked at the Kinko's at the intersection of San Mateo and Academy. Both women went inside the store. An undercover detective did the same.

A second detective stayed inside the unmarked police car and used binoculars to watch Henning and the other woman.

Henning used a false name, Lisa Harding, when she signed in to use a computer inside Kinko's. She had brought along some gold-colored rewritable compact discs and wanted to view the files on them.

As she sat at the store's computer station number two,

Henning realized she was not familiar with the operating system. The computer was a Macintosh.

Henning asked a store employee to show her how to view the files on the "gold discs." As the worker told Henning how to use the system and placed a CD in the CD-ROM drive, he noticed that the CD had two files on it. One of them appeared to be a picture of a building.

While looking through binoculars, the detective outside Kinko's noticed that Henning was speaking on a cellular phone for about five minutes.

After Henning signed off from the computer, the store employee watched her put the CDs into disc holders and carefully wrap them in tinfoil.

Henning was determined not to leave the computer without something else: peace of mind. She twice asked the store employee to check the computer to make sure that the files from the CDs hadn't remained on its hard drive. Each time, the employee assured Henning that they had not.

As Henning paid the $4.80 for her twenty-four minutes on the computer, the employee noticed that the woman with her appeared to be nervous.

The two women left Kinko's at 10:00 P.M. and drove back to Henning's car in Rio Rancho.

Back inside her Honda, Henning drove straight to her town house. She was there for only five minutes.

She next drove to a Motel 6 in northeast Albuquerque. After checking in, she backed her Honda into a parking space before retiring to her motel room.

It had been a long day. The time was ten minutes before midnight.

Henning finally emerged from her motel room at 2:23 P.M. on October 16. Nineteen minutes later, she arrived at That Car Place, the used-car dealership. After spending about a minute inside the office, Henning got back into her car and parked it behind the building. Police watched as she removed items from her Honda and placed them into a 1993 blue Nissan Quest minivan with tinted windows and temporary tags. A few minutes later, Henning drove off in the minivan.

Henning drove through her neighborhood and past her town house without stopping. As she stopped at traffic lights while on westbound Montgomery, detectives noticed that Henning seemed anxious as she peered into the vehicles around her. And she repeatedly checked her mirrors, trying to determine if she was being followed.

As she walked out of an Albertson's grocery store and returned to her van, she looked in all directions. After she returned to her motel room, detectives managed to get the vehicle identification number (VIN) off the minivan.

Early that evening, Henning went to a hotel and used a pay phone in the lobby. Again, an undercover detective eavesdropped while sitting on a couch about twenty feet away. And, again, Henning spoke to a man named Steve. She told him that she was being careful and had not been followed to the hotel.

The sound of a vacuum cleaner made it difficult to hear everything Henning said. But the detective was able to make out parts of Henning's side of the conversation.

Henning assured Steve that she knew what she was doing; then she said that the "harassment" from police was letting up.

"They're looking for tarps," she told him.

On October 17, Henning emerged from her motel room at 5:23 P.M. and drove the Nissan Quest minivan up to the far Northeast Heights and directly past her town house at La Villita Circle Northeast. Eleven minutes later, she entered another residential neighborhood and drove past Bill Miller's home.

Henning ultimately stopped at a movie theater. She walked up to the theater but returned to the minivan three minutes later. She then drove to a health-food market called Wild Oats. After spending eleven minutes at Wild Oats, Henning returned to the minivan and drove back to the Motel 6, returning to her room at 7:38 P.M.

Under twenty-four-hour watch, Henning had kept undercover officers busy for three days.

But the fourth day of surveillance would prove to be her busiest time. And investigators would be closer than she ever imagined.

At 7:30 A.M. on October 18, "Team A," comprised of twelve detectives, two sergeants and two officers, began its shift of watching Henning.

She left her motel room fifteen minutes later and drove to That Car Place, where Harvey joined Henning in the minivan and drove with her to his home. After five minutes inside, the pair returned to Harvey's used-car dealership.

Whether or not she knew she was being followed, Henning apparently managed to elude police.

At 12:20 P.M., investigators contacted the motel to see if she had paid for another night or had already checked out. They learned that Henning was in her motel room at that very moment. A sergeant returned to the motel immediately and located the minivan in the parking lot.

At 12:40 P.M., Henning called the motel's front desk and complained that housekeeping had thrown away her contact lenses. She said she wanted an employee to take her to get a replacement pair. It proved to be a unique opportunity for the surveillance team.

At 1:30 P.M., Henning walked into the Motel 6's lobby wearing a green-and-white-striped shirt and blue jeans. She wore her hair in a ponytail. She also held a Pizza Hut box; upon meeting the man who would drive her to Eyemart Express, she offered him some pizza. The man grabbed a few slices, then left with Henning.

The man who had been introduced as the motel's maintenance worker was actually an undercover officer. As the officer drove Henning to Eyemart Express, she asked him if she could borrow his cell phone. Henning used it to check her pager's voice mail.

Afterward, she spoke about her bad vision and explained that she could hardly see without her contact lenses.

Something unusual played out inside the Eyemart. As she waited to be seen, an employee called out the name Elizabeth a few times before Henning suddenly stood up and answered to the name.

Henning was told that the bill for her new contact lenses was $90. As she reached into her wallet and reached for the money to pay the bill, the undercover officer, posing as a Motel 6 maintenance worker, noticed that she was carrying a large amount of cash.

Henning returned to the motel at 2:26 P.M. Henning thanked the "maintenance man" for the ride to Eyemart.

At 4:50 P.M., Henning wore a white button-down shirt and blue jeans; she had her hair up in a bun as she drove the minivan to a Barnes & Noble bookstore, where she met up with the woman who'd driven the Chevy Cavalier. Police ran the Chevy's license plate and learned that the vehicle was registered to Mary Alice and Mervin Thomas.

An undercover detective went inside the bookstore and noticed Henning and the other woman, believed to be Mary Alice Thomas, sitting inside its coffee shop.

Thomas was about five feet four inches. She had short, curly brown hair and wore glasses and a purple sweater.

At one point, Henning got up and made two calls from a pay phone inside the bookstore.

Driving alone in the minivan, Henning returned to the Motel 6 at 6:25 P.M. Investigators had placed electronic surveillance inside the room while she'd been away. At 12:02 P.M. on October 18, she spoke on the phone with Hossencofft about the possibility of the police finding Girly's body.

The following day, she drove the blue minivan and circled her neighborhood before parking a short distance down the

street from her town house. Henning got out of the van and
ran to her home. Forty-two minutes later, she came out of the
house with a suitcase. She carried it to the van and put it inside the vehicle. She went directly back to the house and returned less than three minutes later with some packages,
which she also put into the van before driving to Thomas's
house in Rio Rancho.

Henning returned to Thomas's home the following night
at 8:25 P.M. The two drove together to Albuquerque and directly past the Valle Grande.

"That's D Hossencofft's wife's apartment."

Henning's words stuck with Thomas.

On October 19, investigators were able to eavesdrop as
Henning spoke on the phone inside her motel room. Although
she was whispering, Henning sounded excited. She mentioned
that she had sold her dolls and had not returned to her town
house.

Two weeks of around-the-clock surveillance ultimately
convinced police that at least one person in Henning's world
could have crucial information about the case and might be
compelled to share it.

On October 25, Detectives Fox and Lescenski went to
Rio Rancho and interviewed Mary Alice Thomas at home.
After the detectives reminded her that she had driven Henning
to Kinko's in Albuquerque to use a computer, Thomas said
she didn't know anything about computers and didn't know
what Henning had been working on.

Thomas said she didn't really know much about the case
because Henning had been advised by her attorney not to
talk about it. But Henning had shared that she thought Girly
had been kidnapped. Thomas said she was also told that
Hossencofft was misunderstood. The investigators sensed
that Thomas was holding back information. Two days later,
they had her before the grand jury.

On October 27, Thomas told the grand jury that Henning
had asked her to hold onto two CDs and a small bottle la-

beled COLON CLEANSER. Thomas said she stored the bottle in her refrigerator and kept the CDs inside a box under the dishwasher.

Thomas also testified that she'd given the CDs back to Henning on October 25, after the detectives had stopped by her home. She added that Henning had asked her to withhold some information from investigators by "pleading the Fifth."

Thomas also said she had seen some Oriental knives in the trunk of Henning's Honda. Henning had mentioned that a sword that belonged to Hossencofft was hidden inside.

And there was something else: Henning had said that Girly had been kidnapped and killed.

According to Thomas, Henning had said the information on the CDs contained Hossencofft's formula for a serum that caused "cell regeneration." Hossencofft had professed that the formula would help planet Earth recover from an alien attack.

Henning had also said that three-year-old Demetri had been kidnapped, killed and decapitated. The boy's head, Henning had explained, had been "cryonically frozen and sent to Malta."

On October 21, 1999, a breakthrough unfolded inside the APD's crime lab.

It concerned a gray hair found on the carpet taken from Girly's apartment. Forensic scientist Catherine Dickey determined the hair's DNA profile matched Hossencofft's.

65

Inside the Tirados' living room, Pedro and Luz now had two pieces of their friend Girly's furniture. It had been given to them following Girly's disappearance.

The furniture included a beautiful Oriental dark green desk with painted images of "traditional" Asian women holding fans.

Upon this desk, Girly had often lit a candle and placed food and drink offerings to Kuan Yin. The audiotape of Buddhist chanting, which Girly had played while praying, was tucked away in the desk's drawer.

Additionally, Hossencofft had sold his laptop computer, which he had often used to get on the Internet, to Luz. She permitted the author of this book to borrow it. On the hard drive, Hossencofft's seven-page curriculum vitae, filled with outrageous claims and misspelled words, remained. There were also a few photos of young Asian women in pink neg-ligees, who appeared to be potential mail-order brides, and a 2½-page e-mail, written by Hossencofft to a woman named Crystal. Dated May 13, 1999, it swirled with Hossencofft's sensational lies.

Obviously intent on reeling Crystal into his web, he wrote lines not unfamiliar to Internet dating:

> *"I have a really nice sense of humor and I love to laugh. . . ."*
> *"One might say that I am a room-service kind of guy. . . ."*

His e-mail said that he had several laptop computers and that some were even waterproof so that he could take them underwater when he went diving.

Like the troubled, brilliant scientist in a B movie, Hossencofft pondered the moral dilemmas that came with his scientific research. He wrote that his creations were for the benefit of the planet, but he was saddened because they could be used as "weapons" to "destroy human life."

Hossencofft finally concluded his e-mail with his address on Moon Street and his telephone number. It had all read much like the letters he'd written to Girly's parents seven years earlier.

66

On October 20, 1999, Bill Miller was back before the grand jury. Under oath, he testified that Hossencofft had twice asked him for his help in killing Girly. Miller said that, on a third occasion, Hossencofft asked Henning and him to "go and get" Girly and bring her to him.

After testifying that day, Miller went to the office of his attorney. At the time, he was represented by Timothy Padilla. While at Padilla's office, Miller secretly recorded a telephone conversation with Henning.

When investigators ultimately learned about the tape-recorded conversation and requested a copy of it, Padilla told a judge that the tape had been misplaced and that he had been unable to find it.

On October 23, a mysterious man called the Albuquerque Police Department.

The anonymous caller said that investigators in the Hossencofft case needed to take a closer look at Henning.

By late October, the forensic scientists at the crime lab had spent weeks analyzing forensic evidence in the Hossencofft case. They'd found Girly's blood, Henning's blood and a gray hair and saliva that matched Hossencofft's DNA. They'd also found animal hair on the carpet from Girly's apartment, on her bloodstained clothes and on the tarp found near Magdalena.

On Girly's carpet, the forensic team ultimately found seventeen natural deer hairs, seven dyed deer hairs, fifty-seven cat hairs, one natural rabbit hair, five dyed rabbit hairs, fifteen dog hairs, two natural feathers and one pink feather.

Investigators already knew that Girly had not owned a pet while living at her apartment, nor had the previous tenant.

On Girly's bloodstained short-sleeved blouse, APD's forensic scientists discovered fifty-six cat hairs and one dog hair.

The taping of the tarp found near Magdalena had paid off, too. Dickey and Arbogast collected 101 cat hairs, 5 dog hairs, 2 dyed rabbit hairs and 2 green feathers. A thorough search of the steam cleaner had also proved fruitful.

Although it had been cleaned, a second chamber used for recycling the moisture sucked up from the carpet contained six cat hairs, twenty dog hairs, fifteen natural deer hairs, and thirty-six dyed deer hairs.

On October 29, police returned to Miller's home. This time, they had a warrant authorizing them to search for, among other items, deer hair.

Miller enjoyed fly-fishing. He had tied his own flies at a fly table inside his garage. In making a good fly, one that fish will bite on, Miller had used deer hair that had been dyed pink. He had also used brightly colored feathers. When police searched Miller's garage, they found deer pelts on the fly table, some pink deer hair and a green feather.

While police were searching Miller's home, they were growing more concerned that Henning might be a flight risk. She was moving around and talking on the phone about plane tickets and passports; police feared she might manage to sneak out of town.

There were now grounds for an arrest. Based on their interview with Mary Alice Thomas, investigators were convinced that Henning had twice lied to the grand jury and had attempted to convince Thomas to commit perjury, too.

In late October, Henning tried her best to avoid surveillance. On October 25, she went to her friend Michael Harvey at That Car Place and traded her Honda for a 1990 Jeep Cherokee. She also checked out of the Motel 6.

On the evening of October 29, Detectives Fox and Lescenski found Henning living in room 160 at the nearby Homestead Village Weekly Studios.

When the detectives knocked on the door, Henning opened it a moment later. The investigators put her in handcuffs and read Henning her rights. She was charged with two counts of perjury and criminal solicitation to commit perjury.

When police searched her room, they found three gold CDs inside a Hershey's chocolate box and a plastic bottle labeled COLON CLEANSER.

67

Steve Zachary knew Linda Henning was not a killer. Hell, she couldn't squish a bug, let alone bring harm to a human being.

Although his poor health prevented him from taking a plane to Albuquerque, Zachary was determined to assemble an impressive defense team.

But Henning refused his help, including his money. And she stopped speaking to him.

"It was a total blackout," Zachary said.

The blackout had been triggered by his earlier comment that Hossencofft was "a lying piece of shit."

Zachary never regretted the remark. Always direct, he felt he couldn't be faulted for his honesty.

And the criticism had been well intended. He wanted Henning to snap out of her fixation for a guy who had been using her. However, Henning was transfixed. Her loyalty to Hossencofft ran deeper than Zachary could ever have imagined. Zachary grew convinced that Hossencofft must have drugged, brainwashed or hypnotized the woman.

"She seems possessed," he said.

* * *

On November 8, 1999, APD's crime lab received an anonymous note. It said that police investigating Girly's disappearance should take a very close look at Henning.

The note arrived sixteen days after the unknown man had
made a similar statement in a telephone call to APD.

On November 12, 1999, Andrew Chew, Girly's brother,
arrived in the United States for the first time. But it was anything but a vacation.

Thirty-six hours and five flights after leaving Malaysia,
Andrew stepped off a plane in Albuquerque. As Andrew claimed
his luggage, he was greeted by Pedro and Luz Tirado. He had
been corresponding with Luz on the Internet and had made
arrangements to stay at the Tirados' home.

Girly had been the oldest of three children. Andrew was
the youngest. In his midtwenties, he was now the family's
official representative to the police and courts concerning
Girly's estate and the investigation into her disappearance.

Andrew stated that his family was prepared "for the worst."

In November 1999, it was becoming evident that Hossencofft
had a number of women in his life.

The Tirados told of a girlfriend who worked at Supercuts
and another who allegedly worked for the Russian Embassy
in Washington, DC. The woman from the Russian Embassy
had called the Tirados' home, stating that Hossencofft had
taken passports belonging to her and her daughter.

So, it was hardly a shock when a man who'd visited the
author's Web site dedicated to the Hossencofft case relayed
the story of another dangerous liaison.

It turned out the man, who wished to remain anonymous,
had briefly rented a room at the Hossencoffts' home on Moon
Street. He said that he had arrived home one day, when the
front door cracked open and Hossencofft quickly handed
him a handwritten letter before closing the door.

It turned out that Hossencofft had entertained a woman inside the house earlier in the day, and Girly had walked in on them. In direct terms, the note informed the tenant that he was to cover for Hossencofft by claiming that the female visitor was his girlfriend.

It wasn't long before the renter moved out. Hossencofft was "a freak," he claimed.

His opinion of Girly had never wavered: "An honest, sincere, hardworking person—I felt sorry for her."

Andrew Chew knew that he had to accept the possibility that his sister had been murdered. But just three days after he arrived in Albuquerque, a ploy arrived at the law office of Bryan Fox and Traci Wolf, the attorneys who had represented Girly in her divorce.

Hossencofft's divorce attorney, Felissa Garcia Kelley, informed Girly's attorneys that her client wished to remain married. He no longer wanted a divorce.

Girly had already been missing for more than two months.

Fifty-six days after it convened, the grand jury made headlines when it indicted Hossencofft and Henning on murder, kidnapping and numerous other charges.

That evening, ADA Paul Spiers and Deputy District Attorney Julie Altwies walked out of the courthouse. The prosecutors had no comment for the reporters staked out nearby. The words would come the following day during a brightly lit news conference.

When Albuquerque police hold a news conference on a high-profile case, it is typically conducted inside the large conference room on the top floor of the law enforcement center downtown. And that's exactly how it played out on the fifth floor on November 18, 1999.

After more than two months of remaining tight-lipped, the police were finally talking. While Spiers and Altwies stood along the side of the room looking on, APD chief Gerald Galvin spoke about the fine work of investigators and the grand jury.

The Hossencofft case was finally a big story.

As important as the news conference had seemed, the real headlines remained in the courthouse, where a judge unsealed many of the documents that same day.

For the first time, crucial details emerged: specific information about Girly's bloodstained clothing and the tarp found near Magdalena; police seizing three guns belonging to Henning; Julie McGuire's sensational story; Bill Miller's testimony that Hossencofft had twice spoken to him about killing Girly.

Miller, though, was not indicted. Not yet.

Henning's attorney also had a piece of new information that he felt compelled to share with investigators on the very day they held their news conference, something no reporter learned that day.

He told police that Henning had hidden a sword above a ceiling panel in her garage.

Police found the weapon exactly where Daryl Cordle had said it was located. It turned out to be a ninja sword with blood on the red handle and steel blade.

The blood on the handle turned out to be Hossencofft's, but the blood on the blade was badly compromised. Someone had apparently tried to clean it off. What remained was not enough to determine its DNA.

Although Girly's body had not been found, 1999 was ending strongly for Paul Spiers. Despite not having a body, he'd successfully helped put two suspects in jail for murder.

For more than three months, Spiers had invested much of his life into the case. Sixteen-hour days had not been uncommon. He'd worked many weekends, too.

Yes, it was good finally to have two suspects in jail.

But that professional success seemed less important one day after Christmas. On December 26, 1999, Spiers's father died in an Albuquerque hospital.

68

Prosecutor Paul Spiers knew that he had a most difficult task. He wanted to prove that a murder had occurred, but the case offered no body. And without one, how could he prove that it was Girly's blood that had been discovered on the tarp and clothes near Magdalena?

Investigators had matched the DNA from that blood with DNA from the wad of hair found inside the wastebasket in Girly's bathroom. It was also identical to the DNA found on Girly's toothbrushes.

But any good defense attorney would be able to produce reasonable doubt, arguing that the source of the hair clump and toothbrush DNA could not be definitively known. Someone else could have tossed their hair into Girly's wastebasket and used her toothbrushes.

Unlikely? Perhaps, but still possible.

"[The situation] presented very real reasonable doubt, a threat to the case," Spiers said later.

The prosecutor hardly wanted to take such a case to a jury. "It would have been fatal," he said.

Spiers had no doubt that Girly's blood was on that tarp and clothing. And he set out to prove it.

He knew that he'd have to get DNA samples from Girly's parents, especially her mother. If it was Girly that had been attacked, then the mitochondrial DNA found in the blood on the tarp and clothing would match Margaret Chew's DNA.

Mitochondrial DNA is found immediately outside the nucleus of a human cell. In a simple metaphor, the nucleus is often compared to the yolk of an egg. Following that example, the surrounding mitochondrial layer is compared to the white of the egg. The nucleus contains the unique blend of each parent's genetic information. But the surrounding mitochondria contains only the mother's DNA profile.

And DNA from Girly's father could prove helpful because it would match characteristics found in her nuclear DNA.

The typically mundane mission of getting a saliva sample from each parent became grossly complicated. The parents lived in Malaysia. Politics, bureaucracy and weather conditions ultimately combined to present a huge roadblock obstructing the effort to get their essential evidence.

The attempt to get DNA standards from Girly's parents began in December 1999.

Ann Talbot, the director of Albuquerque's crime lab, had friends in high places. On December 13, Talbot requested a favor from the Naval Criminal Investigative Service's laboratory. Talbot put Catherine Dickey, her forensic scientist, in contact with the NCIS's David Watson in Singapore. Dickey e-mailed Watson details of the case and requested Watson's help in getting DNA standards from Girly's parents.

Three days later, Watson replied and said that he had contacted the U.S. Embassy in Kuala Lumpur and was coordinating a plan to get the DNA standards from Girly's parents.

On December 20, NCIS supervisory special agent Robert Mulligan made a formal request to the U.S. Embassy's special agent Robert Valente.

But on the day after Christmas, Dickey learned that the U.S. Embassy had denied the request for its help in getting the DNA because of press coverage, presumably unfavorable, that the case had received in Malaysia. Valente referred Mulligan to the State Department's Criminal Investigative Liaison Branch and to Interpol.

But Dickey, hoping to avoid more bureaucratic red tape, sent another e-mail to Watson at the NCIS, explaining that Girly's parents were willing to travel to Singapore to have their standards collected by NCIS. Six days later, Watson wrote back that his superiors were afraid such a move would cause an international incident because it would have bypassed diplomats.

Indeed, the investigators on the Hossencofft case were already sensitive to the diplomacy issue. Spiers wanted the involvement of the State Department or senior levels of the FBI so that the relationship between two sovereign nations would not be disturbed.

On February 1, 2000, Dickey wrote a letter to Interpol, requesting the agency's assistance. The letter was also signed by Albuquerque police chief Gerald Galvin and the New Mexico Department of Public Safety's Sergeant Don Bullis. Bullis was also New Mexico's liaison to Interpol.

Four days later, Bullis wrote a letter requesting assistance to Mike Muth, the assistant chief of Interpol's State Liaison Division.

Two months passed without any reply to Bullis's letter. Spiers knew the clock was ticking, and realizing the importance of verifying Girly's DNA, he decided to use his own connections to make it happen. He contacted an old navy buddy. Back in 1985, Spiers and Thomas L. LeClaire had worked together in Naples, Italy, where both had been JAGs.

LeClaire presently worked as an assistant U.S. attorney and referred Spiers to James T. York, chief of Interpol's Criminal Division's Washington, DC, office. York, in turn, advised Dickey to contact Ralph Horton, the FBI legal attaché at the U.S. Embassy in Bangkok, Thailand.

On April 11, 2000, Spiers fired off a letter to Interpol's United States National Central Bureau:

With reference to communication with James T. York, Special Assistant to The Chief of Interpol, Senior Federal Bureau of Investigation Representative, the United States National Central Bureau is respectfully requested to transmit the text of the following message to: Interpol, Kuala Lumpur, Malaysia.

Spiers's letter explained the details of Girly's case and the need to acquire DNA standards from her parents. On the same day he wrote it, Dickey wrote and faxed a letter to Horton, which also detailed the case and the same request.

The following day, Bullis received an e-mail from Interpol in Washington, DC. It only brought more bad news. The e-mail stated that Counsel General Sylvia Johnson of the U.S. Embassy in Kuala Lumpur had suggested that the prosecutor in the Hossencofft case pay to have Girly's parents flown to New Mexico, where they could provide their DNA samples.

That disappointment, though, disappeared just six days later, when the FBI's Horton sent an e-mail to Dickey stating that he'd spoken with the Royal Malaysian Police and that everything was lined up to get the DNA standards from Girly's parents.

Dickey wasted no time and soon sent Horton the instructions and swabs necessary for getting the samples.

Everything looked quite promising on May 12, 2000, when Jerry Bamel, the FBI legal attaché at the U.S. Embassy in Singapore, used the swabs provided by Dickey and collected saliva samples from Mr. and Mrs. Chew.

Bamel also enclosed a letter explaining that he had been saddened after meeting Girly's parents. They had hoped he'd arrived to tell them that Girly had been found alive.

Although the DNA standards from Girly's parents finally arrived in Albuquerque, more bad news arrived with them. The samples were too deteriorated to yield full DNA profiles. Malaysia's humidity had taken a toll on the saliva.

Consequently, Dickey requested hair samples from Girly's parents. Those samples arrived on December 18, 2000, one year after the effort to get DNA from Girly's parents had begun.

The exhaustive effort had not been in vain, though. The DNA from the hairs of Girly's parents proved that it was her blood that had been found on the tarp and clothing discovered along Highway 60.

Investigators didn't have a body, but they now had proof that Girly was the victim.

69

Located fifty-five miles southeast of New Mexico's largest city, Estancia is a sleepy town of fifteen hundred people along the western edge of the state's windswept eastern and central plains. To the nearby west, the forty-five-mile-long Manzano Mountain Range rises more than ten thousand feet above sea level. The "Manzanos" are a popular destination for nearly twenty species of raptors migrating along the southern Rocky Mountain Flyway.

But any notion that federal inmate Diazien Hossencofft's turbulent life would calm behind the bars of a privately owned prison in Estancia was quickly erased. Among the five hundred inmates were vultures who preyed on the likes of small guys, like Hossencofft, who made big headlines. And, according to his cellmate, Hossencofft soon developed a bitter enemy: Shawn Wilkins.

Wilkins and three other gang members faced murder charges in one of New Mexico's most heart-wrenching criminal cases.

In April 1996, the badly decomposed remains of a young mother, her two tiny sons and her boyfriend were discovered in a remote cabin near the village of Torreón in the Manzanos.

Police said Wilkins and his accomplices were responsible for shooting the mother and her boyfriend, and then leaving her sons, ages three and four, to die of dehydration and starvation.

The bodies were discovered four months later. Near the dead children, investigators found canned food with crude holes in it, caused by the little boys in their desperate effort to stay alive.

According to Hossencofft's first cellmate, fifty-one-year-old Doyle Monk, Wilkins and Hossencofft were soon intent on killing each other.

After reading a newspaper article about Girly's murder, Monk wrote to Detective Fox about Hossencofft's feud with Wilkins.

Monk described Wilkins as a "super punk (gangster)." According to Monk, the friction started when Wilkins and a fellow gang member demanded "rent" from Hossencofft and Monk. Later, Monk said, Hossencofft's anger intensified when Wilkins blocked up sewage pipes with a sheet, prompting Hossencofft to hatch a plan to injure or kill Wilkins with "bean dip."

Monk explained that Hossencofft stole one of his small glass bottles of heart medicine and smashed the glass container into a fine powder. Next, Monk wrote, Hossencofft bought some bean dip from the commissary and then laced it with the powdered glass.

Monk recalled that Hossencofft had planned to serve the dip, tortilla chips and salsa to Wilkins and the other gang members as they watched football on television.

"Luckily for Wilkins," Monk said, Hossencofft was transferred to another cell prior to Sunday's games, so no one had a chance to polish off the dip.

"I could just imagine Wilkins with a bloody asshole," Monk wrote.

Monk had been fascinated with his cellmate. He learned of Hossencofft's affection for Agatha Christie's infamous detective Hercule Poirot and the works of Edgar Allan Poe. But Hossencofft had considered that his crime was much more creative than any misdeed created by the legendary mystery writers.

He told Monk that he'd committed the perfect crime. It seemed to Monk that the cocky bastard flirted with a temptation to revel aloud in the details of his crime.

Hossencofft and Wilkins were two of the most dangerous people Monk had ever seen.

After his transfer to cellblock 1D, Hossencofft wrote a letter to Monk, urging him to request a transfer so that the pair could be reunited as cellmates. In his pitch to Monk, Hossencofft delighted in sharing that his new housing area had two TVs and plenty of tables to play dominoes upon.

Monk hoped that he could get the transfer, even though he knew that Hossencofft, like Shawn Wilkins, was a dangerous man.

Wilkins kills "to prove a point," Monk wrote. Hossencofft kills to "eliminate a problem."

Wilkins's "temper is too bad to stay out of trouble." Hossencofft "thinks he is too clever to be convicted of a crime."

Hossencofft had also spoken about a New World Order and impending doom. Cellmates like Hossencofft didn't come around every day.

He'd even managed to make some "hooch" in their cell, Monk noted. No wonder Monk was disappointed when the prison transferred his mysterious acquaintance to a different pod.

Wanting to learn more about his unusual cellmate, he began to exchange letters with Hossencofft and even wrote to Linda Henning. Monk hoped to learn something significant. Perhaps he could use any new information to negotiate a deal to shorten his own prison time.

* * *

For nearly four months, the news media and public had waited for its first look at Hossencofft following his arrest. The moment finally came on January 14, 2000, the day of his arraignment for murder, kidnapping and other charges related to Girly's disappearance.

The feds planned to drop the phone threat charges against Hossencofft, paving the way for the state to proceed with its more serious murder case.

On March 22, 2000, Hossencofft was transported from the Torrance County Detention Center to the federal courthouse. A judge dismissed the charges related to the threatening phone calls, and Hossencofft was now solely an inmate of the state. His next stop would be his home for the next 1½ years, the Bernalillo County Detention Center (BCDC).

A letter written by Henning to Monk suggests Hossencofft did not receive a warm reception from his fellow inmates.

Henning wrote that Hossencofft had been moved to several pods because the "Mexicans and gangs wanted him out," adding that four inmates had beaten him. What kind of "bastards" would beat up "a little guy with cancer"? Henning wrote.

Henning referred to the trials and tribulations of incarceration as a test from the "High Council." Monk wasn't clear about what that meant, but believed that the High Council was somehow relevant to the New World Order.

According to Monk, Hossencofft and Henning had said that "they" were going to kill everyone on Earth, except people with an A-negative blood type, and claimed to have stored a biological agent in the ground that would contaminate the world's drinking water supply.

In her letters to Monk, Henning wrote that prisons are for profit and that corruption was everywhere. The largest drug dealers were "the Federal Government, George Bush, Bill Clinton, CIA, and local politicians like [State Senator] Manny Aragon."

She added that the "Great War" was coming later that year, promising an end to the "Evil and Corruption."

70

With obvious passion, Linda Henning often voiced—and
wrote about—her belief in various government conspiracies.
She'd even managed to shout out her conspiracy warnings as
she'd been led away from court in handcuffs.

Henning seemed to get satisfaction from an engaged lis-
tener, especially if that person had some perceived stature of
importance. She got just that during the third week of January
2001. And she even got to go to the district attorney's office
for her meetings with Dr. Park Elliot Dietz, M.D.

Dr. Dietz, a forensic psychiatrist, had testified for the prosecution in the trials of some of the most well-known crimi-
nals of the modern era, including Jeffrey Dahmer, Ted "the
Unabomber" Kaczynski, Erik Menendez and John Hinckley
Jr.

For the entire workday of January 23, and most of January
24, Dr. Dietz interviewed Henning and evaluated her psy-
chological profile. ADA Paul Spiers believed Henning was
competent to stand trial, but he wanted an expert's opinion
before driving the case forward.

Spiers believed Henning agreed to cooperate with the
psychiatric evaluation only because of Dr. Dietz's acclaim.

She'd done her background research on the $500-an-hour doctor before meeting with him. In the end, Dr. Dietz determined Henning was both competent and a narcissist.

Later, Dr. Dietz shared his analysis of Henning with The History Channel television program *Dead Reckoning*.

"Linda Henning had a very long history of falling prey to every wacky idea that came down the pike. She was extremely distrustful of everything conventional and ordinary, and would unquestioningly adopt every foolish idea that had to do with nutrition or exercise or UFOs.

"I think it's not an unreasonable way to look at this case, as Hossencofft having brainwashed Henning."

71

It hadn't taken long for Linda Henning to apply her trademark zeal to the crafting of letters. Henning wrote to friends, reporters and enemies. But mostly, she wrote to Hossencofft.

She expressed her devoted love and passion for him. In a response to one of his letters, she wrote that he always made her "so hot" and that she needed his "comfort."

In a February 8, 2000, letter, she informed Hossencofft that he'd always been "like a God" to her, "regardless of these sub-humans." Henning told Hossencofft that his sensual powers were "intoxicating." She seemed to revel in delight as she wrote that she and he both liked "CATSEX."

Their sex life was of little interest to investigators. There was, however, a most serious concern: a threat to human life. It came in a letter written by Henning to Hossencofft, beneath the headline MESSAGE TO ALL CONCERNED.

Investigators intercepted the correspondence and read Henning's declaration that two witnesses in the case, and their families, will "wear the mark of death." She added that the mayor and the leaders of his administration, including the police chief, would also wear the mark of death.

In the same letter, she added a three-sentence edict, stating that once a "final sentencing" had passed, no power on earth could prevent its execution. The judgments, she added, would come from "WARRIOR ANGELS. NO HUMANS WILL BE INVOLVED."

Investigators in Girly's murder case clearly had a mounting concern that Hossencofft or Henning might order someone to cause harm to people associated with the case.

And they feared that "someone" was Bill Miller.

Police and investigators from the DA's office had been investigating Miller for six months, ever since they'd first heard about him during their interview with UFO Group member Rick Carlson. Carlson had said Miller was tight with Henning and Hossencofft.

When the case was barely two months old, Spiers had taken his concerns about a hit to a judge, hoping to cut off all communication between the jailed suspects. On November 18, 1999, Judge Albert "Pat" Murdoch issued a no contact order to Hossencofft and Henning. But it didn't stop the steady pace of letters exchanged between the pair.

Henning and Hossencofft had pulled a common inmate stunt of writing to a third party, then having that person forward letters to the intended recipient. On March 28, 2000, a jail administrator met with detectives and handed over twenty-two letters that had been intercepted after going through a third party, all violations of the no contact order.

In a letter written by Hossencofft, Detective Fox observed the suspect's occasional use of unknown, seemingly self-invented symbols. At times, Hossencofft also arranged letters of the alphabet to form unknown words. Fox believed these were all coded messages. Regardless, much of the letter could be easily read.

Hossencofft had written Henning that he would "inform the council" of her "present situation," and added that he'd received her previous letter that had requested more "(unknown symbol)" for her use against her "assailant."

As the letter continued, he seemed to compliment Henning,

informing her that she possessed more "upgrades" than the last "QN ZYZZYVA," and that Henning was "comparable in size and weight to her." Although Henning's predecessor—"QN ZYZZYVA"—may have had longer hair, Hossencofft added.

Hossencofft wrote that he would tell the "council" that Henning had also requested a "wake up call" for "Jeff R." and "M. Aragon." The names appeared to be more-than-subtle references to District Attorney Jeff Romero and State Senator Manny Aragon.

Hossencofft noted that Henning had also previously asked for a "(unknown symbol)" on an FBI agent.

Detective Fox and ADA Spiers were indeed concerned that Hossencofft and Henning might order a hit . . . on someone.

On May 15, 2000, a jail administrator provided investigators with four more letters that had been intercepted. The name on the return address for a letter written by Hossencofft was Harvey.

Investigators believed Henning's friend and former lover, Michael Harvey, had been a third party who'd initially received it before forwarding it to Henning.

In a letter dated March 22, 2000, Henning had informed Hossencofft that he "must hide the amulet because they will check almost anywhere."

Suspecting that the amulet had belonged to Girly, investigators contacted Andrew Chew in Malaysia. In his June 8, 2000, e-mail, Andrew informed a Bernalillo County Victim Assistance advocate that a necklace and several gold rings, owned by Girly, had yet to be recovered. In following up on his e-mail, Andrew sent detectives photographs of Girly in which she could be seen wearing the jewelry that was now missing.

Armed with Henning's letter about the amulet and Andrew's information about Girly's missing jewelry, Spiers and Fox now had the evidence they needed to get a search warrant.

And on June 28, 2000, they searched both Henning's and Hossencofft's jail lockers. Henning's locker checked out clean.

Investigators made an important find in locker 285, Hossencofft's storage space: the amulet.

72

The resolve of the men and women working the Girly Chew Hossencofft case at the DA's office and at the APD was unwavering.

The Hossencofft story had already become an investigation unlike any case the investigators had ever seen. A woman had been murdered. The body was missing. And the suspects remained smug, aloof and, at times, threatening.

Among those firmly dedicated to the quest for the truth was a soft-spoken, tall man with dark hair and a thick mustache. He had a gentle disposition, but he also happened to be extremely tenacious. Brent Johnson was an investigator for the district attorney's office. For more than 1½ years, Johnson doggedly pursued scores of leads. In time, he came to know the tendencies of the suspects and victim as well as anyone investigating the case.

Jeanette Kiser of Stillwater, Oklahoma, had been one of Hossencofft's targets. She'd met him on an Alaskan cruise in the early 1990s.

Johnson located Kiser and listened to her story.

On the cruise, Kiser recalled, Hossencofft had escorted a

much older woman named Sunny. He'd introduced himself as a heart doctor who had grown up in Japan and had said that he was dying from bone cancer.

Johnson soon recognized the predictable string of Hossencofft's lies. They'd drifted only slightly from the fantastic hogwash he'd been spreading for years.

He'd told Kiser that his first wife died during childbirth. He'd said that he was fifty-eight years old, but would never look older than thirty-five. His grandfather had arranged his second marriage, he'd said, after his wife's father impregnated her in Japan.

All lies, but hardly the end of the deception.

Kiser had remained friends with Hossencofft for several years. On several occasions, he'd visited her in Oklahoma and stayed at her home. In time, though, she'd realized Hossencofft had spun many stories and little truth. In the late 1990s, she'd told him to stop coming to her house. But he persisted, calling her every two weeks or so. In the spring of 1999, the calls stopped.

Not surprisingly, the court system had been aware of Hossencofft for several years. Johnson learned that Hossencofft had been charged with a DWI on April 15, 1999, while driving between Albuquerque and Aztec. Hossencofft's attorney managed to convince a magistrate court that Hossencofft was dying of cancer and had only a few months to live. Consequently, the Sandoval County District Attorney's Office dismissed the case.

Hossencofft's attorney, the one who'd convinced the court to dismiss the charges, had a familiar name. She'd also happened to be his divorce attorney, Felissa Garcia Kelley.

The morning of May 19, 2000, was not an ordinary time in court. The defendant, his behavior, the conduct of one attorney and the circumstances surrounding the case were all odd.

Hossencofft finally found himself on trial, not for murdering his wife, but for allegedly violating the restraining order she'd gotten a year earlier.

In this case, the victim couldn't speak. She'd disappeared eight months earlier and was presumed dead.

Six investigators from the district attorney's office sat in the courtroom's spectator area that day; among them was Brent Johnson. Johnson noticed that Hossencofft appeared to be very sure of himself. He also seemed to enjoy the attention he was getting from the DA's office.

That Kelley was Hossencofft's divorce attorney could not be disputed. But she was not his counsel in the criminal matter before a judge that day. Johnson noted that Kelley and Hossencofft behaved much like two close friends who hadn't seen each other in a long while. They touched each other's arms and exchanged warm smiles.

For some time, the pair spoke softly into each other's ears, separating briefly to acknowledge the beaming affection on their faces.

Kelley had to settle for sitting in the courtroom's spectator area, about four feet from Johnson.

Three times, Johnson noticed Hossencofft shake his hands as if he were holding dice, then pretending to roll the imaginary cubes onto the floor. Each time, he'd smile toward the back of the courtroom, squarely focused on the investigators from the DA's office.

Did Hossencofft think the odds of winning in court that day were good? Did he even care?

After the judge determined that Hossencofft was guilty of violating Girly's restraining order, that announcement was met with a gasp that came from the courtroom audience.

The sudden inhalation came from Kelley, who immediately placed a finger upon her lips and gave Hossencofft a look of disbelief and sorrow.

"How could he have been found guilty?" Kelley asked Steve Long minutes later. Long was the attorney actually representing Hossencofft in court that day. He could see that Kelley truly seemed to be upset.

After the courtroom cleared, Johnson approached Long.

The two men had known each other for many years and had attended school together.

"Be careful," Johnson advised his old friend concerning Hossencofft.

In their brief conversation, Long said that Hossencofft and Kelley had a relationship that extended beyond the typical lawyer/client affiliation.

That afternoon, Johnson caught up with Kelley to interview her about the break-in at her law office, the one she'd reported to police shortly after Girly had disappeared. She'd said a gun had been stolen from her desk drawer.

Kelley seemed surprised by the unexpected visit and asked a coworker to get her attorney on the phone.

Kelley, who'd blamed her brother for the break-in, had never told the grand jury about the burglary.

Johnson had found that odd and asked her why she'd never brought it up.

"Not everything revolves around Diazien Hossencofft," Kelley replied.

Johnson thought he never got a concrete answer to his question.

Kelley's attorney called a moment later. She took the call in a separate room, emerging a moment later and telling Johnson that she'd been advised not to talk to him. Johnson packed up his tape recorder, then leaned up against Kelley's desk, telling her in a soft voice that he didn't want to see her get into trouble.

Did Kelley know where Girly's body was located?

"Do *you* think I know where the body is?" Kelley responded.

"I'm not sure. But when two people are involved with each other, they talk and—"

Kelley interrupted him. "We're not involved."

"I didn't mean sexually, but as friends," Johnson responded. "It was easy to see that you two are, at the least, good friends. And friends talk to each other," Johnson added.

He'd hoped to get Kelley to open up to him. He spoke about the horrors of domestic violence, its effect on family members.

Girly's family deserved closure. They should have the opportunity to pray and say their farewells at a grave site, Johnson told Kelley while noticing that she'd become quiet.

She seemed solemn and did not look him in the eye.

"If your friendship is keeping you from talking to us, it'll be in vain. This prosecution is going forward with or without the body," he told Kelley.

At the next moment, Johnson clinched his hand to form a fist and placed it on his heart.

"Help us, help this family. You are a mother; you understand the need to bring your little girl home."

At last, Kelley turned her gaze toward Johnson.

He observed a woman who seemed sad and helpless. But she said nothing.

In what turned out to be the final months of her life, Girly had determined that it was highly likely that she'd have to fight off an attacker one day, maybe even more than one.

In the summer of 1999, she'd signed up for karate classes and made an unforgettable impression on her instructors at the American Kempo Karate Academy.

Jesse Lucero certainly remembered Girly and the jewelry that she had worn to class. Lucero, a man who seemed to treat everyone with respect, selected his words carefully, too. When Johnson asked if Girly had worn any jewelry, Lucero recalled seeing a gold necklace and a small, bangled gold bracelet with stones in it.

She'd frequently, if not always, worn the jewelry to class, he said.

The interview prompted Johnson to seek out Kelley once again. Earlier in their investigation, police had found a strikingly similar bracelet in Kelley's possession.

She'd told Johnson that Hossencofft had given her the bracelet as a form of payment for her services, adding that its value fell short of covering her actual fee.

When did Hossencofft give the bracelet to Kelley? In the middle of January 1999, Kelley said.

Johnson considered the possibility that Kelley was lying and that she may have actually received the bracelet eight or nine months after the time she'd claimed, *after* Girly had vanished.

He set out to show the bracelet seized from Kelley to several people who'd had contact with Girly in 1999. Lori Gunnare, a paralegal for Girly's divorce attorney, was certain she'd seen Girly wearing the bracelet after January 1999.

Johnson returned to the karate school so that he could show the bracelet to Lucero.

"Yes, that's hers," Lucero said instantly.

Tears appeared to swell in the karate instructor's eyes.

"I saw her wear it. It's hers. I'm sure" was Lucero's emotional response.

Girly hadn't even made her first visit to Lucero's karate school until June 1999, five months after Kelley said she'd received the bracelet from Hossencofft.

Later, Johnson had the bracelet appraised. An expert assessed its value at $1,259. Earlier, Kelley had told Johnson it was worth $450.

Paul Spiers had his own theory about how Kelley had come to possess the bracelet. Shortly after Girly's disappearance, Linda Henning had visited Kelley's law office. Unbeknownst to Henning, Kelley secretly recorded their conversation.

Kelley had wasted little time, starting the recording seconds after Henning entered the front door.

"Let her in, damn it. Christa, don't call anyone," Kelley called out to her receptionist.

Henning entered Kelley's office.

"Hi, have a seat," Kelley began.

"How are you?" Henning responded.

"What's going on?" Kelley asked.

"Well, let me give you *this*, so that you've got (inaudible)," Henning said.

What had Henning given Kelley? Spiers suspected it had been Girly's bracelet.

Kelley had graduated, with honor, from the University of New Mexico in 1995. She'd earned her law degree from the same school two years later.

In 1990, Hossencofft had roamed the same campus and set his sights on a romantic conquest with fellow student Francine Olmstead. Olmstead had studied with Hossencofft at UNM as both prepared for medical school. At the time, he'd called himself Armand Chavez. When he eventually changed his name to Diazien Hossencofft, he told Olmstead that he did so because he wanted to use his grandfather's name.

The friendship persevered, even after the Hossencoffts married. Olmstead had become friends with Girly and had dined with the couple at their home on several occasions. She told Johnson that the final dinner was in December 1998, when the Hossencoffts had seemed a happy couple.

Loose ends bothered Johnson. And not knowing where the bloodied gray tarp had come from was one of them.

On June 8, 2000, he drove by Henning's former town house. She'd lost the home after using it as payment to her former lawyer, Daryl Cordle.

Johnson found a cleaning crew inside the town house,

preparing it for the renters who would soon be moving in. The workers agreed to let him look around. In the garage, he discovered a paint lid with a label on it that said it had come from Home Depot store number 3502. He also discovered a glass jar with paint in it. It had been sealed with duct tape.

Johnson took the paint lid and the jar with him as he left the house and later tagged both items into evidence.

Johnson learned from Home Depot headquarters in Atlanta, Georgia, that Henning had purchased the can of paint found at the town house on June 19, 1999.

Johnson asked Home Depot for any other sales slips or financial records linked to Henning. Two months later, he struck pay dirt. Home Depot informed him that between July 13 and September 8, 1999, Henning had written five checks at its store located on Montano Boulevard.

A sales slip and canceled check confirmed that on September 8, 1999, Henning had purchased a gray tarp that appeared to be identical to the one found near Magdalena two days later.

That was just the tip of the iceberg. Using bank records, Johnson learned that Henning had visited a Wal-Mart store six miles away from her home *on* the night of Girly's disappearance. The store was located 1¼ miles from Girly's apartment complex. At 10:18 that evening, she'd purchased a Mag-Lite flashlight and Rayovac Maximum batteries.

The bank records also indicated that Henning had used her debit card on several occasions at Hobby Lobby. Johnson contacted the store and learned that sales slips indicated that Henning had purchased art sand on February 13, 1999. Art sand had been found on the tarp, in Henning's Honda and inside Girly's apartment.

Girly's boss at the Bank of America, Kathy Freeman (formerly Semansky), knew she couldn't bring Girly back, but she'd do whatever she could to help the investigation. Her digging revealed that Henning had used her bank card four times on the date of Girly's disappearance. Henning had used her card at a Phillips 66 gas station at 12:08 A.M., at a

Walgreens drugstore at 6:33 P.M., at Wal-Mart for an ATM withdrawal at 10:25 P.M., and at a Smith's grocery store at 11:23 P.M.

Had Girly really been killed? One witness believed she'd seen Girly on September 11, 1999, two days after her disappearance.

Dolores DeVargas worked at the Orange Julius store inside the Winrock Center Mall. DeVargas told Johnson she remembered September 11 very well because it was a slow day. The state fair was under way, and that particular Saturday had always been slow during the fair.

The Orange Julius store used the Bank of America's uptown branch, and DeVargas had come to know Girly from her visits to the bank. She recalled that she was standing near the coffeemaker at work when she saw Girly walking by the Orange Julius store.

"Hi, Girly," DeVargas had said as Girly walked nearby. Girly smiled and waved back.

Again, DeVargas stressed that she remembered the encounter because it'd been a slow workday.

But what about the previous Saturday? Johnson wondered.

The prior Saturday had been the Labor Day holiday weekend. Was it a slow day, too?

DeVargas said that it had also been a slow day because many people were out of town for that holiday.

Could DeVargas's brief encounter with Girly have been on September 4, not September 11? Johnson asked. It was possible, DeVargas told him.

Girly had shown up for work at Software Etc. inside the same mall on September 4. She didn't show up for work on September 11.

* * *

To prove that the guns seized in the case actually belonged to the suspects, Johnson launched into another trail of paper and past encounters.

Through interviews, an ATM transaction and a receipt, he learned that the Smith & Wesson nine-millimeter had been purchased by Henning at the state fairgrounds in Albuquerque on October 3, 1999. Twelve days after she purchased it, police found the weapon with her longtime friend Michael Harvey in his car during a traffic stop.

The task of learning the history of the black nine-millimeter Taurus started on Indian land. A man who lived on the Santo Domingo Pueblo, north of Albuquerque, had owned the weapon in 1988. An interview with him and the gun's subsequent owners ultimately produced a receipt signed by Bill Miller. Miller paid $200 cash for the weapon on May 4, 1999.

His work as a handyman also captured Johnson's attention.

On September 9, 1999, an Albuquerque woman had written Miller a check for $75 for some handiwork he'd done at her house. During that time, the woman had also had a local company working on her swimming pool.

Johnson imagined a frightening scenario, prompting him to contact companies that sold pool acid. One company had an outdoor solar pool that was used for evaporation. It was 25 percent acid. Johnson was told that, on occasion, "birds fall in and are gone in a week."

Employees at one store told Johnson that if pool acid was used to get rid of Girly's body, it would have required fifteen to twenty gallons to cover her. Once the acid had evaporated, only white powder would remain. The entire process would take about two weeks.

It was suggested to Johnson that lye could also have been used.

* * *

Heather Phillips worked at the *South Side Newspaper* in Ontario, Canada, and was no stranger to Hossencofft's monstrous tales.

She'd heard him brag that he could get away with murder, boasting that he'd read many books on mass murders to "learn how they did it." Without a body, he claimed, he could not be prosecuted.

Hossencofft said he'd have no problem making a body disappear. He'd just put it in a bathtub, cover it with lye and eventually watch it "all go down the drain."

Johnson caught up with Phillips in December 2000. She explained that she'd met Hossencofft on the Internet around November 1998. He'd even stayed at her home in Canada that same month, and while wearing a jade pendant that looked like a Life Saver candy, he asked for $50,000 to "repair his damaged laboratory." Phillips didn't give him $50,000, but she did send Hossencofft $100 a month for several months.

Phillips became engaged to Hossencofft. He was supposed to be moving up to Canada to marry her. But in the fall of 1999, his e-mails no longer arrived.

Phillips feared Hossencofft had been killed by the government. She'd telephoned Pedro Tirado, but it was his wife, Luz, who answered the phone.

Luz explained that Hossencofft was not dead, but he had been "taken care of," a reference to his arrest. Phillips searched the Internet and learned of her fiancé's arrest, and much more.

He'd been married. He had a girlfriend named Linda Henning. His estranged wife was presumed murdered. And the body hadn't yet been found.

The paper trails in the Hossencofft investigation had revealed concrete information, providing specific details regarding the whereabouts and activities of the suspects. It was hardly sensational, but the knowledge would prove to be extremely valuable to the prosecution.

During the course of the investigation, several people

came forward with shocking stories. Johnson spoke with many of them.

One informant claimed that Hossencofft had confided "we killed her." The source said that Hossencofft divulged that Girly had been killed "over money."

Hossencofft had also allegedly boasted that no one would ever find the body because it had dissolved.

The tipster recalled three exact words alleged to have been uttered by Hossencofft: "I used acid."

A second informant was not happy to be talking to police. This person claimed Henning had confessed to Girly's murder.

Johnson wrote down the words Henning had allegedly said: "Girly is food . . . good spaghetti sauce. . . . They won't find the body. The little bitch got what she deserved. . . . She hated the boy. . . . She didn't care for the boy."

The informant had more to tell, claiming that Henning had said that Bill Miller knew what had happened to Girly.

"Long time in planning," Johnson continued to write down the words allegedly uttered by Henning.

"He (Miller) carried Girly into the house and put her in the chair. . . . Girly was tied to the chair and was killed in the chair. . . . Mats had been placed on the floor for blood. . . . They cut her."

According to this informant, Henning had also said that Girly yelled and cried as Miller carried her into a house. The informant claimed to have been told that Hossencofft was there, too, and had stuffed something into Girly's mouth.

According to this informant, Henning suspected that Miller had raped Girly before bringing her to the house, adding that Henning loved Hossencofft and the duo had eventually planned to put out a hit on Miller's life.

The informant also said that Hossencofft had a plan to escape from jail. He was going to dress up as a woman, put on a wig and walk out.

A third informant was an inmate inside the Bernalillo

County Detention Center. Twenty-seven-year-old Lynn Marie Crouch had been housed in the same jail pod as Henning. Crouch had an extensive criminal history.

Johnson asked her what she wanted in exchange for her information.

"Nothing . . . what happened to that girl was wrong," Crouch replied, referring to Girly.

Crouch said Henning had written her several letters. They usually were coded within Henning's poetry; a few lines of nonverse would appear within the poem.

Johnson wanted to look at those letters. Crouch explained that she'd left the letters from Henning at a house in Clovis, where she'd lived after her release from jail in March 1999. But after several weeks, she'd had a falling-out with her roommate and moved out.

At Johnson's request, a representative of the district attorney's office in Clovis visited Crouch's former roommate. The roommate told the investigator that she'd been very upset with Crouch and had thrown out all of her property.

Crouch's story surely would have been valuable to the case, if only it could have been verified with Henning's own handwriting. She said Henning had spilled the beans, admitting that she and Hossencofft had killed Girly. Henning had wanted Girly dead and was glad the deed was done, Crouch said.

Crouch said she remembered Henning saying that Girly's body and clothes were in two separate locations, the body not far from where the clothing had been discarded, but a Jeep would be needed to get to Girly's remains.

Crouch said Henning told her the story several times, and each time, the story never changed.

And it had sensational elements. Henning had allegedly referred to herself as an alien queen who had to fight Girly (but never said how or why), and she'd joined Hossencofft and a man named "Joseph" in knocking out Girly inside the apartment.

They done it for the insurance money, according to Crouch.

Speaking of money, and this claim certainly meshed with the truth as Johnson had come to know it, Henning had also allegedly said that she'd paid for everything that she and Hossencofft had done together while preparing for the kill.

But the most frightening scenario came toward the end of Crouch's interview with Johnson. According to Crouch, Henning had said that she and Hossencofft were like the *Highlander* character:

"You have to take their head."

73

Police suicide is one of the most disturbing experiences that a law enforcement department can encounter.

And on June 9, 2000, it struck the Albuquerque Police Department when off-duty detective Nick Gonzales died from a self-inflicted gunshot to the head. Gonzales was a ten-year APD veteran and was less than three weeks away from his thirtieth birthday.

As one of the original investigators in the Hossencofft case nine months earlier, Gonzales had made a momentous decision in the early phase of the case. He had decided to remove the entire carpet from Girly's apartment. Had police only removed the three large, bleached sections, they would likely have never discovered four tiny drops of blood, two belonging to Henning and two from Girly.

After his death, people who knew Gonzales well said that his decision to kill himself stemmed from difficulties at home.

Linda Henning had another explanation. In her letters written from jail, Henning took credit for the illnesses and deaths of people connected to the case and their family members. She wrote that those responsible for inflicting "injustice" upon her would pay a price. After Gonzales's death, she told all who would listen, "I told you so."

It had been about 270 days since Girly had disappeared. Over that time, investigators had made small reconnaissance missions to the Magdalena area.

By June 2000, they were secretly preparing for the first large-scale search for Girly's body. The effort to locate her remains would involve a great variety of resources: money, an airplane, helicopters, horses, dogs and more.

And, in addition to the simple fact that the clothes had been found west of Magdalena, a credible expert's opinion heightened hopes that Girly would soon be found.

Ronald P. Walker, Dr. Park Dietz's associate, told Spiers that a victim's body is almost always left within twenty to twenty-five miles of her discarded clothing.

The first planning meeting for the search was attended by several people at the Gold Street Café in downtown Albuquerque. A second meeting unfolded June 14, 2000, at the district attorney's office. But before it even started, a decision was abruptly made to change the approach drastically.

While driving to the meeting, APD's public information officer, Detective John Walsh, listened to a 770-KKOB radio report that a major search for Girly's body would soon take place near Magdalena.

Investigators, while disappointed that their plan had been leaked to the media, decided to roll with the punches and to use the opportunity to set a trap.

ADA Paul Spiers, Detective Mike Fox, Deputy District Attorney Julie Altwies and other investigators decided that they'd hold a news conference, blasting details of their search across the local airwaves and in newspapers.

The reason for revealing their hand was quite simple. No doubt the media reports would catch the interest of Hossencofft and Henning. The investigators hoped it would spark some communication between the two primary suspects, knowing the duo was not likely to stay mum about such a public spectacle as it related to their possible handiwork.

The trap was set. And investigators were not disappointed.

74

The dutiful course of investigation revealed more than evidence. As it nearly always does, a study of the suspects in the Hossencofft case exposed their habits, passions and hobbies.

Linda Henning had enjoyed art. Diazien Hossencofft had been something of a clothes designer, having made impressive outfits, including Halloween costumes for Girly and Demetri, in happier times.

Henning firmly believed that aliens existed in outer space and here on our planet. Hossencofft had played the role of alien in prior scams, but he now had the perfect pupil.

Art and extraterrestrials converged on a common ground for Henning and Hossencofft. It fueled her allegiance to him, an engine that maintained warp speed even while she was imprisoned. Their many hundreds of jail letters to one another included numerous drawings of alien creatures.

In one drawing, Henning sketched the upper body of a vicious, fanged creature with wings on its back. Its body was heavily scaled. The face was narrow with human characteristics, but it also resembled a reptile. Instead of hair, the scalp was bald with deeply ridged rows of flesh or bone extending from the forehead to the back of the neck, like stripes on a watermelon.

Henning's handwritten notations appeared around the drawing with arrows pointing to various parts of her creation's body.

A remark written near the wings stated "Breeder's workers"; another, near the hand, said, "4 fingers."

Before mailing the drawing to Hossencofft, she wrote that she wished for him to finish the lower part of the drawing, adding that what she had drawn was all "I can remember. . . . How accurate is it?"

But the winged alien was not the only drawing on the page. To the left of it, she had drawn what appeared to be a dinosaur or reptilian egg. Below the egg, another oval-shaped drawing had what looked like a tomato stem attached to its top and a hollowed bottom. It looked more like an eggplant than an egg. And to the right of that drawing, now directly below the winged alien, Henning had drawn the head of a bewitchingly beautiful woman with her shoulder-length hair pulled straight back, thin and raised eyebrows over cat-like eyes and full, attractive lips.

Together, the egg, woman and alien, laid out on the page in a circle, strongly suggested that Henning had depicted the life cycle of her alien, beginning with an egg, reaching human form and finally transforming into the winged reptilian life-form.

Henning's drawings were not limited to reptilians. A vast assortment of male and female humanoids had much softer features and sported everything from horns to molelike snouts to ridges of extra skin running down the center of the face and across the brow to form a crosslike pattern.

Henning wrote that, over billions of years, animal species had evolved into humanoids and that the origin of the oldest extraterrestrials were cats.

Unconfirmed celestial domains appeared beside each drawing: "Kaser 5," "Felen 5," "Dylar 3," "Merna 4" and the "unisex" creatures from "Unari 3."

The creatures looked like characters straight out of *Star Trek: The Next Generation*.

A few of Henning's drawings appeared far more menacing: for example, the facial image of a "Class 1 Drone," a ferocious beast with "razor sharp teeth" and spikes protruding down the center of its wide head. She noted that a secretion gland produced a "bio-weapon." The thing looked like some sort of hybrid of pop culture's the Blob, Swamp Creature and Sleestack.

Henning's masterpiece, however, was a full-bodied skeletal drawing of an unnamed creature capable of growing up to "7.6 feet." This being had extremely long fingernails for "tearing and shredding," "hard to break fused wrists," a "large scalpel bone" that "protects organs, supports wings" and a nose with "secretion glands" that "paralyzes victims."

She wrote that the alien gained thirty pounds after feeding on "humans, eggs, birds, well, anything!!"

The quirkiest remark came at the bottom of the page. After writing that the alien could run the forty-yard dash in 3½ seconds, she added, "Advice: throw marbles."

On Sunday, June 11, 2000, nine months after Girly's disappearance, ADA Paul Spiers traveled to Magdalena with a friend, Drug Enforcement Agency (DEA) agent Mike Marshall. The two men wanted to scout the area prior to the upcoming search.

Spiers considered the lonely patch of wilderness west of Magdalena to be the closest thing to a grave site for Girly.

For two hours, Spiers and Marshall chatted intermittently as they drove the hundred-plus miles to Magdalena. But it was still another 7.1 miles to the site west of town where Girly's clothing had been found with the tarp, tissue, washcloth and duct tape.

The conversation in the car between Spiers and Marshall faded. Just as in previous trips made by investigators to the site, those last seven miles passed silently, a natural consequence of human minds swept up in the possibilities of Girly's fate.

Find her. The thought wouldn't let go of Spiers's mind.

He wouldn't concede to the fatal notion that her body might never be found.

75

In what looked like a bumper-to-bumper convoy, vehicles of all sorts arrived from the east on Highway 60: APD's large mobile crime unit, ATVs, horse trailers and more. These rolling hills hadn't seen such a procession since the famous cattle drives to Magdalena a hundred years earlier.

At 10:25 A.M., APD's detective John Walsh began to address the media assembled at the command post and matter-of-factly announced the long list of agencies taking part in the search: the Bernalillo County Sheriff's Office, New Mexico State Police, U.S. Customs, Bernalillo County District Attorney's Office, the Department of Public Safety, Bureau of Land Management, Forest Service, graduate students from the University of New Mexico's Anthropology Department, the Southwest Trackers organization, the Albuquerque Metal Detectors Club and representatives from the National Guard.

Walsh also said that investigators from the state's office of the medical investigator were on-site and available "if needed."

Walsh next introduced the man in charge of the search.

Exuding confidence and speaking in the vernacular of

law enforcement, Detective Damon Faye provided insights into the role of each component of the search team.

"We're primarily using pedestrian reconnaissance. That's actual ground searchers," Faye explained.

Detective Faye outlined the role of the aircraft, without exactly saying that they're equipped with technology that can detect a rotting corpse.

"From the air, units are flying in support to check with forward-looking infrared. They can check for thermal differentials in the ground, calling coordinates to us. Then we can send in a different team, intelligent-cadaver sniffing dogs."

The press was eager to learn more about the cadaver dogs, and Raymond Rogers had some answers. Rogers was a member of the Los Alamos Mountain Canine Corps.

The gray-haired gentleman sporting the cowboy hat was the owner of Brenda, an eight-year-old coonhound. Brenda was one of four cadaver dogs provided by the Los Alamos Mountain Canine Corps for this search. Rogers, like other members of the Corps, volunteered his time when law enforcement requested his assistance.

And he patiently answered a reporter's questions.

Nine months had passed since Girly's disappearance; would the dogs ever find Girly's remains?

"Oh, that's no problem at all," Rogers said.

Turns out, nine months is as good as yesterday. Rogers explained that Brenda had previously done exceedingly well in a mock search that tested her ability to discern human flesh and bone from dead animals. With assistance from a physical anthropologist, Rogers continued, the test included spoiled pork and beef, some human samples taken from cadavers three years earlier, some cast bones and some much older human remains. One piece of human cadaver was 750 years old, taken from some ruins in the Four Corners area.

"Brenda alerted very easily on the seven-hundred-fifty-year-old remains," Rogers said.

Brenda had never "alerted" on the animal meat or plastic, he explained. Those would have been "false positives."

Rogers revealed that some things can make a search for humans extremely difficult. "One thing that will kill a scent is automobile exhaust, diesel exhaust."

Some "human products" will confuse the dogs, too. "If there's a couple of used Kotexes in some place or one of these Port-A-Potty bags . . . particularly if there's a couple of used Kotexes in it, the dogs just can't discriminate, except by the intensity of the scent."

Like Detective Faye, Rogers seemed secure in the knowledge that his team's abilities were up to the task at hand.

"[The bones] get denuded of all flesh in New Mexico, maybe in something like six months," Rogers said. "It depends, of course, [on] the weather, the moisture, the exposure, how many animals are around, things like that. It wouldn't be a problem to find human bones unless they have been *chemically treated* somehow."

Wearing tight-fitting white T-shirts, camouflage hats, and backpacks, two search teams of men and women set out on foot from Highway 60 and Cat Mountain Ranch Road. One team headed south, the other west.

And far from the command post, APD's horse patrol searched for any sign of Girly in "the farthest region that we think these people could have gone in the disposal of the body," explained Detective Walsh.

The beaming confidences from Detectives Walsh and Faye only added to the optimism that Girly's remains were about to be located.

"Now we can get rapid response with the helicopter. We've already seen a series of things on the ground that are suspicious," Detective Faye told reporters still gathered at the command post. "The area's about nine to eleven square miles that we're searching today. This is an area that we can easily cover in one day. We can do it substantially, comprehensively."

But the investigators also considered the daunting possibility that Girly's body might be inside one of the countless abandoned mine shafts in the area. DA investigator Rudy Checkle explained that, in preparation for this search, organizers discovered that several of the mine shafts were not even listed with the Bureau of Mines.

As the search teams went about their jobs, members of the media did their best to pass the time beneath the hot desert sun with little to no cover in sight.

Investigators kept reporters and photographers herded along Highway 60. Cat Mountain Ranch Road was now off limits to the press.

DA investigator Brent Johnson offered to show the media exactly where state highway worker Raymond Gabaldon had discovered Girly's clothing, the tarp, the duct tape, the hair, the washcloth and the twisted bits of tissue paper soiled with Girly's saliva and mucus.

After walking a few hundred yards from the command post to the site along the south side of Highway 60, Johnson pointed to the slope that rises from the southern edge of the highway. This was where Gabaldon made his discovery.

A seemingly benign moment occurred at the command post when Channel 7's helicopter landed next to it. But instead of a news crew, firefighters stepped out of the chopper. No one seemed to be asking what their arrival was all about, but the pieces of the puzzle started falling into place.

The first clue came from Raymond Rogers after he returned from his search with Brenda that afternoon.

"How has it gone today?" he was asked.

"Well, we worked all over the place and, of course, all the dogs will do, or can do, is give an indication. Then we call the investigators if we get an indication," Rogers said.

It seemed apparent he was unwilling to reveal directly any news of a discovery, but he did lay out protocol. "The proof of the pudding is what [investigators] say. So, I suggest you ask them," Rogers said politely, while deferring to the top brass like an old pro.

Moments later, a police helicopter landed momentarily smack in the middle of Highway 60, then lifted off, its nose lowered as the craft gained altitude, but it never seemed to rise more than a few hundred feet. The chopper flew westward and ducked over the top of a nearby hill, its apparent destination a short distance away and just south of Highway 60.

This was too much to bear. Rogers had all but said the cadaver dogs alerted on human remains. Now APD's helicopter was suddenly on the move.

"Tomorrow morning we'll be resuming the search shortly after daybreak, and we'll be looking down into a specific site," Detective Walsh explained to the media at the command post.

"We'll be bringing equipment on to shore up or to render this area safe for a closer look by the AFD personnel. It will be quite an operation, and we'll be on-site for several hours tomorrow."

Walsh initially didn't tip his hand to reporters. He didn't explain that three out of the four cadaver dogs alerted on the mine earlier in the day. The dogs' reaction prompted investigators to call for the Albuquerque Fire Department (AFD) team that specializes in securing old structures before rescuers move in. Only this was a possible recovery operation.

"Is the fact that you're coming back tomorrow an indication that you've found something down there?" asked Channel 7 reporter Rod Green.

"No," Walsh responded without hesitation. "It is not that we've found anything of any specific nature. It certainly is intriguing enough that we want to take a closer look."

76

The quest to get to the bottom of the old, abandoned mine shaft began at 8:30 A.M. on Sunday, June 25, 2000. Day two's search for Girly's body involved far fewer people than Saturday's major operation. But there was no less anticipation—perhaps there was more.

Instead of nine to eleven square miles, this search was focused on a hole in the ground, three feet by five feet, its depth a mystery. The abandoned shaft had a lot of debris stuffed down its throat.

One haunting question was on everyone's mind that morning: was Girly's body at the bottom of this decrepit mine shaft out in the middle of nowhere?

For several hours, the sound of saws and pounding hammers filled the air as the AFD guys executed their task of shoring up the shaft with precision and patience.

There's no such thing as a rush job when reinforcing a century-old mine shaft. Cut corners and you might die.

About two feet below the top of the shaft, the firefighters constructed their first brace against all four sides of the shaft, applying to the entire lengths four customized and freshly cut two-by-fours so that they met end to end, forming a rectangle. For added support, a fifth two-by-four bisected the brace.

Once the top of the mine was secured in this fashion, a tethered firefighter could descend a few feet into the shaft, then reach down and grab large pieces of debris, then hand it up to the men standing on firm ground just above. Most of the debris turned out to be large, twisted pieces of long-rusted metal, quite possibly the outer walls and roof of some building in a bygone era.

Once the firefighter inside the shaft cleared out the nearest debris, he could be lowered a few more feet, then begin building another rectangular brace to secure that section of the narrow passage. The job of removing twisted sheets of metal, some of it about ten feet long, then securing the shaft, went on for six hours.

"Hendricks! Want to come out?" a man peering down into the mine yelled out. "You've been down there for about an hour."

Less than ten minutes later, the team reached the bottom of the shaft.

The firefighters, the police investigators, prosecutors and their investigators formed a circle around the top of the shaft. While looking down into the darkness, they all seemed to be having a quiet discussion about what they had found inside.

Had they just discovered Girly's body? The scene almost looked like a quiet eulogy, a sacred moment for those who'd come so far and dedicated so much time in the pursuit of justice and closure for Girly's family.

It turned out that the searchers found something dead, all right. But it wasn't Girly. The firefighters discovered parts of a dead animal at the bottom, an elk.

That seemed odd. How long had the animal been dead? After all, if it had died recently, then it seemed that all of

those old twisted sheets of metal would have had to have
been placed in the shaft *after* the elk parts entered it.

Detective Walsh would say only that the elk would likely
be taken to the University of New Mexico's Anthropology
Department for further analysis.

The high-profile search for Girly's body on the weekend
of June 24 and 25, 2000, involved scores of people and cost
thousands of dollars in police overtime and resources; it also
benefited from the generosity of numerous volunteers. And
it all unfolded more than a hundred miles from Albuquerque.
The investigators knew it was unlikely that they'd ever be allowed to conduct a similar search in this investigation again.
Not to sound heartless, but their bosses could easily argue
that this was just one missing woman. And she was only *presumed* dead. Albuquerque had no shortage of violent crimes.
The time and money could be better spent.

As the firefighters put away their tools and prepared to head
home, prosecutors Paul Spiers and Jack Burkhead, along with
Mike Marshall, took turns digging at what seemed like a
random soft patch of ground. It wasn't a desperate act. Just a
hopeful one. The men knew this day was slipping away and
hated the thought that Girly's body could be nearby and left
undiscovered.

77

At 5:15 A.M. on July 7, 2000, investigators planned to search the area around the abandoned house in the remote desert northeast of Magdalena, near the home of Bill Miller's friends Geneva Liddon and Randy Bell.

Unlike the high-profile search west of Magdalena two weeks earlier, this exploration would pass under the media's radar.

Among the search party of fewer than ten people was a woman speaking words of encouragement to her dog, Miranda. Wendy Brunish said the Heeler-Doberman mix had originally come from the Santa Fe Animal Shelter. Brunish and Miranda were one of two teams from the Los Alamos Mountain Canine Corps who had volunteered to help search that morning.

Moments later, the other team, Mike Warren and his dog, Jasper, ventured into the old house. They came out a few minutes later, having found no scent of human remains.

Investigators had visited the dilapidated adobe dwelling months earlier. With no sign of Girly inside the house, this search focused on the nearby land. The immediate property included an old corral about thirty-five yards southwest of the house.

The surrounding terrain included an arroyo to the east. The trees and scrub plants that lined its path appeared fluorescent in the morning light. Nearby, large and rolling hills appeared to the north, east and west. Was Girly's body out there?

The search party, which included ADA Spiers, Detective L. T. Gunther and Investigator Rudy Checkle, hoped to answer the question, once and for all.

Gunther, wearing a black cowboy hat and duster, appeared determined to round up any nearby clues.

The single-story structure, with large windows to each side of its front door, looked as if it had once well met the needs of life in this far-off place. The debris scattered upon the entry room's floor included a coiled box spring long removed of any thread or fabric. The flimsy remains of a wooden door also stretched across the floor.

A small storage room now had a curious assortment of things inside: stacks of cow manure, empty shotgun shells, old Shasta Cola cans and empty cans of Vienna sausage and Franco-American spaghetti.

Rodent pellets in the corners of the room were covered with some sort of white powder. A wasp nest hung from the ceiling. The adobe walls had been badly chipped away, exposing chicken wire. In other areas, holes in the adobe appeared to have been made by bullets.

If not for the specter of Girly's vanishing, the abandoned house simply would have appeared to have been a place where teenagers had goofed off or hunters had found shelter.

That was quite likely the extent of its history in recent years. But one had to wonder.

The sight of stacks of cow manure in the tiny room was a puzzle. Most people stored firewood, but cow manure burned, too. Had someone stored it here while making plans to hide out?

The ultimate question also tugged at the minds of the investigators. What if they had just walked away from or even over her?

But there was no sign of Girly Chew Hossencofft that morning.

In August 2000, a grim reminder of Girly's death arrived a half a world away.

Its brown paper wrapping showed signs of wear, but it was familiar to Girly's parents.

It was the care package that Mr. and Mrs. Chew had sent their daughter eleven months earlier.

Never opened, it still contained the cookbooks, curry powder, dried curry leaves, audiotapes of Buddhist chanting to Kuan Yin and one piece of red skirt.

The only major change was the unavoidable, single word now written across the top of the package.

In capital letters, it simply said, "DECEASED."

78

For some unknown reason, what had been a relatively rare form of cancer only twenty years earlier had become the fifth most common cancer in the United States. And now it had a firm grip on Ron Koch's life.

The debilitating effects of non-Hodgkin's lymphoma on Hossencofft's attorney were taking their toll. Weakened by the illness, Koch underwent chemotherapy. The chemo had caused his thick black hair to fall out. In court, he'd shown up wearing a brimmed hat upon his bald head.

Koch had been a bear of a man. Now he was fighting for his life.

By October 3, 2000, any hopes that Koch would be able to continue representing Hossencofft had faded. But the murder suspect had a solution.

Appearing in court that day, Hossencofft told Judge Richard Knowles that he wanted to represent himself. The court called for a twenty-minute recess.

"What would be the advantage of *pro se,* the legal term for representing one's self?" the author asked Hossencofft during the court's recess.

"I will never take the stand. Rule 514," he said, matter-of-factly, would protect him from testifying during trial.

It was no mystery that he'd been studying law in jail. And it was no surprise that he wanted to show off a little of that knowledge. Hossencofft admonished the work of investigators. As far as he was concerned, they were a collection of Keystone Kops. He emphatically stated that the thirteen-month-long investigation had produced no evidence implicating him in the disappearance and murder of his estranged wife.

"They didn't find any piece of me anywhere. . . . They (prosecutors) stuck this pig, and they want to see if it squeals," he said with mounting intensity in his voice.

A moment later, his tone softened as he shared that he was writing a book about the case. He'd decided on a title, too: *The Last Days of Tomorrow,* based on what he said was the state's intention to have him killed by lethal injection.

It was easy to see where a steam cleaner had passed over the carpet.

Much like a vacuum leaves a light-colored path after passing over a dirty rug, the steam cleaner had left a track. A strong cleaning agent, probably bleach, had lightened the color of the carpet taken from Girly's apartment. The cleaner had been used in a confined area, and it appeared to have been pushed back and forth in random directions.

To Catherine Dickey and Donna Arbogast, it looked like a rush job.

But the cleaner had left a trail in more than one way.

Steam carpet cleaners work on a relatively simple principle. The cleaning solution is released from a reservoir and into the carpet. The cleaner also sucks the spent fluid out of the carpet and into a second reservoir. Investigators had not been surprised to find the cleaner in a relatively clean condition.

Shortly before moving to South Carolina, Hossencofft had loaned it to his neighbor John Deyber. After using it, Deyber had cleaned it before returning it to Hossencofft on September 7, 1999.

Early in the investigation, the crime lab had tested the thin film of residue found inside the dirty-water reservoir for any sign of human blood. The leucomalachite uranium and luminol presumptive tests had both come back positive.

But Dickey was never able to get any DNA out of it.

Now, more than a year later, the investigation into Bill Miller had linked him to deer hair, prompting Dickey and Arbogast to revisit the residue found in the cleaner.

On December 7, 2000, Arbogast telephoned Detective Fox and said that she'd found deer hair in the steam cleaner. She added that some of the hair was natural in color and some of it had been dyed pink. That had also been the case with the carpet from Girly's apartment. The residue inside the steam cleaner also contained a piece of pink Mylar, between one and two millimeters wide. That discovery only heightened Fox's interest.

Hadn't he seen Mylar on Miller's fly-tying bench a year earlier?

On December 12, 2000, Arbogast telephoned Fox with the answer. She reported that she had revisited items taken from Miller's house on October 29, 1999, including evidence taken from Miller's fly-tying table. It included a piece of clear Mylar that was about one-sixteenth of an inch wide.

As a result of the Hossencofft case, Detective Fox had studied fly-fishing and had learned that deer hair and Mylar are commonly used for tying flies. The deer hair could be dyed a variety of colors, including pink. Mylar used for tying flies was typically about one-sixteenth of an inch wide.

Arbogast's revelations convinced Fox that he was closing in on something he felt was long overdue: an arrest warrant.

On December 14, 2000, Albuquerque police returned to

Miller's home. In stating what police were searching for, their latest warrant read unlike any other:

> *IN THE STATE OF NEW MEXICO, COUNTY OF BERNALILLO THERE IS NOW BEING CONCEALED CERTAIN PROPERTY, NAMELY: Any and all fibers. Any and all materials used in fishing, hunting, gaming, or tying flies for fishing to include but not limited to deer hair and Mylar. Any and all trace evidence to include but not limited to glitter.*

Police did not leave empty-handed. They seized a silver-and-blue tackle box, additional fishing items and hair samples taken from Miller's two cats. When police noticed Miller reading the search warrant, they saw that his hands trembled.

After finding deer hair in Miller's home, Arbogast set out to compare its DNA with the deer hair found in Girly's carpet and inside the steam cleaner. She had her results four days later.

On December 18, 2000, Arbogast informed Detective Fox that the DNA of pink deer hairs found in Girly's carpet and in the steam cleaner was "consistent" with the pink deer hairs found in Miller's home.

Seven weeks later, Arbogast telephoned Fox and shared a rundown of animal hairs found at various locations in the Hossencofft case:

1) Girly's living-room carpet:
- Sixty natural cat hairs
- Fifteen natural dog hairs
- Eighteen natural deer hairs
- Six dyed deer hairs
- One natural rabbit hair
- Five dyed rabbit hairs

- Eleven natural feathers
- One pink feather

2) Tarp recovered from Highway 60:
- One hundred and one natural cat hairs
- Five natural dog hairs
- Two dyed rabbit hairs
- Two dyed green feathers

3) Girly's blouse recovered from Highway 60:
- Fifty-six natural cat hairs
- One natural dog hair

4) Steam steam/carpet cleaner:
- Three natural cat hairs
- Twenty natural dog hairs
- Fifteen natural deer hairs
- Thirty-six dyed deer hairs

5) Standards collected from Miller's home during search warrant:
- Natural and dyed deer hairs
- Natural and dyed feathers
- Natural and dyed rabbit hairs
- Natural cat hairs

On Monday, February 12, 2001, the SWAT team was secretly staking out Miller's home. Some houses had even been evacuated. Investigators feared a shoot-out.

Investigators were simply waiting for a judge to sign an arrest warrant before moving in.

Miller emerged and went to the Wild Oats Market and sat alone at a table near the front of the store. An employee noticed that he had a spiral notebook.

At 9:40 A.M., a judge signed the arrest warrant. Five minutes later, he signed warrants authorizing police to search Miller's home and truck. Immediately afterward, Detective Fox contacted the Miller surveillance team and informed its members that they were good to go. The warrants had all been signed.

As Miller exited the Wild Oats Market, he noticed the uniformed SWAT officers in the parking lot and did a quick about-face and reentered the store.

Undercover officers, already inside, closed in and arrested him.

As Miller was taken into custody, the store employee noticed that his spiral notebook had been left beneath the table. She gave it to police.

Miller was charged with first-degree murder, kidnapping, tampering with evidence, and other crimes.

Immediately after arresting him, investigators took Miller to the nearby police substation. While Miller's hands were cuffed in front of him, the detectives left him alone in a holding cell as they stepped into an adjacent room to discuss the arrest.

Detective Fox placed a VHS tape inside a VCR that was hooked up to a security camera focused on the holding cell.

Fox next went back into the holding cell and asked Miller if he wanted to speak to his lawyer before going to jail. When Miller said he did, the detective went to find a cell phone so that his prisoner could speak privately with an attorney.

What happened next was an absolute surprise.

Investigator Brent Johnson and Detective Pete Lescenski looked up at the surveillance monitor and witnessed Miller taking business cards out of his wallet and eating them. He also stuffed papers into his socks.

Johnson and Lescenski rushed into the holding cell. Johnson managed to make Miller spit the partially eaten cards out of his mouth.

Miller's arrest paved the way for a much broader search of his home. In addition to any more fishing items, police had a warrant allowing them to search for guns and ammunition.

The search began at 11:20 that morning. Detectives were busy bringing boxes out of Miller's poorly lit garage so that a police photographer could photograph them.

Nan Miller slipped in and out of sight as she went repeatedly in and out of the home's front door.

While it was difficult to see what police had found, the search warrant's inventory detailed a large cache of weapons, ammunition and more.

Items Seized from Miller's Home

- Ammunition magazines
- Duct tape
- Green canvas bag
- Two black bags with ammo
- Shotgun barrel
- Maps
- Notebooks
- Document
- Blue bag with mags
- Smith & Wesson .38 Special
- Twenty-two-caliber Beretta with mag model 21A-22
- Remington sawed-off shotgun model 870
- Rossi .22-caliber long rifle
- SKs 7.62 x 39 rifle with attached bayonet
- Ruger M77 Mark II .30-06 with soft case
- M14S .308 rifle with soft case
- Smith & Wesson model 3000 shotgun 12-gauge
- Remington model 600 .243 Winchester
- .22-caliber long-rifle revolver
- American Arms Co. Revolver Smith & Wesson, barrel cut
- Beretta 9mm model 1934
- Remington 870 shotgun 12-gauge
- Winchester model 47 .22-caliber
- Ruger Mark II semiauto .22-caliber
- Browning .22-caliber semiauto
- Smith & Wesson model 686 357 revolver
- Savage model 5 .22-caliber rifle
- Ruger Mark II target .22-caliber long rifle

• North American Arms .22-caliber revolver
    Items Seized from Miller's 1986 Ford Pickup
• Carpet
• Drapes
• Cushion covers
• Maps

Miller had the arsenal that police had feared he'd use against them.

While the investigation of Miller had intensified, forty-nine-year-old Ron Koch had fought to stay alive. On December 19, 2000, the cancer that had attacked his lymph nodes claimed his life.

79

Just as he had done on the outside, Hossencofft never hesitated in jail to boast about his brilliance.

In time, he came to know fellow inmate Jeffrey Padilla.

Padilla, twenty-nine, was hardly just another jailbird. And it wasn't simply because he was charged with two murders. Police believed Padilla was the leader of Los Padillas, the oldest and most sophisticated gang in Albuquerque. Deeply rooted in the nearby South Valley, members of Los Padillas had also been connected to a drug-smuggling and distribution ring connected to two of Mexico's largest drug cartels.

Los Padillas symbolized family and power. It controlled the primary flow of black tar heroin out of Mexico and into Albuquerque.

In April 2000, Padilla helped convince a corrections officer to go to the jail's lobby and retrieve a sack that had just been dropped off by a woman. Padilla and his cellmate said they were hungry for food from the outside and that the sack contained burritos.

With a coworker nearby in the lobby, the corrections officer apparently had a last-minute change of heart and decided